# Storytwisting

## A Guide to Remixing & Reinventing Stories

**"Concise and evocative,** Storytwisting challenges this traditional teller to look at stories differently. The authors not only provide teaching aids, but speak to the meaning of stories, both culturally and ethically. All this wisdom—combined with simple fun in making stories that excite contemporary audiences of all ages—delivers a must-read for storytellers ready to engage their imaginations to create lively stories."

—DOROTHY CLEVELAND, co-author, *Beyond the Sword Maiden: A Storyteller's Introduction to the Heroine's Journey*

"The authors, who perform together as 'The Storycrafters,' are the balloon artists of the American Storytelling Revival. They take an ordinary story, stretch it, fill it, and turn it into a work of art. This generous book illuminates their method, offering **something for everyone: students, teachers, scholars, and storytellers.** But to get the best of this book, add your own imagination. Read aloud the many excellently twisted stories included here, then spin the dial. Jeri and Barry give you all the tools you need to 'do the twist.'"

—DAVID NOVAK, storyteller, National Storytelling Network Circle of Excellence Oracle Award recipient, instructor, East TN State University's Graduate Storytelling Program.

"Anyone who has ever heard The Storycrafters tell their twisted tales in concert has wondered, **'How do they DO that?'** This book provides the answer, taking you deep into their storytwisting magic, peeling back the layers of thought, research, creativity and craft that produce their entrancing and thought-provoking stories. Jeri and Barry explore their process step by step, illustrated with clear and relevant examples that will inspire many a twisted tale! This is a generous gift to storytellers, teachers, and lovers of story."

—SHERRY NORFOLK, storyteller and co-author of *Social Studies in the Storytelling Classroom*

"*Storytwisting* **is a brilliant piece of work.** Read this book, any chapter in this book. You will suddenly find yourself creating astonishing new tales, spinning diamonds out of kelp, and morphing mountains into molehills!"

—WILLY CLAFLIN, storyteller, author, National Storytelling Network Circle of Excellence Oracle Award Recipient

# Storytwisting

## A Guide to Remixing
## & Reinventing Stories

# Jeri Burns & Barry Marshall
## The Storycrafters

Parkhurst Brothers Publishers

MARION, MICHIGAN

**www.parkhurstbrothers.com**

Parkhurst Brothers books are distributed to the trade through the Chicago Distribution Center, and may be ordered through Ingram Book Company, Baker & Taylor, Follett Library Resources and other book industry wholesalers. To order from Chicago Distribution Center, phone 1-800-621-2736 or send a fax to 800-621-8476. Copies of this and other Parkhurst Brothers Inc., Publishers titles are available to organizations and corporations for purchase in quantity by contacting Special Sales Department at our home office location, listed on our web site. Manuscript submission guidelines for this publishing company are available at our web site.

Printed in the United States of America

First Edition, 2017

2018 2019 2020 2021 2022 2023 17 16 15 14 13 12 11 10 9 8 7 6 5 4 3 2 1

Library of Congress Cataloging in Publication Data: [Pending]

ISBN: Hardback 978-1-62491-096-8

ISBN: Paperback 978-1-62491-097-5

ISBN: e-book 978-1-62491-098-2

Parkhurst Brothers Publishers believes that the free and open exchange of ideas is essential for the maintenance of our freedoms. We support the First Amendment of the United States Constitution and encourage all citizens to study all sides of public policy questions, making up their own minds. Closed minds cost a society dearly.

All URLs in this book are being provided as a convenience and for informational purposes only; they do not constitute an endorsement or an approval by the publisher of any of the products, services or opinions. Parkhurst Brothers Publishers bears no responsibility for the accuracy, legality or content of linked sites or for that of subsequent links. Contact external sites for answers to questions regarding their content.

| | |
|---|---|
| Cover, interior art and design by | Linda D. Parkhurst, Ph.D. |
| Proofread by | Bill and Barbara Paddack |
| Acquired for Parkhurst Brothers Publishers and edited by: | Ted Parkhurst |

012018

# DEDICATION

*This book is dedicated
to the creative energy that resides in all of us
and to those who harvest its power.*

# ACKNOWLEDGMENTS

WRITING A BOOK IS LIKE EMBARKING ON A FAIRY TALE JOURNEY. There are many helpers along the path. Even the tiniest gestures helped us in enormous ways.

**The Fairy Godmother**—Tresca Weinstein, writing group member, whose loving commitment to the book (and us) never flagged for an instant. She was there from the book's inception to hours before we pressed the send button. From global philosophical ideas to missing hyphens, her stellar contributions and positive spirit reside in these pages and forever in our hearts.

**Johnny Appleseed**—Karin Weule, whose sagacious inquiries and heartfelt reactions caused deep pondering and reassessment that bore much fruit. Like her namesake, Karin's generosity knew no bounds (but unlike him, she never wore a pan for a hat). Her steady involvement was tree-like. We gratefully took refuge in her caring, nourishing shade whenever the going got tough.

**The Mad Hatter**—Beth Horner, whose gift of time, immense wisdom, and organizational smarts was critical to this book. Beth's "mad" sense of humor is always appreciated, but was especially valued during a couple of looooong SKYPE sessions. We were graced and honored to have this storytelling national treasure involved in our project.

**The Mad Hatter's Tea Party**—A jumble of generous storytellers helped us with various portions of the book. We are deeply grateful to each of them for their time, expertise, and brainpower. Anne Goding, Debbie Gurriere, Margaret Read MacDonald, Sherry Norfolk, Antonio Rocha, Gayle Ross, Penninah Schram, Denise Valentine, and Csenge Zalka.

**The Seven Dwarfs**—Audience members at the Falcon Ridge Folk Festival, Clearwater's Great Hudson River Revival, and the Flurry Festival. Their enduring support helped us mine the depths of twisted tales for intergenerational audiences over many fun-filled years.

**Mama Bear**—Bobi Burns, who lovingly acted as reader, listener, and all around caretaker (though she never made a pot of porridge in her whole life, and never will).

**The Trickster**—Zack Marshall, our son. His sheer presence in our lives caused us to play with stories. Zack can always be relied upon for brilliant commentary, unexpected ideas, and playful observations. His mind moves in "smirkful" and mirthful ways—he is our greatest teacher.

**Goldilocks**—Carin Quirke de Jong, a writing group member, who cheerfully spoke her mind and helped make the book's voice "just right."

**Zeus** (without a thunderbolt)—Ted Parkhurst, who decided to give this book life after it sprang forth from our heads. His wise, guiding hand gentled our ideas into being.

**The Boy who Drew Cats**—(okay the girl who drew cats), Linda Parkhurst, whose artistic eye and graphic skills transformed every component of the book—from plain blocks of text to the cover design—into something simply pleasurable to gaze upon.

**Snow White**—Devyn Whiting, our niece, who had nothing to do with the book, but inspired us when we wrote the acknowledgments. She always wanted to be Snow White, and now she is.

**Magic Beans**—Fern Bradley, who helped at the very start of this journey.

**Spectators in the Emperor's Parade**—Family, friends, workshop folks, students, storytelling festivals, colleagues, Lewis Carroll and our kitty. We couldn't have done it without you!

**The Pied Piper**—Wendy Nowlan, an educational visionary who hired us to teach and to help develop a graduate storytelling program. This is where the book's foundation was first developed.

Our deepest gratitude to each and every one of you.

*Jeri & Barry*

# TABLE OF CONTENTS

# PREFACE

Storytwisting is our signature approach to storytelling. It wasn't the plan, but serendipity never is. While we love writing and performing quirky retellings of traditional stories and well-known fairy tales, our longstanding commitment to this writing style was instigated by our audiences.

There are several folk and music festivals at which we are honored to perform nearly every year. Like holidays, they are cherished, family rituals. Our family has grown up at these festivals and with those who attend them. Likewise, the families and adults who attend have grown up with us.

The first time we performed a *fractured* story at one of those festivals, the audiences clamored for more. Because we knew the audiences and they knew us so well, we listened.

We soon learned that festival audiences were not the only ones to love our reimagined stories. They were also a hit with schools, libraries, professionals, general family audiences, children, and adults. People of all ages appreciate them, and everywhere we go, they ask us to tell them. We perform these stories to meet contemporary audiences and satisfy their hunger for this type of story. And we are delighted to share our process for writing such tales so that you can develop this style of story too.

## About Collaboration and How We Wrote this Book

We, Barry and Jeri, are a team in all regards—life partners, work partners, and a performance duo. We have performed together as *The Storycrafters* since the early nineties. However, we discovered early on that division of labor makes our work process smooth as pudding—and keeps our relationship sweet as pudding.

Barry is the business side of The Storycrafters, the art and graphics department, Webmaster, and general marketing whiz. Jeri is head of development and the all-around writing slug. Although we both teach adults and kids, Barry does more arts-in-education workshops in schools and Jeri teaches more college classes. He is the recording engineer and Jeri is a public radio essayist and blogger. This divide-and-conquer strategy helps us manage our Storycrafters work and benefits the life-partner side of our existence, including raising and homeschooling our son and kitty, while maintaining our (way too big) yard and garden.

But we are not always separate! Performances, rehearsals, most workshops, event-producing responsibilities, and our beloved healing storytelling sessions with psychiatric patients always include both of us.

And the writing of our pieces? Every piece is different. Generally speaking, we start with something on paper. Whether it begins as an oral telling, such as a family story, or if it comes from several versions of a folktale or myth, one retelling is drafted. This same process occurs for storytwisting pieces. The story draft is written by Jeri. It's in her job description (writing slug). Jeri has this to add:

> Barry is also a sounding board for my quirky writing ideas and an editor extraordinaire—he cuts text faster than a chef cuts vegetables. He is also my haven for writer's block trauma. His shoulder is perfectly sized for my head to tuck into whenever I stare at blank screens.

Despite our divide-and-conquer approach to the Storycrafters business, we are collaborators through and through. Rehearsals occur on the couch while swapping foot massages. Brainstorming sessions and conceptual discourse happens in long car rides to gigs (which is indie artist slang for booked performances). Our performed stories are completely collaborative, spoken word duets—he speaks, she speaks, he speaks, etc., with some unisons thrown in for fun—often accompanied by music of our own making.

The presentation of this book mirrors our creative and performance style. We employ the point of view of first-person plural to reflect our collaboration. Sometimes, however, we share personal anecdotes or content that is in one of our voices.

While the Storytwisting approach and all of the stories were created by Jeri and Barry, it is more efficient for one person to write a book. Jeri drafted it and integrated Barry's content, his cuts, and revisions.

One writing voice is easier to read than two.

# A WORD TO THE WISE

THE FOURTEEN STORIES THAT APPEAR IN THIS BOOK are *authored works with copyright protections*. While they are based in folklore, these tales were written by Jeri Burns and Barry Marshall, The Storycrafters. They are original compositions and/or adaptations.

*If you want to tell any of these tales in live performance,* you must obtain permission directly from Barry and Jeri, The Storycrafters.

*If you want to record* or adapt any of these tales for any other forum (including but not limited to audio, video, all forms of print, online, digital, interactive, gaming, or other forums that exist and have yet to be invented), you must first obtain permission from The Storycrafters *and* Parkhurst Brothers Publishers.

Thank you in advance for your ethics and professional courtesy.

*Jeri Burns and Barry Marshall*

www.storycrafters.com
The Storycrafters on Facebook
Twitter: @storycraftersx2
info@storycrafters.com

Parkhurst Brothers Publishers
PO Box 356
Marion, MI 49665
231-215-0488
ted@parkhurstbrothers.com
www.parkhurstbrothers.com

CHAPTER ONE

# An Eye•Opening Experience

A NUMBER OF YEARS AGO, we offered a series of storytelling workshops to adults in England. After sharing guidelines and tips for how to learn a story to tell, we gave students several short folk tales to peruse. Each selected a favorite. As it happened, an Irish teller selected a Jewish story complete with a rabbi, Jewish school, Yiddish words, and challah. After spending workshop time on technique and practice, each participant had an opportunity to tell his or her tale for the rest of the group. When the Irish teller performed his story, the classic Jewish folk tale did *not* pop out of his mouth. He transformed it into a full-blown Irish story, complete with parish priest, church, Irish whiskey, soda bread, and a touch of the Irish language.

The workshop participants delighted in his story and the storyteller delighted in telling a tale that burst with Irish humor. It was a joyous performance, but not just because the story was well told. First, the story was transferred to a cultural context that was more familiar to the teller and his audience. Second, because the expected story was altered and set in an unexpected place, it was particularly intriguing for those of us who knew a more traditional version.

Was the story he told the same as the one that he read on paper? The plot of the story remained the same and the basic meaning of it was unchanged. However, the setting and the characters were as different as could be. In a discussion that followed the presentation, the Irish teller maintained that he loved the story as it was written, but he knew that telling it as a Jewish tale would not be as meaningful to his audiences as it would be with his added Irish accents. By making changes to the tale, he translated it from one culture to another while preserving the basic essence of the story.

The storyteller could have chosen to present a Jewish story to his audiences, educating them with new cultural information to offer a multicultural experience. Instead he made a different choice. He chose to relate the essence and humor of the tale without the cultural clothing. He believed that the familiarity of the Irish setting would invite his listeners in and allow the humor of the story to be featured more prominently. It occurred to us that the process we witnessed in the workshop was comparable to the way many traditional stories have been passed among people for millennia.

But this experience opened our eyes to something else.

Where the other listeners enjoyed a humorous Irish tale, our experience was different from theirs even as we laughed right along with them. Every Jewish element that was transposed to Irish culture took us by surprise. It was like walking down a familiar street only to discover that all the trees and flowers were planted in new places and the houses were different colors. Experiencing old and new at the same time is an intellectual and emotional adventure.

Not only was it great fun to hear his tale, it also taught us a great deal about Irish culture and values. You see, every alteration in the story was significant to those who knew the Jewish version. With our expectations shaken up, each narrative change was a red flag that commanded our attention. Our grasp of new cultural information and the meaning of the story were both amplified because his altered version was overlaid on one we already knew.

The natural human tendency to change stories for different audiences, coupled with the powerful connections such stories offer listeners, is the impulse behind this book. Change is integral to the oral tradition. Storytwisting channels change to craft new stories from traditional ones.

There are multiple ways to denote the alterations made to traditional stories—they are told, retold, adapted, based on, fractured, adapted and retold, to name a few. According to storytelling and folklore scholar Margaret Read McDonald, if a story is *told* by someone, it is spoken in the words of an indigenous storyteller or transliterated from that teller's words when written down.

### Definitions of Key Terms Used in this Book

When read in order, this list sheds light on ideas that are relevant to storytwisting.

**Traditional Story**–a tale in the oral tradition. Some examples include folktales, myths, legends, fables, urban legends, and older, literary fairy tales that have entered (or re-entered) the oral tradition.[2] Traditional stories are in the public domain.

**Retold or Adapted**–a traditional story that is composed in a storyteller's own words. The terms "adapted" and "retold" are interchangeable.

**Straight Retelling**–a retold or adapted tale that is faithful to the plot and story elements of a traditional story. Compare to twisted or storytwisted, below.

**Adapted Retelling**–a straight retelling of a traditional story that contains a sustained transformation of a story element, such as a shift from prose to rhyme or a change in setting. There is no expectation that the audience will recognize the source tale(s).

**Intertextuality**–the reverberant echoes of a pre-existing story in a new tale; a conversation or dialogue between the story being told and the tale upon which it is based.[3]

**Fractured**–a story that carries a sustained twist or transformation of one or more story elements. It also contains implied or explicit social commentary, intertextuality, shaken expectations, and/or is self-referential about stories or storytelling process.

**Storytwisted or Twisted**–an umbrella term for an adapted retelling or fractured story with a sustained twist or transformation of one or more story elements, purposely altered to resonate with audiences. Compare to straight retelling, above.

**Parody**[4]–pokes fun at a tale type, such as fairy tales, or a specific story, like Cinderella.

**Postmodern**–refers to a contemporary style of art and literature that incorporates parody, intertextuality, and self-reference; often reinterprets social and literary thought.[5]

**Mash-Up**–when story elements from two or more pre-existing stories are included in a single new tale.

**Personal Folktale**–a term we coined to describe a storytwisting tale type where a folktale is told as a personal story, as if it happened to the storyteller.

**Story Rap**–a traditional story told in rap style. Story rap is the term we use to designate rap versions of stories.

**Historical Fiction Folktale**–a term we developed to describe a traditional story that is reset in a time period of the past.

**Wordplay Story**–a traditional tale retold in a number of playful, linguistic formats, such as puns or spoonerisms (where the speaker transposes the initial sounds or letters of two or more words–a pack of lies vs. a lack of pies).

A story is *retold* when a platform storyteller or author hears or reads a story and recasts it into his or her own language. Finally, McDonald indicates that the words *adapted* and *retold* are interchangeable.[6] For storytwisting purposes, there is a need for an additional category, to denote stories with an intermediate degree of alteration, tales that are less than fractured and more than adapted or retold. The term *adapted retelling* fulfills that need. Further discussion of adapted retelling follows.

For purposes of this book, we distinguish storytwisted from straight or untwisted tales. Straight stories are adapted or retold tales in a storyteller's own words. A storytwisted tale is defined as an adapted or retold story whose function goes beyond a straight, faithful rendering of a folk or fairy tale. Storytwisted tales with intertextual recognition, self-awareness, shaken expectations, and/or implied or explicit social commentary are fractured. Storytwisted tales devoid of such intentions are adapted retellings. Generally speaking, storytwisted tales differ from untwisted stories in one important way. Where straight retellings present an intact tale, storytwisted ones, like fractured stories and adapted retellings, carry a sustained twist or transformation of at least one story element, purposefully altered to heighten the story's resonance with audiences. For more discussion about retelling, see Chapter Two: "Storytwisting Strategies".

## Storytwisting: A Transformational Process

When stories are told, stories are changed. This is the essence of the oral tradition. If the changes are subtle, the integrity of the traditional story is preserved in each retelling. Over time, this process yields a body of beloved stories that are familiar across generations and sometimes across cultures.

But when a familiar tale undergoes significant change, it is sometimes defined as a fractured tale. Fractured tales are familiar stories told in unexpected ways. They carry new messages, updated content, or offer a cockeyed view of beloved stories. Often humorous, sometimes poignant or searing, fractured tales pay tribute to tales of the past while winking at life in the present.[7] A straight, un-fractured retelling represents a story in much the same way that a painted portrait represents the likeness of a person. In contrast, a fractured story is more like a Picasso, with a rearrangement and exaggeration of features that are re-formed into an unexpected, artistic whole.

Fractured stories work best when based on source stories that are familiar to the audience and the storyteller, such as cultural stories told within a culture. When fractured stories are told, the comfort of the familiar tale juxtaposed against the revelations of a reimagined version offers cultural insights that resonate with audiences. They often also make us laugh.

But what about stories told in multicultural settings?

While there are no specific tales that are native to every world culture,

---

### Fractured Stories vs. Fractured Fairy Tales

When stories are fractured, people often think about fairy tales, partly because famous childhood stories were humorously reimagined in an old cartoon segment called "Fractured Fairy Tales" from the *Rocky and Bullwinkle* television series. According to the scholar Ruth B. Bottigheimer, fractured fairy tales are based on traditional fairy tales. She further explains that parodies and fractured fairy tales are similar, but parodies have a different purpose. Whereas "parodies mock individual tales and the genre as a whole, fractured fairy tales, with a reforming intent, seek to impart updated social and moral messages."[8] Scholarly thought about fractured fairy tales is very important for storytellers to review, but the term itself is a bit confining. In addition to fairy tales, other story types can be fractured, like local legends, Aesop's fables, urban legends, and tall tales. For that reason, when we use the term "fractured story," we mean any story type that was or will be fractured or parodied, including fairy tales.

---

there is, for better or for worse, a body of stories that cross cultural and national borders. To borrow a term used by the scholar Donald Haase, these stories are transcultural.[9] Many cultures know them. They form the canon of European-derived folk and fairy tales told in America.[10] Filling library bookshelves, these stories are taught in schools, are depicted on stage and screen, and appear in the visual arts in Western culture. "The Tortoise and the Hare" and "Cinderella" are two examples of that sort of tale. Etched into the popular imagination, these stories are recognized by people of many different cultures and age groups. Because they are familiar to many people, they make excellent fodder for fractured stories.

The story-making approach for fractured tales can work equally well on unfamiliar stories. As our Irish storyteller demonstrated, audiences enjoyed his tale even though they didn't recognize the tale upon which it was based. They heard one story while we heard two. Furthermore, although there was one dominant message of his story, audience members experienced different story genres. Those who did not know his Jewish source listened to what we call an adapted retelling. Those of us who knew the source tale heard a fractured one.

Both tale types result from a transformation process, a process we call Storytwisting. While that process is the same for both, the difference between them lies in the intention. Fractured stories are a meta experience—both the older story and the new one are recognized by the audience. Reverberant echoes bounce from story to story to storyteller to story listener. In contrast, adapted retellings have no submersed agenda, no self-referential content or in-jokes. There are no reverberant echoes to excite or distract listeners. This critical difference, the awareness of one story or multiples, affects the composition and performance of such tales.

At its heart, reverberant echoes are what literary scholars call intertextual dialogue,[11] or *intertextuality*.[12] A fractured tale is characterized by a dialogue or conversation between two or more texts at once, the one being told and another source tale.[13] A writer or performer is aware of this "double exposure"[14] from start to finish. Like a tour guide at a history site, the performer highlights connections with grand flourishes or sedate subtlety. Audience members in the know are privy to nuanced meaning through explicit and implied narrative commentary in the new piece.

When an *unfamiliar* story is transformed in this manner, the result isn't a fractured story with intertextuality. But it isn't exactly a straight retelling either. To borrow a word used by the great folklorist Vladmir Propp,[15] the story's "function" in that case is not to create intertextual dialogue and make social or literary commentary. It serves other functions.

One might choose to alter an unfamiliar tale for many reasons. A storyteller may want to make the story's cultural context more familiar to an audience, as the Irish storyteller did. In the classroom, a teacher can set a story in a new era and stitch historical context and content right into a pre-existing narrative to deepen a history lesson. At home, a father can pique his daughter's interest in language and change the animals in a classic story to her favorite critters. Families may personalize a folktale as if it happened in their neighborhood as a homeschooling exercise or project for a family reunion. That secondary function, the one beyond the perpetuation of a story, is embedded in the way the new tale is written.

## Use of Terms

For purposes of this book, when we use the term audience, it refers to story readers and/or listeners and applies to performing storytellers, students, and writers. When we specify listeners, the content targets storytellers who tell stories at live events.

We use a bevy of terms to describe the storytwisted tales and the stories upon which they are based. Our choice of multiple terms is not a result of indecisiveness. It reflects our desire to employ a variety of words for reader interest and to specify nuanced meaning when necessary. In some instances, we refer to storytwisted products by specific names, such as story rap, wordplay story, mash-up, or one of our own invention—the personal folktale. The words that appear in the table below, beneath the heading of *Base Tale*, refer to stories and texts like "Rapunzel" and "The Gingerbread Man." While every story created through our approach is storytwisted, there are additional terms that we use to denote such tales, and those terms appear under the heading *Storytwisted Tale*.

### *Terminology*

| Base Tale | Storytwisted Tale |
| --- | --- |
| Traditional | Reimagined |
| Well-known, widely-known | Revised |
| Familiar | Re-envisioned |
| Root | Fractured, Fractured retelling |
| Familiar | Reinterpreted |
| Old or older | Reconfigured |
| Classic | Newfangled |
| Prior | Postmodernized |
| Pre-existing | Adapted retelling |
| Foundation | Remixed |
| Source | Reinvented |

## The Legalities and Ethics of Storytwisting

We are not legal experts and cannot provide professional guidance on these matters. Even so, these issues are important to raise.

It is up to you to determine that your source story is free and clear of copyright restrictions. You don't want to waste your time working on material that others may think they own. You don't want to get either yourself or your clients into legal trouble. If there is any uncertainty, we would advise you to seek permission from the copyright holder.

Teachers, for whom there are fair use exceptions, may have greater latitude in what they can do with copyrighted materials in a classroom setting. We suggest you check with professionals at your school or where you obtained your degree for advice.

---

### Origins and Originality

The array of terms that we use to describe base tales purposely excludes the word original. It is not possible to identify one original piece in the world of folk and fairy tales. Folklorists spend lifetimes tracking stories. Ethereal and hard to hold, they are passed by word of mouth, written down, lifted out of print and back to the oral tradition, integrated into popular culture, and find their way back to print again. Even an iconic story in the classical canon, like Charles Perrault's "Little Red Riding Hood," didn't originate with him. The story is rooted in folklore. While the Perrault story might serve as the sole source of a storytwisted piece, it is not correct to refer to it as the original "Red Riding Hood" tale.[16] The word original pertains more to twisted stories. A world of creative thought, language, integration, and ideas come together to produce such tales, and while it is true that they are based on a pre-existing source or sources, they can sparkle with originality, wit, and thoughtfulness.

---

One way that some storytellers approach this is to abide by *the rule of three*, a guideline associated with Margaret Read McDonald. If you can find three different versions of the same folktale, the common wording and shared narrative framework are probably in the public domain.[17] A number of folktale collections are in the public domain. Other texts, such as fractured versions of stories that are based on folktales, are not folktales themselves. They are original pieces with copyright protections.

Just because a book, television show, song, story, or movie suggests that a tale is traditional, it doesn't mean that the entirety of its contents is in the public domain. Fairy and folk tales have wended their way into popular culture, and while some of that content is public domain, some of it is the intellectual property of individuals, businesses, or institutions. It is up to you to create ethically. Stories abound with adaptive promise, it takes time and focus to discover what will work for you. Protect yourself against copyright violations. Research your sources to make sure they are in the public domain. If there is any doubt, seek permission from rights holders.

## Ethics and Culture

There is a saying, "You can't hate someone whose story you know."[18] To this we would add, *you can't hate a people whose stories you know.*

In our own storytelling work, one reason we share traditional folktales, myths, and wonder tales is to promote dignified, cultural understanding across cultures.[19] Because such tales are not widely known, we present them straight, not as reimagined retellings. We choose words, musical accompaniment, and linguistic ornamentation that respects the culture of origin. Filtered in this way, through a storyteller's authentic voice and performance style, the oldest stories can resonate with modern audiences.

*Stories beget understanding.*
*Understanding begets respect.*
*Respect begets justice.*
*Justice begets peace.*

*That is the power of Story.*
Antonio Rocha [20]

Storytellers who share traditional tales proudly connect audiences with the rich tapestry of culture and history that is woven in and around them. To do so responsibly and ethically, culture and story are researched with an eye to understanding language, cultural symbols, and meaning.[21]

In addition to studying multiple versions of the tale whenever possible, storytellers learn about cultures and story meaning directly from members of those cultures.[22] Storytellers also evaluate their sources. Was the story collected and rewritten by someone who didn't understand the culture? Was it respectfully retold by a conscientious storyteller or folklorist? Was the tale gathered and promulgated by the people who tell it? Finding and confirming a story's provenance pays homage to its culture of origin. It also allows us to make informed, sensitive choices about stories so that we can represent values, images, and symbols with respect.

The sharing of cultural stories is complicated.[23] While the well-researched sharing of folktales from other cultures is acceptable in many circumstances, there are also situations when storytellers must refrain from telling cultural tales without permission. Not every culture wants its stories told by outsiders.

Here is an example from the United States. In Native American traditions it is widely expected that professional storytellers ask a culturally knowledgeable tribal member's permission to tell any of its stories.[24] But for many, that is not enough.

Native American history is a powerful and poignant demonstration of the wholesale exploitation of peoples and the appropriation of their cultures by outsiders. Hundreds of nations have had to fight for the right to dignity, to speak for themselves, and govern their lives.[25] For that reason, when well-meaning outsiders request permission to tell a story, even though the request is intended with respect, it can still feel like an imposition—or even an invasion—to Native peoples. To outsiders, making the request may feel like we are honoring Natives voices, but to insiders it can be perceived as yet one more attempt to silence Native voices and substitute our own.

When we ask for permission to tell a story, we ask one person to speak on behalf of a whole culture. Speaking directly with tribal members to learn about their cultures and then asking permission to tell a tale is a step in the right direction. But it is *not* enough—an interview does not build a relationship with the community to whom the stories really belong.[26]

When permission to tell a Native American tale is offered, cultural respect doesn't end there. The storyteller must honor the gift of permission by telling the story as it was given, not by recreating it anew. *In situations like these, we do not believe that Storytwisting is acceptable.*

Our goal is to share thoughts for your consideration. Only you can decide what feels ethical and proper. Only you know your cultural identity and what tales you can carry respectfully. Ultimately, it is the responsibility of every tale-teller to determine the acceptability of telling another culture's tale, to seek permission to do so when needed, and to find a different story to tell if permission is denied.[27]

## So What Stories Can We Twist?

As in all things, it is the personal decision of each writer/storyteller to determine what stories to twist. Our own storytwisted pieces typically derive from our personal heritages. We are selective about which traditional stories we alter to support our desire to respect and impart cultural understanding. Generally speaking, we twist tales from our personal Euro-American ethnic traditions, local tales, American stories, tall tales, urban legends, and most frequently, the broad-based "famous" traditional fable, folk and fairy tale canon that is shared across many cultures and communities. Like any guideline, there are exceptions. In Chapter Five, our faithful retelling in sonnet form of a Buddhist Jataka tale, "The Quail Sonnet", demonstrates such a case. It is important to note that whenever we make an exception, we carefully consider the cultural and historical implications and the effects on meaning if reinterpretation or parody come into play. There are many stories out there that we would never twist.

## Structure of the Book

This book is designed to be used by storytellers, writers, educators, home-schooling families, and older students. You can read it from start to finish, skip over the sections that define literary terms if you already know them, or read the chapters in any order you wish. (The story types in Chapter Three, "Fracture Point: Setting" and Chapter Four, "Fracture Point: Point of View" are easier to execute than those of later chapters.) If you choose to play reader hopscotch, we urge you to review the second chapter first so that you understand the underlying Storytwisting philosophy and principles.

Along the way, you will bump into quotes from Lewis Carroll's *Alice in Wonderland*. They illustrate the parallels between Storytwisting and Alice's experience of the upside down and unexpected world of Wonderland. Carroll's rich language expresses how there is method in madness and meaning in mayhem. These are emblematic components of the Storytwisting process.

This introductory chapter offers a basic idea about the book and describes its structure and dominant terminology. Chapter Two, "Storytwisting Strategies" describes the Storytwisting approach and provides a philosophical and theoretical background for this storytelling model.

The balance of the book offers stories, ideas, and tried-and-true techniques for crafting and telling twisted tales. These how-to or practical chapters touch upon the interplay of six literary elements: *setting, point of view, rhyme, wordplay, character,* and *mash-up.*

The practical chapters feature one to three stories each. While every chapter has different topics and issues, there are consistent sections throughout:

*Twist the Focus*—Each chapter begins by describing the literary or story element that will be fractured or twisted.

*Do the Twist*—We explain the process for writing a featured type of story with some suggestions and guidelines.

*Storytwist*—A sample story of our own creation is featured.

*Twisting Tips*—A section where we provide additional suggestions and guidelines targeted to the featured story type.

*Twist for Thought*—Every chapter concludes with a discussion about relevant, applicable issues, such as memorization training, cultural sensitivity, and storytelling with social awareness.

The following features also appear throughout the book:

*Insets*—These highlighted boxes accentuate content that digs deeper into particular ideas.

*Teaching Twists*—These highlighted boxes and sidebars contain content or exercises for educators.

*General Twisting Tips*—These boxes and sidebars bring attention to tips that refer to the use of this book or to the general process of Storytwisting. Because these important considerations can apply to any and all types of twisted tales, they are sprinkled throughout the book.

There is a cultural imperative to re-create stories.[28] With the imprimatur of generations and cultures, many stories form the narrative foundation of childhood. As adults, these tales reside in overflowing, antique trunks in the attics of our memories. Opening those trunks and trying on the old stories in a new day and time is as fun as dress-up games and as instructive as a good TED talk.

# NOTES

1. Lewis Carroll, *Alice's Adventures in Wonderland*, Full Text of *Alice's Adventures in Wonderland*, August 12, 2006, accessed July 10, 2016. https://archive.org/stream/alicesadventures19033gut/19033.txt

2. Not all literary fairy tales are purely original works. Many were probably influenced or inspired by tales already in the oral tradition.

3. "Double vision" is the title of a chapter of a fairy-tale history book that carries the meaning of intertextuality—and then some. Marina Warner, *A Short History of the Fairy Tale*. (Oxford: Oxford University Press, 2014), 146-157.

4. Linda Hutcheon, *Theory of Adaptation*. (Abingdon, Oxon: Routledge, 2006), 3. Hutcheon indicates that a relationship to prior texts is a key characteristic for parodies and fractured stories, but they differ in an important way. Fractured stories proclaim a relationship to a particular text whereas parodies are not as direct about that relationship.

5. Postmodernism is a literary style that is very complex indeed. One fabulous condensed definition of the concept is this: "Make it new, then make it newer. Differently." John Sutherland, *How Literature Works: 50 Key Concepts*. (Oxford, New York: Oxford University Press, 2011), 139.

6. Margaret Read McDonald, e-mail message to author, February 23, 2016.

7. This is one way that we describe a "fractured story." The definition of the term is as variable as the ways that a single story can be fractured. For an intriguing and in-depth scholarly treatment of what makes a fractured fairy tale, see Vanessa Joosen. *Critical and Creative Perspectives on Fairy Tales: An Intertextual Dialogue between Fairy-Tale Scholarship and Postmodern Retellings*. (Detroit: Wayne State University Press, 2013), 9-48.

8. Ruth B. Bottigheimer, "Fractured Fairy Tales," in *The Oxford Companion to Fairy Tales: The Western Fairy Tale Tradition from Medieval to Modern*, ed. Jack Zipes. (Oxford, New York: Oxford University Press, 2010), 172.

9. Fairy and folktale expert Donald Haase notes that it makes sense to be "thinking of fairy tales transculturally, as they exist across conventional geographic, linguistic, and cultural borders." Donald Haase, "Decolonizing Fairy-Tale Studies," *Marvels & Tales* 24, no.1, 2010: 31. Accessed May 20, 2016. http://digitalcommons.wayne.edu/marvels/vol24/iss1/1

   While Haase focuses much of his discussion on fairy-tale translations and collections, it is not unreasonable to extrapolate his idea to folktales as well. The thrust of his argument is that it makes sense to add a third analytic orientation to fairy tale studies. In addition to two longstanding—and somewhat opposing—approaches: a) viewing stories as socio-historical products of cultures, and b) universalism—which focuses on the common features of stories—Haase argues that their translations from one language to another, their proliferation across different forums (such as literary or stage), and their re-settings in new cultures makes them *transcultural* products, which begs for a transcultural analytic approach.

10. Scholars often refer to these stories in short form as the European canon. We sometimes make use of this shorthand in the book as well. But not all storytwistable tales fit in that category. See "Storytwisting: A Transformational Process" in this chapter for a discussion on this.

11. Maria Nikolajeva, *Children's Literature Comes of Age: Toward a New Aesthetic.* (New York and London: Garland Publishing, 1996), 153, 181-186.

12. The term intertextuality was coined by Julia Kristeva, a European theorist who is renowned in several fields of thought. See Julia Kristeva and Toril Moi, "Word, Dialogue, and Novel" (1980), in The Kristeva Reader (New York, NY: Columbia University Press, 1986), 37.

13. We use this term broadly. Since there are multiple versions of most traditional stories and fairy tales, or even multiple types of sources (such as literary and oral versions), it is up to the writer to identify which source or sources are to be used as the foundation for a reimagined tale.

14. Cristina Bacchilega,. *Fairy Tales Transformed? Twenty-First-Century Adaptations and the Politics of Wonder.* (Detroit: Wayne State University Press, 2013), 31.

15. Vladimir Propp, *Morphology of the Folktale*, second ed., revised and edited by Louis. A. Wagner. (Austin & London: University of Texas Press, 1968). Originally published in Vladimir Propp, trans. Laurence Scott, *The Morphology of the Folktale.* (Bloomington: Research Center, Indiana University, 1958). Propp is known for his study of the constituent parts of folktales, like characters, their actions, and their functions in fairy tales; his work was seminal in the field of folklore analysis. Our use of the term is technically different than his because we apply it to a whole story, not its component parts. But the underlying meaning is consistent.

16. See generally, Alan Dundes, *Little Red Riding Hood: A Casebook.* (Madison: University of Wisconsin Press, 1989). Catherine Orenstein, *Little Red Riding Hood Uncloaked: Sex, Morality, and the Evolution of a Fairy Tale.* (New York: Basic Books, 2002). Jack Zipes., ed., *The Trials and Tribulations of Little Red Riding Hood*, 2nd Edition. (Routledge. 1993).

With so many versions of the same story swirling about in literature, the oral tradition, and popular culture, scholars have developed new terms to characterize the multiple media in which stories exist and are transmitted. For example, Cristina Baccilega presents us with a visual and compelling term, the "fairy-tale web" in Bacchilega, *Fairy Tale Transformed*, 18. To describe the wide range of printed media for folktales and the way that we use them, Donald Haase uses the word "hypertext." Donald Haase, "Hypertextual Gutenberg: The Textual and Hypertextual Life of

Folktales and Fairy Tales in English-Language Popular Print Editions." *Fabula* 47, no 3-4 (2006), 222–30

17. Kendall Haven and MaryGay Ducey, *Crash Course in Storytelling*. (Westport, CT: Libraries Unlimited, 2007), 102.

18. To the best of our knowledge, this is a proverb.

19. For an excellent read on promoting cultural understanding through story, see Melissa Heckler and Carol Birch. "Building Bridges with Stories." In *Storytelling Encyclopedia: Historical, Cultural, and Multiethnic Approaches to Oral Traditions Around the World*, ed. David Adams Leeming. (Phoenix, AZ: Oryx Press, 1997), 8-15.

20. Used with permission. Antonio Rocha, digital message with the author, June, 28, 2016. Antonio Rocha is a prominent storyteller, originally from Brazil, now residing in the United States, whose beautiful storytelling work carries him across the globe.

21. Anne Goding, *Storytelling: Reflecting on Oral Narratives and Cultures*, 2nd ed.. San Diego: Cognella Publishing, 2016.

22. Heckler & Birch, "Building Bridges with Stories," 12.

23. See, generally, Goding, *Storytelling: Reflections on Oral Narratives and Cultures*, 2016, Heckler and Birch, *Building Bridges*, 1997, and the work of Susan O'Halloran, a storyteller whose expertise is devoted to culture and diversity, http://susanohalloran.com/.

24. A person who is a member of a culture does not necessarily have the understanding to interpret stories and give permission to outsiders to tell them. It is up to you to determine if the person whose permission you seek is culturally knowledgeable.

25. In 2007, the United Nations published an important document in consultation with Native peoples. The United Nations Declaration on the Rights of Indigenous Peoples. Article 11.1, states: "Indigenous peoples have the right to practice and revitalize their cultural traditions and customs. This includes the right to maintain, protect and develop the past, present and future manifestations of their cultures, such as archaeological and historical sites, artefacts, designs, ceremonies, technologies and visual and performing arts and literature." United Nations Declaration on the Rights of Indigenous Peoples, p. 9. Accessed 5/21/16, http://www.un.org/esa/socdev/unpfii/documents/DRIPS_en.pdf

26. Gayle Ross, telephone conversation with the author, May 15, 2016. This section of the book is infused with Gayle's expertise.

27. Gayle Ross kindly gave us permission to tell a Cherokee tale many years ago. The language and meaning of our version is very similar to hers. It is a straight retelling; it is not fractured or an adapted retelling. But we altered one thing to make the story "ours." We incorporate musical accompaniment, and received her permission to do so.

28. Jeri Burns and Barry Marshall, "Revitalizing Traditional Stories: A Cultural Imperative." Paper presented at Ananse SoundSplash Storytelling Conference and Festival, Kingston and Montego Bay, Jamaica, West Indies, November 19-25, 2014.

*Alice: "Would you tell me please which way I ought to go from here?"*

*Cheshire Cat: "That depends a good deal on where you want to get to."*

LEWIS CARROLL[1]

CHAPTER TWO

# Storytwisting Strategies

STORYTWISTED TALES ARE A GREAT WAY TO MAKE CONNECTIONS with audiences and to re-connect with our own experiences of traditional literature. As we write this book, we are working up a fractured version of the "Snow White" story. It is the first time we have attempted this tale because Jeri harbored disdain for the title character ever since she was a child. But the writing process broadened her relationship with Snow White. Jeri puts it this way:

> I never liked Snow White. But, through fracture and twisting, I've learned that there is more to her than petulance and a desire for indentured servitude to dwarfs or princes. These characteristics offended me when I was growing up, and when we started telling stories, I didn't want to imprint another generation of children with them. But our Snow White is different.

Thanks to the Storytwisting process, we are no longer constrained by the paternalistic themes of the widely-known version. A new side of the Snow White character has emerged. We never would have seen our way to reinterpreting the story for modern times *without* twisting the familiar tale. Without twisting it, we never would have made peace with this fairy tale and found a fun new way to tell it.

When we tell stories straight, we exert ourselves to preserve their cultural integrity as fully and faithfully as we can. But the ones that are storytwisted— from quirky odes to word nerds to the simplest retelling of a tale in a new time or place—those are the tales that carve a special place in our hearts because we've gone through the journey of creating a reconfigured piece. Storytwisting changes our relationship with those stories. The novelty that we, as creators, perceive when we develop a new story impacts our connection to it and stays with the story from conception to performance on stage. It invigorates our work as artists.

We have twisted many tales. Yet every time we start a new one, we are as surprised about the process as we were the first time. Traditional stories and fairy tales are rich fountains of image and meaning, and they have perpetuated for good reasons. They touch the human condition and resonate with cultures all over the world.

Transformations and twists can be applied in a multitude of ways to any public domain story. Although creativity and intuition are key components, it helps to have guidelines. While teaching workshops, graduate, and public school classes, we developed a set of usable tools, drawn from our writing experience, that help others craft their own twisted tales. Not only is Storytwisting useful for reimagining traditional folk and fairy tales, it can also be used in educational settings to teach the literary elements that form the architecture of narrative.

## A Way to Look at How Stories Fracture: The Rock Metaphor

The term *Storytwisting* connotes flexibility. Although bending and shaping story material is certainly part of the process, it is not as taffy-like as that sounds. Whether the new tale is a wildly re-envisioned parody, a faithful rendering in a historical setting, or a prose tale told entirely in rhyme, all storytwisted tales begin with a *fracture*, which we call *the fracture point*.

We thought seriously about this the year that our son took earth science. He bubbled about his science labs at supper. One night, he recounted the process of breaking rocks into new forms. "Dad, if you hit a rock just right, a piece of it breaks off and makes it look like a baby version of the first rock." Then he pulled some rocks out of his backpack and poured them on the supper table. "You see?" He pointed to a pair of rocks, one smaller than the other. "I broke that small one off!" he said proudly.

"Look!" our son continued, "The two rocks look like each other. That's how we know that the little one came from the big one." He explained that a resemblance between rocks is crucial to identifying the new rock as one that was fractured from the old.

A fractured rock exposes material that was embedded in the "parent" rock. So does a fractured story. After the fracture, something new is brought to light, something that couldn't be seen when the pieces were fused together. Like tiny windows into time, the newly exposed side of a story offers a glimpse into cultural life of the past and how it applies to the present—or how it doesn't. It is like a blank page, waiting for explanatory words and images.

The rock analogy made a world of sense to us. But what sealed the deal was when our son continued his earth science lab story. "The teacher told us that the best way to make a baby rock is to use a tool." He smiled. "I chose a hammer." Then he raised an imaginary hammer high over a dinner biscuit. "Mr. Nightingale told us that we have to aim carefully when we hit the rock, or we won't get a nice, new one." Zack guided his hand down through the air and broke the biscuit in two.

A tool helps to break rocks without shattering them. A tool starts the process that produces a baby rock. A tool can also be used to find a tale's fracture point. For us, this tool is Storytwisting.

**Retelling**

Before sharing strategies for Storytwisting, it is helpful to review what it means to retell traditional tales. Myths, legends, and folktales are windows into the past and snapshots of culture. Telling these tale pays tribute to human history and world culture; it also encourages folklore to persist.

In addition to developing cultural knowledge, traditional stories offer primal, prototypical story vocabulary. Understanding the structure, symbols, and meaning in traditional tales improves the writing and telling of all stories, including fractured ones.

How does one retell a story? Retelling a story means restating the basic plot points and images of a traditional story and representing them so that listeners recognize the retold story as a version of a literary or oral tale told throughout time. Retelling creates faithful renderings of stories. Nevertheless, it is not a copy-and-paste process.[2] Professional storytellers evaluate several versions of the same traditional story to find common threads. After careful consideration, new language is composed to convey those commonalities. That is retelling in a nutshell.

Memorization of a story's text is not the same as retelling it. There are some storytelling traditions where stories are passed intact from one tradition bearer to another.[3] This bardic process of traditional cultures requires words *and* storyline to remain exact.[4]. In contrast, retold stories, as we define them, have an intact storyline with words composed and arranged by the storyteller.

## An Example

When telling a story like "Goldilocks and the Three Bears," particular events must be there for it to be a faithful rendering of the widely known tale. It features three bears, porridge served in three bowls, and Goldilocks. After the bears leave to take a walk, Goldilocks enters the house, tests the porridge, chairs, and beds, before falling asleep in the smallest bed. The tale ends when she runs off upon the bears' return.

What we have presented are recognizable elements of this tale, which storytellers affectionately call the story *bones*. In addition, there are iconic phrases about the porridge being "too hot" or "too cold," and the chairs and beds being "too hard, too soft, and just right." Furthermore, there are repeated refrains, like "someone's been sitting in my chair," "someone's been eating my porridge," and "someone's been sleeping in my bed."

This content forms a very basic storyline gleaned from reading or hearing multiple versions of the story.[5] They are the common threads. With original language woven around these common threads, a new retelling of "The Three Bears" is crafted. If the tale is lifted out of its usual forest setting and placed in another time or place, the resulting story is what we define as an adapted retelling. If instead, we reverse roles so that a baby golden bear enters a girl's home, that is an example of a fractured story. Both fractured stories and adapted retellings are produced through Storytwisting. (See Chapter One inset, "Definitions of Key Terms Used in this Book")

## The Storytwisting Process

Articulation of the Storytwisting Method first occurred while we were teaching graduate storytelling classes. Our students wanted to learn how to fracture stories, so we conceived a model to teach different ways to accomplish it. We quickly realized that it was more than an academic exercise. It could be of practical use to storytellers, writers, and others. As it became a regular feature of our workshops and classes, we christened the method Storytwisting, after our storytelling recording series, *Classics with a Twist*.

Storytwisting starts just like a board game. Imagine a game dial or spinner, like the one from the classic game called Twister. Its appearance is similar to an analog clock or watch. Instead of a circle of numbers for telling time, however, the Twister dial is framed with a circle of colors. It also has a pointer, like a clock's hand. With one spin of the Twister dial, the pointer goes round and round until it rests on, or selects, one color. The dial tells the player what color is selected for action in the next turn.

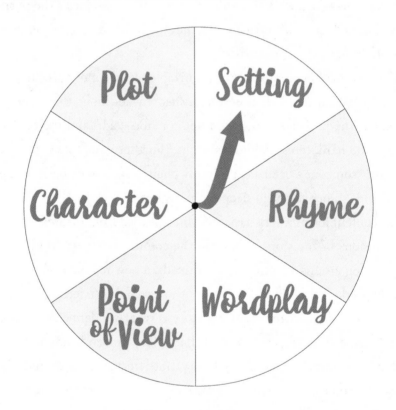

The Storytwisting dial is a conceptual tool that works just like game dials. Before twisting a story, we spin this imaginary dial to guide our intention. Instead of colors or numbers, however, our dial is framed with several classic literary elements of stories. Every twist of the dial highlights or selects a different literary element. When we speak about spinning the Storytwisting dial, we speak figuratively. Instead of spinning an actual pointer, we consciously select one literary element—the fracture point—for our new story.

Six literary elements appear on the Storytwisting dial, though there certainly could be more. Entire books and in-depth websites are devoted to defining narrative literary elements. Such compilations are encyclopedic in scope. Despite the wide array of options in the literary marketplace, it is generally agreed that all stories have certain basic components, like *plot, character,* and *point of view.* In addition to those, the Storytwisting dial also includes *wordplay, rhyme,* and *setting.* We selected these because they are the six literary elements that we twist the most.

Suppose we decide to storytwist the tale of Rapunzel. Our first step would be to twist the dial and choose a story element. Let's say that we select point of view as the fracture point. Instead of telling the story in the voice of an impartial, third person narrator, we tell it from the perspective of the tower. With that intention, we are now ready to begin the writing process.

We begin with a review of the basic Rapunzel storyline. Confined by a witch in a door-less tower, Rapunzel's only means of human contact occurs when she lets down her legendary, golden, hair. It is so long that her step-mother the witch climbs it like a rope to Rapunzel's window. One day, a prince discovers the secret and develops a relationship with the young woman in the tower. Trouble ensues. After banishment, blindness, and twin babies, many versions of the story conclude with a happy reunion between Rapunzel and the Prince.

Once we start writing, we enter a trial and error phase. To determine what other parts of the story need to change, we engage in literary massage therapy, twisting plot, motifs, and messages to fit the new story. Periodically we stop and scrutinize the tale like a rock under a microscope. By turning it this way and that, we study the surfaces of the newly formed story to see what we learn about the reimagined tale and how it can inform the writing. We continually look back at our source Rapunzel tale(s) to see what insights the fracture and twists reveal when compared against the widely-known story.

Some changes are decided consciously in advance. Others are revealed through writing. There is no stiff formula about what must or must not change.

Every shift does not have to be related to point of view. The new story does not have to rigidly adhere to every detail in the familiar Rapunzel narrative. Compositional decisions are guided by a *focused creative intention* on point of view and the story's function. Additional details, characters, and/or actions may have to change for the tale to work from the perspective of the tower. That is where twisting and flexibility comes in.

When it is complete, a new version of Rapunzel, "The Tower's Story," will be cohesive in its own right. But we are not done. We review every narrative alteration, alone and in combination, to make sure that the new tale still echoes the prior rendition. A storytwisted tale stands on its own *and* in harmony with its source. Making this work is an exciting tightrope walk.

### Twisting Tip

Intertextuality, a word that comes straight from the heart of the academy, captures an important concept related to storytwisting. As we describe it in Chapter One, intertextuality refers to the *reverberant echoes* between two or more stories, when one story subtly or boldly alludes to another. While "reverberant echoes" is an image-based phrase—a preferred mode of storytellers—intertextuality, an academic word, is ironically, more concise. That is why it is used frequently throughout the book. Since intertextuality is not a commonly known term, this definitional reminder is included for your convenience.

Twisting the dial on literary elements is a surprising process, just like fracturing rocks in an earth science lab. One hit with the hammer, and a piece of the rock breaks in an unexpected direction. It could just as easily have broken off in another. It is the same way with stories. Although we target a story element when we point the dial, we don't know what new side of the story will emerge after fracture. We can't guess all of its permutations. The unexpected makes the writing process revelatory, and as adventurous the story itself.

The Storytwisting Method focuses intention on one fracture point. In addition to fostering intertextual resemblance, the method serves another important purpose. The sea of possibility is endless when considering all that can be changed in a story. To behold the boundlessness at the shore of this sea is exciting! But it can be paralyzing. Storytwisting offers a way to navigate those waters.

## THE KITCHEN SINK ISSUE: AVOIDING PITFALLS

### Overtwisting

Whenever we do Storytwisting workshops, excited participants fracture the living daylights out of stories. Freed from the strictures of "how it is supposed to go," their creativity is unleashed. But this comes with a cost. Faced with limitless options, a newfangled story can run away like an off-leash dog. Free and independent, it embarks on a twisty journey, making unexpected detours, exploring uncharted terrain, and arriving at new destinations. The trouble is, sometimes it gets hopelessly lost.

Creativity is a wonderful thing. As great ideas pour forth, it is natural to want to use every one. But problems arise with overzealous creativity in fractured tales. We call it the kitchen sink issue.

After a glorious idea spree, it is tempting to put "everything including the kitchen sink" into a revised piece. But think about this. Every new idea represents a tweak or shift in the older tale. The more shifts there are, the harder it is to recognize a familiar story.

Furthermore, as the number of narrative tweaks increase, it becomes more and more difficult to incorporate them cohesively. A multitude of changes complicates the Storytwisting process. It can also make the writing process a stressful, managerial morass. Selectivity is paramount.

This is not to say that kitchen sink tales are invalid. Many brilliant, beautiful narratives arise from such inspired beginnings. But fractured stories are different animals. They contain more than a kernel of recognition or a few random pingbacks to a source story. When a legion of changes makes a new tale diverge significantly from its source, it is no longer a retelling of a story with reverberant echoes of a traditional source tale, but a parody of a genre.[6]

### Meaning

The kitchen sink issue manifests itself in yet another way. Students of storytwisting have an overarching desire to be clever. On one hand, that is to be expected. Such stories often *are* clever. But cleverness alone can't launch a story into someone's heart. Meaning is required.

Familiar stories have well-known themes and messages. They reflect societal issues and values in symbolic form. To mask that under a veil of cleverness imperils meaning. Most importantly, a loss of meaning severs the shivery connection that occurs when one is immersed in two stories at once.

To make meaning conscious, we now introduce another conceptual tool in the storytwisting toolbox, the Post-it note. Whenever we work on any type of story, we carefully craft language to describe our interpretation of the story's dominant message.[7] We affix that message, like a little Post-it note, to a written version of our story, or we commit it to memory. Before writing and rehearsing, we refer to that message. We keep it in mind throughout the entire creative process. The story's meaning influences the composition of language, imagery, characterization, and most everything else in our tale. Our goal is to be consistent with that idea, reinforcing the message with gentle linguistic brushstrokes as we go. If we retell "Cinderella" with a message about rags-to-riches, a consistent presentation would align descriptions and figurative language with a contrast between a state of poverty and affluence. If our dominant message is about hope, the text of our retelling might include words and imagery associated with trust, desire, and wishes. For storytwisted tales with intertextuality, we compose separate Post-it notes for the familiar tale and the remix. This is a challenging but rewarding part of the process for us and for our students.[8]

Think about it. Every source story is about something meaningful. A fractured tale reflects, restates, or twists that meaning and carries it to a new place. But a reimagined story only reaches that new plateau when an audience recognizes the location where the journey began.

The Storytwisting Method pushes back at the Kitchen Sink Issue by focusing on one fracture point at a time. Although it can't completely harness the tendency to over-create around a fracture, it sets limits. Over-creation is akin to scarring because it draws attention to the fact that a change occurred. It's usually best to let the change speak for itself. Furthermore, all storytwisting strategies set forth in this book prioritize meaning—as reminders to channel creativity in the service of the story, not the storyteller.

## The Rock Metaphor Revisited: Additional Considerations

Rocks with multiple fractures produce many new rocks. They can also be pulverized to powder. This makes it challenging or impossible to identify an original portion of rock in the rubble. It is also difficult a to detect a resemblance among rock pieces when one can no longer recognize which is the parent or child.

Novelty is certainly wrought from rock shards. Earth science teaches us that through heat or pressure, one rock can be transformed into another. But after so much processing, the new rock is not the same type of rock as its parent, the original rock. It falls into a different rock category altogether.[9]

The same thing happens with stories. A new story can be built from the pieces of wildly fractured pre-existing stories. The result might be an original, modern fairy tale, a brilliant epic parody, or a postmodern pastiche, but it won't necessarily be a storytwisted tale.[10] The resemblance between a re-envisioned piece and its traditional source connects the dots of meaning in ways that manifest a meaningful new tale, and a manageable one at that.[11]

It is not impossible to fracture stories in multiple ways at once. But unlike novels or full-length movie adaptations, where there is space for edifying and sifting through the instructive rubble, the relative brevity of folk and fairy tale length pieces makes it more challenging to manage multiple fracture points with elegance and coherence. Jessica Tiffin refers to this issue as "narrative insecurity."[12]

Our book is designed to help users achieve success, or—with a nod to Tiffin—*narrative security*. That is why we usually recommend a single fracture point and connection to a recognizable root tale. As you gain experience with the process, you can explore more advanced styles of Storytwisting.

## How it all connects: A Duncan Williamson Story

We must now share some wisdom that we received a long time ago. It has given us purpose in how we approach faithful retellings of cultural stories and storytwisted tales as well. Running like a seam of gold throughout our career, this wise conundrum was shared by a gentleman named Duncan Williamson.

Some years ago, we were invited to several festivals and events in the UK. At a festival in Northern Ireland, we were overjoyed to meet the fabled Duncan Williamson. He was a Scottish Traveller and storyteller whose education was built entirely on folktales and life experience. A walking library with over 2000 folktales swimming through his busy brain, Duncan Williamson was a tradition bearer and traditional storyteller par excellence.

Seizing an opportunity to learn from his expertise, we decided to ask him a question that burned in our storytelling hearts. We wanted to know his opinion, as an indigenous tradition bearer, about how much of a story must be kept intact for a story to be considered the same story, and how much could be changed.

We were standing outside a pub one evening when we cornered Duncan and asked. He gazed down at us and his watery blue eyes glistened. Duncan said in his rolling, musical Scots accent, "My dears, there are three things you can never change when you tell a story—the beginning, the middle, and the end. Other than that, you can change anything you want." To seal the deal, he beckoned us to share pints in the pub, along with secret sips of his very strong potcheen on the side.

Like a thought-provoking riddle tale, Duncan Williamson's wisdom offers a beautiful conundrum. That conundrum has been the bedrock of our storytelling craft ever since. Whether we retell stories straight or reimagine them in wacky ways, we follow his sage advice. Even when we change endings or muddle with story middles, his words always guide our work and our hearts.

And that, dears, is our conundrum for you.

## Twist for Thought: Reflections About Mirrors and Rocks

The image of a fractured mirror is one way to understand what fractured stories are like. When gazing into a fractured mirror, aspects of one's countenance are distorted or masked by breaks in the glass and the angles at which the shards repose. Just as a mirror reflects a face, a fractured story reflects a previously existing story or tale type. When we look into mirrors, we are aware that we are gazing at our reflections. Likewise, fractured stories trigger a bit of cultural memory. Just as looking into a shattered mirror results in our seeing parts of ourselves, examining a fractured story results in our seeing parts of a pre-existing story and the connotations of that story. When you—as a storyteller or writer—fracture a story, you expect your audience to accept that you are referencing the source story's content and connotations. At the same time, you and the audience understand that those references are implicit in the reimagined tale along with original meanings.

The mirror metaphor is useful for looking at what makes a fractured story, but it has limitations for compositional purposes. When a mirror is fractured, glass may crack in only one or two places, leaving the mirror mostly intact. Or, it may shatter into many pieces. Breakage is seemingly random. While you can deftly rearrange the glass shards into a new creative work, you cannot directly influence the size of each piece or how many there are. The scatter of glass is produced by many factors beyond your control. Moving back to the realm of narrative—like mirrors, stories can be mildly or wildly fractured products. However, the fracturing *process* deserves consideration as well.[13]

Building a coherent, multi-faceted story is usually *not* the result of a hit-or-miss approach to writing. Similarly, fracturing a story is seldom a haphazard process. One might say that it is comparable to building demolition. Engineers blow buildings up—but not randomly. Explode and destroy, action movie style, is not their intent. To ensure city safety, engineers cause the building to implode upon itself and collapse almost neatly. Their process is *artfully designed.*

*E.L. Doctorow once said that writing is "like driving a car at night. You never see further than your headlights, but you can make the whole trip that way."*[15]

If we transfer the mirror metaphor to the realm of narrative, it correctly implies that stories can mildly break, wildly shatter, or scatter their shards into the wind. But the more we shatter mirrors or stories, the less we can discern a reflection. The more a source story is shattered, the more difficult it is to recognize the root tale in its new form. For these reasons, we do not recommend placing intertextuality and story integrity at the mercy of a random fracturing process.

The mirror analogy is one way to think about the fractured story as a product.[14] But we need a way to think about process too. That is why we developed the metaphor about rocks.

Like mirrors, rocks fracture, producing two or more distinct things— rocks, fragments, shards, particles. Although a rock is different than a mirror, opportunities for reflection, distortion, and referential-awareness remain. Instead of mirror-like reflections, fractured rocks present alternative facets of the original. Each sliver of rock tells the observer something about the original, or *parent* rock. Size and surface dis-similarities between the original rock and its own remnants present a similar idea of distortion. Also like the mirror, the split or shattered rock presents newly-revealed aspects of the original rock, which may be displayed in new configurations.

The rock metaphor for fracturing stories suggests tools for a teachable process to create engaging stories. There is design in the fracturing of rocks because the elements of a rock, the minerals, often break in predictable ways. Like rocks, stories have elements. Rather than smashing story elements with reckless abandon, methodical writers will target one element at a time, thereby stewarding a new story into being.

The rock analogy offers other important ideas for story assembly, shaping, and drafting. When a rock breaks, a new side of the source rock is exposed and a new rock is born from that fissure. Just as the geologist studies shards or drills cores to learn about the source rock, writers and those who craft stories will find new aspects of a source tale by exposing its facets through fracture. We can dig and learn and share something brand new while reflecting on a shared connection to something that came before.

The rock and mirror analogies both allow a writer to compare a source to a fractured product but the rock metaphor carries the creative process one step further. The new rock or shard may be rough around the edges, particularly where it broke off from its source. Its jagged facets can be smoothed and refined and the entire rock can be polished. Similarly, a fractured story requires creative attention to smooth, refine, twist, and polish it for sharing with others.

Finally, the fracturing process can also be applied to other styles of story adaptation. While adapted retellings do not usually incorporate the fractured story's signature characteristics of intertextuality and self-reference, they do share another one. There is some distortion when an adapted retelling is compared directly against its pre-existing source because the new tale carries a sustained transformation. But unlike fractured tales, the distortion of an adapted story pertains more to a story's structural characteristics than to its meaning.

Creativity and artful design are at the heart of storytwisting. After a story is fractured from its source, it is "taken in hand." Like a rock, it is twisted and turned so that it can be evaluated from all sides. Artistic choice determines which edges to sculpt, what to leave raw and natural, and where sharpening or polishing bring artistic vision to light. Imaginative ingenuity and knowledge of narrative structure work in tandem to transform that new piece into a meaningful tale. This exciting process is experimental, intuitive, creative, and brilliantly fun. Welcome to the fascinating world of Storytwisting.

# NOTES

1. Lewis Carroll, *Alice's Adventures in Wonderland*, full text of *Alice's Adventures in Wonderland*, August 12, 2006, accessed July 10, 2016. https://archive.org/stream/alicesadventures19033gut/19033.txt

2. The scholar Jack Zipes differentiates between "duplicates" and "revisions." A duplicate of a story is not intended to rethink a pre-existing source, but to replicate its images and content. This idea corresponds to some degree with the idea of a straight retelling. A revision, on the other hand, involves a conscious re-orientation of meaning or ideas to conform with contemporary times and/or the viewpoint of the creator. This roughly corresponds to our term for storytwisted tales, including fractured and adapted retellings. See Jack Zipes, *Fairy Tale as Myth/Myth as Fairy Tale*. Lexington: University Press of Kentucky, 1994, 8-11.

   Amie Doughty embraces a similar term in her study of updated children's tales. "Revisions of folktales, however, are versions of folktales, usually written, that take traditional tales, often well-known ones, and alter them in a much more elaborate manner than retellings." See Amie Doughty. *Folktales Retold: A Critical Overview of Stories Updated for Children*. Jefferson: McFarland, 2006, 11.

3. Anne Pellowski, *The World of Storytelling: A Practical Guide to the Origins, Development and Applications of Storytelling*, exp. and rev. ed. (Bronx: H.W. Wilson Company, 1990).

4. Richard Bauman, *Verbal Art as Performance*. (Prospect Heights: Waveland Press, Inc., 1997). Bauman's seminal study was influential in the world of folklore and the study of the variability of performances. He documented that even when the text remains the same from performance to performance, there were differences in how they were performed, from performance to performance.

5. Folklorists study how folktales vary and remain the same over time and place. But the term *mulitvocality* is sometimes used in among fairy tale scholars to describe how fairy tales can be told with different voices, like feminist revisions of a Brothers Grimm fairy tale in which the older tale and the revision "enter into dialogue" with one another. Donald Haase, ed., *Fairy Tales and Feminism: New Approaches*. (Detroit: Wayne State University Press, 2004), 24.
Heteroglossia, a mouthful if ever there was one, means substantially the same thing as multi-vocality (it is translated as *multi-voicedness*). The term doesn't only pertain to the multiple voices within a literary work or between works however, but with

the multiple social and philosophical meanings attached to the language itself. John Sutherland, *How Literature Works: 50 Key Concepts*. (Oxford, New York: Oxford University Press, 2011), 140-143.

6. This is where the definitional *mush factor* gets active. Some storytwisted tales are parodic, but not all. A pure parody might not, as discussed in Chapter One, announce itself as such, whereas a fractured one makes that plain. Furthermore, all storytwisted tales are not parodic or fractured. Adapted retellings have neither of these features. See Chapter One, "Definitions of Key Terms Used in this Book"

7. There are many ways to refer to the main message of the story: moral, theme, core idea, heart, essence, dominant message. Choose one that works for you. For further reading, see Robert McKee's use of the term "controlling idea." Robert McKee, *Story: Substance, Structure, Style and the Principles of Screenwriting*. (New York: HarperCollins, 1997), 114-118.

8. It cheered us to discover recently that Paddy Chayefsky, the acclaimed screenplay writer, taped a physical note to his typewriter that clearly stated the core theme of the movie of the movie he was writing. All of his writing for the movie connected back to the idea on that paper. Robert McKee, *Story: Substance, Structure, Style and the Principles of Screenwriting*. (New York: HarperCollins, 1997), 118.

9. There are three basic categories of rocks: sedimentary, igneous, and metamorphic. Rocks with particular properties fall into one of those three categories. Rock transformations occur after an original rock, or *protolith*, is metamorphosed through high heat or pressure and becomes a new type of rock. For example, sedimentary-to-metamorphic transformations include limestone to marble and shale to slate. When a *protolith* undergoes transformation, the newly produced rock no longer fits into its old category—the rock that once was sedimentary is now categorized as a metamorphic rock. "Protolith." *Oxford English Dictionary*, accessed May 23, 2016, https://oed.com/Protolith and William S. Fyfe, "Metamorphic Rock," *Encyclopedia Britannica Online*, accessed May 24, 2016. http://www.britannica.com/science/metamorphic-rock

10. In her analysis of postmodern film adaptations of traditional fairy tales, Jessica Tiffin found that characters dangle without the structure of their source stories, and this threatens the meaning of the film(s). While she indicates that there are times when a pastiche works, she believes that it is hard to balance meaning and a myriad of story elements divorced from their foundational tales. Jessica Tiffin, *Marvelous Geometry: Narrative and Metafiction in Modern Fairy Tale*. (Detroit: Wayne State University Press, 2014), 228-232.

11. This is not to say that we believe parodies or pastiches to be free of meaning. On the contrary, they can be extraordinarily rich narratives. It has been our experience that storytwisting guidelines offer a manageable process for crafting new pieces with meaning, both with or without parodic intent.

12. Tiffin, *Marvelous Geometry*, 231.

13. Our approach happens to be consistent with Linda Hutcheon's theory of adaptation, which defines adaptation as more than a product, but a process as well. Linda

Hutcheon, *A Theory of Adaptation*. (Abingdon, Oxon: Routledge, 2006).

14. For an alternative description of the mirror analogy, see Cristina Bacchilega, *Postmodern Fairy Tales: Gender and Narrative Strategies,* (Philadelphia: University of Pennsylvania Press, 1997), 5-10.

15. E. L. Doctorow, "The Art of Fiction No. 94," *Paris Review*, 101, Winter 1986, accessed May 28, 2016., http://www.theparisreview.org/interviews/2718/the-art-of-fiction-no-94-e-l-doctorow.

Chapter Three

# Fracture Point & Setting

Stories unfold in a particular place and time.[2] Traditional folktales are set in geographical locations that often correspond to the surroundings of those who tell them. Fairy tales are set in long ago and far away kingdoms. And some stories, like legends, occur in specific points in history.

Without setting, a story is untethered, with characters and events dangling like misplaced commas. The setting anchors a story's characters to something knowable. When we understand where characters live and breathe, we make better connections to them and to their story.

Like a theatrical set, setting creates a physical context for the story's events. But setting is much more than that. Setting evokes mood. To embed a story in a dark, shadowy forest imparts a feeling of mystery or danger. There is an air of adventure or a veil of the unknown. Forests shimmer with expectation, excitement, or fear of what is to happen there. An amusement park or farm offers a completely different mood.

Narrative delights abound when a story setting shifts. Stories can travel through time and space. Tales can be dressed in the garb of ancient Rome or revolutionary America or told in an updated, contemporary neighborhood. They can be transposed to a desert, rain forest, city, farm, or to your local school or library.

## Twist the Dial: From One Setting to Another

When we hear certain stories, like fairy tales, we imagine them in an ethereal place of "once upon a time"—a place where magic and fantasy spring to life. But what happens if that same story is told in a contemporary setting? What if it is localized to where you or your audience lives, or to a school? What happens if the story shifts to a brand new natural landscape or a different historical time period?

A shifted setting can reveal nuances in a story or time period that remain obscured when the setting stays intact.[3] It can also show us something about our own lives.

In this chapter, we offer three stories: "Milk Bottles," "I Need Quiet!" and "The Sleepy Fairy." Each story displays a different way that settings can shift. The first is placed at a particular time in history, the next is an updated, contemporary rendition of an older folktale, and the last story is an example of how a story moves to a new geographical location. In addition to describing how we transformed setting in each tale, we provide suggestions for how to make the new settings believable. In this chapter, the setting-oriented Twisting Tips section appears after we discuss all the stories.

## HISTORICAL FICTION FOLKTALE FEATURING "MILK BOTTLES"

### Do the Twist

"Milk Bottles" is the tale of a mysterious woman who visits a store night after night to obtain bottles of milk. She is a stranger who doesn't speak. The shopkeeper grows curious. One night, he and some friends follow her. She disappears in a graveyard, near a freshly dug grave. They open the casket to discover her dead body, with a living baby cradled in her arms. This stunning ghost story about a mother's love is told all over the United States.[4]

### Why We Did the Twist

People love ghost stories, particularly upper elementary and middle school children. Since we perform frequently in schools for these age groups, this tale is an excellent addition to our repertoire.

As arts educators, when we twisted this story, we wanted to offer educational content along with the story's creepy yet heartwarming message. To accomplish this goal, we adapted the tale with setting as our fracture point. Then, we transposed the story to our hometown in the late Nineteenth Century. In so doing, we created what we call a historical fiction folktale. Useful in any setting and for any audience old enough to hear it, the historical dimension provides a taste of history while meeting a fourth grade New York State curriculum requirement to cover New York State history. "Milk Bottles" has become a staple in our school repertoire. Students and teachers love it.

Historical fiction folktales, like "Milk Bottles," have three component parts: (1) Facts, (2) Fiction, and (3) Folktale. First, we will discuss the facts, which represent the historical part of historical fiction folktales. Then we will tackle the fiction, or creative modifications that are made to the source story. The folktale, summarized above, is self-explanatory. Our storytwisted version of this tale is not fractured. It is an adapted retelling, so the structure and meaning of the folktale is intact. (See Chapter One, "Storytwisting: A Transformational Process" and Chapter Two, "Retelling")

**How We Did the Twist: Facts—Research**

Researching a historical fiction folktale is like falling down Alice's rabbit hole. It is an adventure packed with delightful and irksome surprises. But before we could embark on that journey, we had to evaluate the feasibility of this writing choice. Could a story about milk bottles be set in the era we chose? Were bottles in use in the late Nineteenth Century? Once we discovered that

---

### Seven Steps for Adapting Historical Fiction Folktales

**1. Conduct a feasibility check**–Characters, patterns of action, and other details from a traditional story may not work in every historical setting that you choose for your twist. Determine feasibility before beginning the research and writing process.

**2. Research location**–Learn what you can about the geography, climate, architecture, people, and cultural traditions of the location where your new story is set.

**3. Research historical time period**–Identify its technological advancements.

**4. Story bone consistency**–Make sure that the new story bones are consistent with the new setting, are expressed in a cohesive manner, and that they have fidelity to the source story.

**5. Creative modifications**–Make creative modifications to fit the new setting to the structure of the traditional story and to match facts about the setting and the era.

**6. Inventive writing**–Use as needed to modify the story to fit the new setting.

**7. Accuracy**–Double check the accuracy of imagined details. Additional research also develops more historical connections for a historical fiction folktale.

milk bottles were in use at that time, we started our research.

Our next task was to learn more about the history of our town, the location for our twisted story. Philmont, New York is a tiny mill town. Located a hair's breadth away from Massachusetts, it is technically not a New England village. But in spirit, Philmont thrived in the late Nineteenth Century along with many New England mill towns.

---

### Twisting Tip

*Embrace trial and error as an integral part of the storytwisting process.* Or as we say to ourselves, "Trust and adjust." This tip fits all aspects of storytelling. Nothing novel is accomplished without it. Go back, try again, make adjustments, explore. You lose nothing when something doesn't work, save time. What you gain is a better story; you also learn something that aids all of your writing. View errors or failures as your friends; they are not negatives but opportunities to learn and improve.

---

As time went on, our little village fought an uphill battle with circumstances. Economic downturns and devastating fires wiped out the mills. By the 1990's, Philmont's Main Street was littered with abandoned empty storefronts like discarded match boxes. People still visited Philmont, but only to get gas on their way to a more attractive destination. Thankfully, things changed. Today, the village is rising from the ashes of struggle. Those once-empty storefronts house lovely restaurants, a hair salon, a real estate office, a general store, and the waterfall that powered the mills is now a beautiful hiking destination. While many details unearthed in our research did not make the final story draft, they contributed depth to our understanding of the story, authenticity to our resultant work, and confidence in our writing and performance of the polished piece.

After learning Philmont's overall history, we delved further into the time period to glean the aura of the era in which we wanted to set our story. We discovered that Philmont's mills were textile mills. There was a general store and a train that stopped at the depot in town. We learned about the lifestyle and habits of the people who lived here. Careful research helped us paint an accurate picture of old Philmont and its general store, the when and where of our storytwisted tale.

To determine if we were finished with the research, we inserted the bones of the traditional story into our newly researched setting to check for gross inconsistencies or historical incompatibilities. In our experience, tiny details or even large chunks of a source folktale won't fit into a storytwisted tale without certain modification. For example, in many versions of "Milk Bottles," the bottles are stored in a refrigerator. That was impossible in a Nineteenth Century version of the tale because refrigerators weren't in use at the time. To make our tale believable, McKinley's shop needed an ice box, not a refrigerator.

### Teaching Twist

*Reset a favorite folktale in a historical period of your choice. Invite students to research the era for a feasibility check. Suppose you choose to work with the "Puss in Boots" story. Clothing is of central concern in this tale about a trickster cat who dresses up in human garb to help his owner win a princess. Guide students with questions for research. If the tale is placed in Roman times, for example, are boots acceptable footwear? Encourage students to research the era's attire to describe the clothing of all characters. This activity will also build vivid pictures of the new story's characters for descriptive writing.*

*An ogre and his castle are features in the Puss tale. What type of Roman-era building could play the part of the castle? Were ogres feared during that time period? If not, what monstrous creatures were? Perhaps princesses are not relevant to your selected time period. Is there another high status designation or role for women of that time?*

*If there are no historically accurate substitutes for main story components, choose another era or try a different story. Time spent doing a feasibility check is not time lost, but time spent learning.*

This bit of information hurtled us back to the library to learn about ice harvesting on the Hudson River and how ice was stored. Along the way we discovered that ice-harvest bonfires were important events. They took place on the shores of the lake that feeds the falls that powered the Philmont textile mills. We incorporated this information in our story, creating a textured piece for contemporary audiences with setting-oriented, bite-sized educational details for school audiences.

ಶ

## Fiction: Creative Modifications

Next, we added fiction to fact to make the storytwist work. Whether a traditional tale is an exact synonym for fiction is a matter of philosophical debate that is beyond the scope of this book.[5] For our purposes, let us assume that all folktales are fictional. In addition to the folktale itself, other fictions figure into the new story to facilitate the tale's translation from one setting to another. With the storytwisting dial positioned on *setting*, we didn't alter plot, characters, or point of view. We transferred the intact bones of the traditional ghost story into our reimagined tale.

The placement of a pre-existing tale in a new setting creates idiosyncrasies. Not every part of the source story fit our adaptation. To make the new tale work, we twisted parts of the traditional story to fit the particulars of our new setting.[6] For example, several fictions were added to the story. We imagined the way the town's old roads intertwined to get to the forest, as there is no forest in town today. The daily village council meetings at McKinley's shop are purely fictional. Tiny though they are, these and other fictions helped embed the setting's facts into the structure of the traditional story.

Our story's shopkeeper, McKinley, was also a man of our own invention. Or so we thought. Once, after we told the story, a Philmont resident named Dot Bowes approached us. "I enjoyed your story, but for more reasons than you would guess. My grandfather's name was Yerick. He owned Philmont's general store back in those days." Dot's eyes twinkled as she continued, "He was just like your McKinley."

We shivered. It was as if she was the one who had just told a ghost story. Somehow, we invented a historical person who also happened to be real. Was it a happy accident? The power of the imagination? Or do spirits really live in ghost stories? Maybe a little bit of all three.

☙

## Storytwist

### *Milk Bottles*

Adapted retelling by Jeri Burns and Barry Marshall
Copyright 2004, 2018 The Storycrafters

We live in Philmont, a sleepy little village in the Hudson Valley of New York. But at the turn of the Twentieth Century, it was a thriving mill town. Textile mills flourished and trains carried salesmen and merchants into town to do business with the mills and the shops on our once bustling Main Street. In the heart of it all was a general store owned by a man named McKinley.

McKinley was a well-known figure in Philmont who lived in an apartment over the general store. He opened his shop every day at 6:00 a.m. and closed every night at 11:00 p.m. His business ran like clockwork. Philmonters counted on McKinley's shop for bread, milk, flour, coffee and other basic necessities for life in a mill town.

One night, in late October, McKinley was preparing to close up shop. It was 10:45 p.m. He wasn't expecting anyone to come in because the mill workers lived an 'early to bed, early to rise' schedule. No trains were due. He was wiping down the counters and doors of the iceboxes when the bell over the front door jingled.

McKinley looked up from his work. A woman entered the shop. He didn't recognize her. While it was unusual for a woman to be out alone at that time of night, what was even stranger was that she wore a thin white summer dress against the late October chill. Her hair was her only cloak.

The woman walked over to the icebox and opened it. She took out two bottles of milk and made her way over to the cash register, her dress swirling about her ankles as she walked. She placed the bottles down on the counter and gazed at McKinley. He told her how much the milk cost.

In response, the woman silently raised her right hand up to her right ear. Then she removed a gold earring. She gazed at it before setting it down. When the earring clinked on the countertop, McKinley felt a shiver run up his spine. Without saying a word, the woman picked up the bottles of milk and opened the door.

McKinley stared at the earring. By the time he came back to himself, she was gone. He stepped outside to talk to her, but she was nowhere in sight. McKinley entered the shop and locked the door, put the earring into the cash register, and went upstairs to sleep for the night.

The next morning, he opened the shop at 6:00 a.m. He ran the shop normally and nothing unusual happened. The earring sat in the cash register all day. He didn't tell anyone about what happened. It seemed almost too strange to mention.

That night, at 10:45 p.m., the woman in the summer dress returned. She selected two more bottles of milk. At the counter, she gazed at McKinley. Slowly, she raised her left hand to her left ear, and removed the matching gold earring. The woman placed it on the counter as payment and McKinley felt that shiver run up his spine again. As she left the shop he called, "Stop!" But she walked off into the night.

I should summon the police, he thought. But that didn't make sense. She hadn't underpaid for the milk. In truth, she overpaid. So, once again, McKinley locked up the shop, placed the second earring in the cash register, and went upstairs for the night.

The next day, he opened the shop at 6:00 a.m. and waited impatiently. Every day, the members of the village council met at a table in the front of McKinley's shop at noon, drank coffee, and discussed the affairs of the village. On this particular day, McKinley told them everything that happened for two nights running. He brought them into the shop. When he put the earrings on the counter, everyone felt a shiver run up and down their spines.

The men made a plan to discover the woman's identity. Every member of the village would gather in the alley next to McKinley's shop later that night. If the woman came again, they would follow her.

Sometime after 10:00 p.m., the men huddled in the alley. It was pouring rain. They looked like drowned rats. McKinley stayed in the shop, cleaning scales and shelves. At precisely 10:45 p.m., the woman entered the shop. Her thin summer dress was soaked—it clung to her as she crossed the shop with two more bottles of milk. At the counter, she raised both hands up to her neck and unclasped a gold necklace. She gazed at it before setting it on the counter. McKinley felt that familiar shiver run up his spine. Then she picked up the milk bottles and left the shop.

McKinley and the council members followed her down Main Street, staying about three quarters of a block behind. She stepped in puddles. Water and dirt splashed onto her dress. She walked for two blocks and then turned right on Church Street. They followed.

In those days, Church Street wasn't paved. As she walked down the hill, mud and gravel soiled her dress. Near the bottom of Church Street, she turned right and walked into the woods with the men in pursuit. Leaves and sticks stuck to her dress as she walked through the woods. When she reached the end of the woods, she disappeared into the Mellenville Cemetery.

The men lost ground as they tried to stick together in the bramble-filled woods. When they reached the edge of the cemetery, they lost sight of her. They combed the entire cemetery with no luck. The men turned back toward the woods when they heard a sound coming from a freshly dug grave. It was a plaintive, high-pitched cry.

The men high-tailed it out of the cemetery and went home for the night. But none of them slept very well. When McKinley opened his shop at 6:00 a.m., the council members were waiting impatiently for him. They held an emergency meeting of the village council and passed a proclamation that gave them permission to go to the cemetery and dig up that grave.

Armed with pick axes and shovels, the entered the cemetery. When they reached the grave, they heard the cry. With trembling arms, they dug down to the lid of the coffin. The sound was definitely coming from inside.

When they opened lid, the woman was there. She was dead. She was wearing the summer dress. It was soaking wet and covered with mud, sticks, and leaves. Down at her feet were open, empty milk bottles. And in the crook of her arm was a baby—alive—crying for more milk.

## UPDATING A FOLKTALE TO A CONTEMPORARY SETTING: "I NEED QUIET!"

### Do the Twist

We were invited to tell Jewish stories for an autumn gathering. The sponsors asked us to include a story for Sukkot, the Jewish harvest holiday. But we couldn't find stories to fit the parameters of the gig and the audience. Instead, we adapted "It Could Always Be Worse," a beloved story in the Jewish folkloric canon, and transformed it into a holiday story.

The story features a distressed family member who repeatedly seeks a rabbi's advice about noise at home. The rabbi cleverly advises the family to bring a different farm animal into the home, day after successive day. The cumulative effect is that the house gets noisier and noisier. When the rabbi advises the removal of the animals, the house is restored to its original noise level. In comparison to when the animals were in the house, things seem very quiet indeed.[7]

*Teaching Twist*

*Update a favorite folktale to a local neighborhood. Make other changes only when they are necessary for the new story to make sense. The objective is to learn all about setting.*

**Why We Did the Twist**

Our initial instinct was to transpose the story from an Old World Jewish village set in an unspecific time and place to an Old World Jewish village during its annual Sukkot festival. But on further thought, we wondered how the tale would resonate with audiences if it were set in an everyday, familiar time and place. So we spun the storytwisting dial to *setting* and updated the old tale. Instead of an old world village, our tale was set in a contemporary, suburban setting, just like the neighborhoods of our audience members.

Rather than create a family of strangers from whole cloth, we told a story about some friends who lived in a suburban neighborhood on Long Island. Every time we visited them, we witnessed their humorous interactions. The husband, Andrew, was often upset about something. He complained about this or bemoaned that, and with a swift word or action, no-nonsense Cara came to the rescue. We always giggled while watching them and they laughed at themselves. Their real life dynamic is featured (and exaggerated) in this offbeat piece.

As with "Milk Bottles," we started with the feasibility check. And that was where we got stuck.

**How We Did the Twist**

Our plan was to transpose the folktale from an old-world Jewish village to a modern Jewish community. We wanted to tell it straight, without implied social commentary. As it often happens, the story had different ideas.

## Feasibility Check: Philosophical Choices—Messages and Tradition

In the traditional story, "It Could Always Be Worse," the wisdom of a rabbi is sought to solve a problem. In our tale, a Long Island mother plays the rabbi's role of wise advisor. With just one tiny bit of gender swapping, our innocent little story became a feminist revision of an old tale. Such a change is charged because it reassigns power. The wise character role shifts from a man to a woman, from a community leader to a mother in a home.

Before we walked this path, we carefully considered the cultural consequences of this choice. Traditional stories reflect cultural values and norms. Jewish folklore often spotlights knowledgeable, revered men, like rabbis, and traditional male heads of household, which reflects the importance of wise men in the culture.[8] If our new story placed a woman in the classic rabbi role, it would depart from older versions of this tale. Would such a change mean a significant departure from Jewish tradition? Would it violate cultural values?

> ### *Twisting Tip*
>
> *Make sure that your twisted story aligns with its untwisted predecessors.* The "Storytwisting Dial" introduced in Chapter Two helps the writer maintain story alignment and encourages intertextual play. Like a literary GPS, the dial keeps the story—and writer—on track by aiming altered content to the fracture point. Evaluate every change you make to ensure that it fits your fracture point—character or setting, point of view or rhyme—wherever your story dial points. As we note in Chapter Two: "The Kitchen Sink Issue: Avoiding Pitfalls", indiscriminate changes to multiple story elements threatens the meaning or narrative security of the new piece.

With an eye to answering these questions, we researched Jewish folklore and identified a number of Jewish tales and story collections that feature the wisdom of women.[9] With folkloric precedent for wise women in traditional Jewish stories, we decided that our fractured variant was consistent with a body of Jewish folklore.

A wise woman in a leadership role is also consistent with modern Jewish life. Today, there are women rabbis. Jewish women are independent, working professionals. Most are not confined to the limited range of roles they once were. Our new story emphasizes a modern truth that harmonizes with traditional stories of the past. Telling an old story in a contemporary context is an opportunity to speak to the past while also speaking to the present.

A straight retelling of this folktale typically includes a male rabbi in the advisor role. But ours is not a straight retelling. When we selected the modern setting as the fracture point, new options were revealed. Despite the updates and holiday-specific content layered into "It Could Always Be Worse," our storytwisted version respects Jewish culture. It also reflects the time-tested message of the older story, that it is wise to have perspective.

### Nuts and Bolts: The Remaining Creative Process for "I Need Quiet!"

Once the tale passed our feasibility check, we moved on to the next stages of research. In contrast to our process for "Milk Bottles," we didn't need to learn about a particular locality because "I Need Quiet!" is set in a generalized, archetypal suburb. There was no need to research the setting in detail. We both grew up in the suburbs and regularly visit family and friends.

But we did need to learn about the Sukkot holiday. We researched the symbolism of the Sukkah itself, a tiny hut designed to remember the fields and pastoral nature of farming. Decorated with the fruits of the harvest, the Sukkah is a quiet, contemplative space that honors the holiday.

Next, we checked the bones of the traditional tale for consistency in our new setting. We identified a sticking point. Most suburban settings are barnyard free. Cows and chickens are not typical residents in Long Island neighborhoods near New York City. The details of the story's setting must ring true, especially when setting is the fracture point because setting is the scaffolding upon which the rest of a story is built. If the foundation is flawed, the story won't stand.

Adjustments were necessary. We brainstormed details about our friends' lives, how the children interacted with each other, what they did after school, and so on. We wrote lists of noisy objects or critters in typical suburban homes to help us write creative modifications. One item leapt off the page, *Andrew's daily commute*. This detail could serve a double function. A long, crowded commute is a factual detail that contributes to the authenticity of the contemporary suburban setting of the story. Furthermore, it is logical for a stressful commute to increase Andrew's need for the tranquil comforts of home upon his return from the frenzy of city, work, and trains. Though subtle, the stresses of modern life lent credence to Andrew's story problem and contributed important details that painted a believable picture of the new setting. It was also consistent with Andrew's character, the meaning of the holiday, and the traditional story theme.

Step by step, we twisted each "nut" into place and bolted together a story—like a backyard Sukkah—to tell for the Sukkot holiday.

## STORYTWIST

### *I Need Quiet!—A Tale for Sukkot*

By Jeri Burns and Barry Marshall
Copyright 1998, 2018 The Storycrafters

One autumn, the Klein family was very busy. The children, Jenna and Deanna, had just started school, Deanna for the very first time. Every afternoon when they came home, they blew their mother Cara a kiss as she worked at her computer, ate a snack, and went outside to play in their grassy yard. At first, they got along, but by the time their father Andrew came home, they argued, "You did it, no you did it, no you did it!"

Andrew would hear them and cry "Enough noise already! I need *quiet!*"

Things changed on the weekend before Sukkot. Cara and Andrew reminded the girls of the coming harvest celebration. They explained that they would remember the houses of the wandering Jews of long ago by building a sukkah. Then they went outside to build it.

It was a very exciting weekend. The girls unrolled the canvases that would hang as the walls of the sukkah. While their parents erected poles, Jenna and Deanna gathered branches and twigs for the roof. Then together, everyone tied canvases to the poles. Branches were placed on the roof, leaving enough space for the stars of night to shine down upon them. The girls hung carrots, apples, and pears from the branches for decoration. Then the family sang a Sukkot song together.

On Monday, when the girls came home from school, they blew their mother a kiss, ate a snack, and went outside to play in the sukkah. When their father came home from work, he sat in the sukkah. He heard squirrels nibbling on the fruit, the wind whistled around the walls of the sukkah, and his children argued: "You did it, no you did it, no you did it!"

Andrew cried, "Enough noise already! I need *quiet!*"

He went in the house to ask Cara what to do.

"I work all day in the noisy city. I come home to rest. Sukkot is a celebration of agriculture, of the country. It's supposed to be peaceful in the country. I need *quiet!*"

Cara nodded her head. Then she said "Things can always be worse."

Andrew groaned "How can things be worse than this?"

Cara said "I can solve your problem. Bring out the popcorn maker tomorrow. Make popcorn for the girls to hang from the branches of the sukkah."

"Are you sure?" he asked.

"Trust me," she said.

The next day, Jenna and Deanna came home from school, blew their mother a kiss, ate a snack and went outside and played in the sukkah. When Andrew got home, he went out in the yard with the popcorn maker. He plugged an extension cord into the outdoor electrical socket and popped popcorn. Squirrels nibbled at the sukkah, the wind whistled around the walls of the sukkah, his girls argued "You did it, no you did it, no you did it!" and the popcorn popper went pop pop pop.

Andrew cried, "Enough noise already! I need *quiet!*" He went into the house and spoke to Cara.

"I did just as you told me, I brought the popcorn popper into the sukkah. What a racket! How can I find the peace of country living this way!"

She listened to him and said "You know, things can always be worse."

Andrew shook his head and groaned, "How can things get any worse?"

"Listen" she said, "I can solve your problem. Bring the dogs out into the sukkah. It will help."

"Are you sure?" he asked.

"Trust me," she said.

The next day, the girls came home from school, blew their mother a kiss, ate a snack and played in the sukkah. When Andrew came home, he brought the dogs into the sukkah. Squirrels nibbled at the sukkah, the wind whistled around the walls of the sukkah, his girls argued, "You did it, no you did it, no you did it!" The popcorn maker went pop pop pop, and the dogs barked ruff ruff!

Andrew cried "Enough noise already! I need *quiet!*" He went into the house and spoke to Cara.

"I did just what you suggested and brought the dogs into the sukkah. It is horrible in there, worse than the train at rush hour."

"Things can always be worse" Cara said. Andrew shook his head and groaned.

"Listen," she said, "I can solve your problem. Tomorrow, bring the lawn-mower out into the sukkah. The grass is too high and it bothers the girls."

"Are you sure?"

"Trust me."

The next day, the girls came home from school, blew their mother a kiss, ate a snack and played in the sukkah. When Andrew came home, he brought the lawnmower into the sukkah. He started the motor. Squirrels nibbled at the sukkah, the wind whistled around the walls of the sukkah, his girls argued "You did it, no you did it, no you did it!" The popcorn popper went, pop pop pop, the dogs barked, ruff ruff! and the lawnmower growled, vroom vroom.

Andrew cried "Enough noise already! I need *quiet!*" He went into the house and spoke to Cara.

"I just can't stand it anymore. How are we going to have a peaceful supper celebration tomorrow in the sukkah with all the noise? We will never hear our prayers over all that racket."

Cara nodded and said "I can solve your problem. Put the lawn mower in the garage, bring the dogs back inside the house, and return the popcorn maker to the kitchen."

"Are you sure?"

"Trust me."

So the next day, the girls came home from school, blew their mother a kiss, ate a snack and played in the sukkah. When Andrew came home, he went outside and sat in the sukkah. Squirrels nibbled at the sukkah, the wind whistled around the walls of the sukkah, his girls argued, "You did it, no you did it, no you did it." It was quiet. It was peaceful. It was wonderful. It was just like the country.

That evening the Klein family started the eight-day Sukkot celebration. In addition to the traditional Sukkot prayers, Andrew added one of his own. He gave thanks for being blessed with such a wise and caring wife.

ॐ

## Re-Setting a Folktale to a New Geographic Location: "The Sleepy Fairy"

**Do the Twist**

It is lovely to follow a set of guidelines to write a story, but it is also lovely to follow raw instinct. Our next story was written by accident. We were in the middle of a week at a family dance and music camp when the program coordinator approached us right before our late afternoon workshops.

**Why We Did the Twist**

"We have a Wednesday evening tradition here at camp. The children gather in the middle of the woods without their parents. Then the storyteller shares a bedtime tale. It shouldn't be too long, maybe five minutes or so. The kids love it when there is music. We love it when it is related to the beautiful, natural setting. Everyone adores this tradition. We know you will do a great job." As she departed, a group of children approached. "Oh, we heard you are telling the story in the woods. Please make it scary!" But the smaller ones begged, "No, not scary, please!"

We looked at each other. Neither of us could think of an appropriate tale to tell to a large group of three-to-twelve-year-olds in the woods at night. Without their parents. Right before bed. Our workshops had to run until dinner, so we figured we'd discuss it later. But just as we started teaching, we realized that we couldn't wait. It was Wednesday.

When faced with tricky situations like this, being "two storytellers for the price of one" comes in very handy. Barry took the lead in the workshops while Jeri hovered helpfully in the background. Some comments from Jeri:

> I racked my brain for classic story structures and patterns, pairing some, discarding others. It felt like I was trying to remember a password to an online account. Haphazard as it was, this process produced gold when a random pairing reminded me of a folktale that I could adapt on the fly.[10]

## How We Did the Twist

With the storytwisting dial pointed to *setting*, a folktale from a village setting was placed in the very forest where Wednesday night bedtime stories happened. Farm animals became forest critters and humans became a fairy daughter and her father. Over supper, we discussed sound effects while passing the mustard. During dessert, we wrote a simple, sweet lullaby. With harp in hand, we walked to evening activities and decided how to divide the narration. Then, nestled in the woods, with utter faith in the enduring structure of the traditional folktale, we told that newly adapted piece. The harp was sweet, the singing sweeter. Children loved it. Counselors loved it. The sponsors loved it. We did too and it became an expanded, popular piece in our repertoire.

"The Sleepy Fairy" is a storytwisted version of "It Could Always Be Worse." Our twisting function was not parody or social commentary. We borrowed a tried-and-true story structure to tell a humorous story for a wide age range. That is adaptation at its simplest.

---

### *Teaching Twist*

*Challenge students to learn about adaptation by transferring a story from one geographical place to another. "The Three Little Pigs" is a wonderful specimen. Not only do the animals change in a new setting, but so do the materials for house building. This encourages the study of flora, fauna and environmental variables, like climate. Students can research the predators and prey that can fill the roles of wolves and pigs, find location-specific alternative building materials for the houses, and write an old story anew.*

---

❧

## STORYTWIST

### *The Sleepy Fairy*

Adapted retelling of a Jewish folktale by Jeri Burns and Barry Marshall
Copyright 2009, 2018 The Storycrafters

A fairy and her father lived in a little house in the forest. One night, her father tucked her in, pulled the moss blanket up to her chin, and kissed her good night. He sang her favorite lullaby before tiptoeing out of the room.

*When the night is dark and deep, close your eyes, go to sleep.*

The breezes were blowing, the raindrops were falling, and the fairy tried to go to sleep. She tossed and turned. She wiggled and wriggled. Finally, she sat up in her bed and cried, "Too much noise."

It wasn't long before her father's loving footsteps tapped through the house. He entered the room, folded his arms, and said, "What's the matter, powder puff?"

"Well Daddy, it's bedtime right? And when it's bedtime, you are supposed to go to sleep, right? Right?"

"Right!" said her father.

"Well Daddy I hear sounds. I hear woosh-woosh and sprinkle-sprinkle. How can I sleep with all that noise?"

Her father's mind tossed and turned. Finally, he said, "I have an idea! Why don't you go outside and bring an ant into bed with you?"

The fairy considered this. She had two aunts. "Would you like me to bring in Aunt Dolores or Aunt Vivian?"

Her father laughed. "Not your relatives, honey. An insect."

The fairy skipped out into the night. It was easy to find an ant in a forest. She bent down, stretched out her hand, and a little ant put its leg in her hand. They walked hand in leg, leg in hand back to her room. She tucked the ant into a guest bed in her room, pulled a guest moss blanket snug around him, and tucked herself back in bed. To make them both comfortable, the fairy sang the lullaby.

*When the night is dark and deep, close your eyes, go to sleep.*

In the darkness of the room the fairy heard whoosh-whoosh, sprinkle-sprinkle. Then she heard the ant's antennae squawk like a siren, doodle-doo, doodle-dee. The fairy tossed and turned. She wiggled and wriggled. Finally, she sat up in her bed and cried, "Too much noise."

It wasn't long before her father's loving footsteps banged through the house. When he entered the room, he folded his arms, smiled sweetly, and said, "What's the matter, lovebug?"

"Well Daddy, I tried to go to sleep. But I heard whoosh-whoosh, sprinkle-sprinkle. Then I heard doodle-doo, doodle-dee. It sounds like a garbage truck is backing up into my room. What if all that trash falls on my head? It's the stuff of nightmares, Daddy."

Her father's mind tossed and turned. Finally, he said, "I have an idea! Why don't you go outside and bring a caterpillar into bed with you?"

"A caterpillar? But Daddy, will it purr? That noise will keep me up. Can I get a dogarpillar instead?"

Her father laughed. "Caterpillars are soft and silent honey. Now go get one."

The fairy skipped out into the night. She saw a caterpillar nibbling on a leaf. She stretched out her hand and the little caterpillar put its leg in her hand. They walked hand in leg, leg in hand back to her room. She tucked the caterpillar into another guest bed in her room, pulled another moss blanket snug around him, and tucked herself back in. To make everyone comfortable, the fairy sang her lullaby.

*When the night is dark and deep, close your eyes, go to sleep.*

In the darkness of the room the fairy heard whoosh-whoosh, sprinkle-sprinkle, doodle-doo, doodle-dee. Then she heard the caterpillar's legs rumbling, ba-da-ba-da-ba-da-ba-da-dum.

The fairy tossed and turned. She wiggled and wriggled. Finally, she sat up in her bed and cried, "Too much noise."

Soon her father's loving footsteps pounded through the house. When he entered the room, he folded his arms, smiled sweetly, took a calming breath, and said, "What's the matter, potato chip?"

"Well Daddy, I tried to go to sleep. But I heard whoosh-whoosh, sprinkle-sprinkle. Then I heard doodle-doo, doodle-dee. Then I heard ba-da-ba-da-ba-da-ba-da-dum. Daddy, it sounds like a whole gym class is dribbling basketballs all around the room."

Her father's mind tossed and turned. Finally, he said, "I have an idea! Why don't you go outside and bring a chipmunk into bed with you."

"But Daddy, aren't monks spiritual people, like priests or rabbis or imams? Why would you want me to chip one? Wouldn't that hurt?"

Her father laughed. "A chipmunk is a tiny, furry animal with fat cheeks and stripes down its back. Now go get one."

The fairy skipped out into the forest. A chipmunk was near a tree nibbling a nut. The chipmunk put its foreleg into her hand. They walked hand in foreleg, foreleg in hand back to her room. She tucked the chipmunk into yet another guest bed in her room, pulled another moss blanket snug around him, and tucked herself back in.

*When the night is dark and deep, close your eyes, go to sleep.*

In the darkness, the fairy heard whoosh-whoosh, sprinkle-sprinkle, doodle-doo, doodle-dee, ba-da-ba-da-ba-da-ba-da-dum. Then she heard the chipmunk squeak, "hoo-wee, hoo-wee." The fairy tossed and turned. She wiggled and wriggled. Finally, she sat up in her bed and cried, "Too much noise."

Her father's loving footsteps boomed through the house. When he entered the room, he folded his arms, smiled sweetly, took a calming breath, looked at his girl and said, "What's the matter, daffodil?"

"Well Daddy, I tried to go to sleep. But I heard whoosh-whoosh, sprinkle-sprinkle, doodle-doo, doodle-dee, ba-da-ba-da-ba-da-ba-da-dum. Then I heard hoo-wee, hoo-wee. It sounds like a broken bicycle. That makes me think of the beach. And the beach makes me think of ice cream. So now I'm hungry. Can I have some milk and a pizza?"

Her father's mind tossed and turned. "I have an idea! Why don't you take all the animals back to their own homes?"

So the fairy and the animals skipped into the forest. She left the ant at an anthill, the caterpillar by a leaf, and the chipmunk near a tree. When she got into her bed, she pulled the blankets up to her chin.

*When the night is dark and deep, close your eyes, go to sleep.*

In the darkness of the room, the fairy heard whoosh-whoosh,

sprinkle-sprinkle. And in no time at all, the father fairy heard his little fairy snore.

## Twisting Tips

### Setting Storytwisting Tips

*Take the time to research your settings.* Understand how the meaning of the traditional tale might be altered when you transpose it from one time and place to another. If you decide to move a tale from one geographical location to another, be sure that your understanding of climate, geography, plant and animal life are consistent with that place.

*Include true details of time and place in a historical story.* Your tale must pass a history buff's muster. There are always people in the audience who know when fiction masquerades as fact. And they will correct you. Even if they don't, those who notice historical errors will momentarily lose the thread of the story because of an inconsistency or mistake. They might lose confidence in the story and stop paying attention altogether. Ultimately, stories and their truths are far more striking when fiction is embedded in fact.

*Expect the research process to be ongoing.* Just when you think you are finished with research, new details crop up that require double checking. Even after you think your historical fiction folktale is completed, audience members may ask questions that cause you to do additional research. Welcome these questions! They are learning opportunities for you. What you learn will make the story better.

*Gather more material than you think you need* to write your story. Diving deeply into your research on setting pays off in many ways. It helps with descriptive detail, draws authentic character motivations, forges links between old and new story, and offers fodder for additional, unplanned twisting. It is also one, gigantic writing prompt.

*Avoid over-description* (or avoid overwriting) in your final product. Adapting a story for a new setting requires research and inventive writing. It is tempting to include every idea in your new, twisted tale. Don't. If you do, your tale will sound like a history text, a tour book, or a meandering, newbie novel. This distracts you and your audience from the narrative. To choose among all the goodies, ask yourself if the audience must know a detail for the story to make sense in its new setting. Include it only if the answer is a resounding yes. For example, one of the details we discovered in our research for "Milk Bottles" is that our village's original name was Factory Hill. It was a fun detail to discover, but it never made it into the story.

## Teaching Twist

*Using this table as a guide, start a new column and place the same story in your school. Encourage students to write their own version of the story using the items in the Story Element column. See "Appendix B" for a reproducible copy of this chart for students.*

| STORY ELEMENT | TRADITIONAL | TWISTED SUKKOT | TWISTED FAIRY |
| --- | --- | --- | --- |
| Upset character | Old woman/man | Andrew | Sleepy Fairy |
| Advisor character | Rabbi | Cara | Father fairy |
| Everyday house noise | Rocking chair, snoring, cat | Girls arguing, squirrels, whistling wind | Rain and breezes |
| First addition to the house | Goat | Dogs | Ants |
| Second addition to the house | Chicken | Popcorn maker | Caterpillar |
| Third addition to the house | Cow | Lawnmower | Chipmunk |

*Research and write more than you need to tell a good story* during the crafting process. None of that work is wasted. Every tidbit thrives in the internally imagined picture of the story's time and place. This lends depth to writing and performing.

*Write about settings that you know firsthand.* When you change a story's setting, it helps to really know the place. Choose places that you have lived or those you have visited. The creative process is not only rich and very enjoyable to write, but easier to accomplish because the settings are vivid and real. With time and experience, you may leap to unfamiliar locations.

## Twist for Thought: Cultural Sensitivity When Changing a Story's Setting

Storytellers are a respectful bunch. Like fervent, folksy ambassadors, we share traditional tales in order to open hearts and minds to cultural understanding. Yet even with the purest of intentions and most honorable preparations, we sometimes make mistakes. Because adaptation is a slippery slope for cultural miscues and storytwisting is an adaptive writing method, we have pondered the issue deeply. This essay is an overview of the reasons why we think it is best to avoid changing a story's setting to a different culture without an insider's view of that culture.

When we twist settings in our Storycrafters' work, we focus on time period and location, as "Milk Bottles" and "The Sleepy Fairy" demonstrate. Though rare, when we change a story's culture—as we do to some extent by moving an Old World Jewish story to a modern, American, suburban neighborhood in "I Need Quiet!"—we have strong ties to the culture in which the tale is reset. Suburban America is where we both grew up. Furthermore, the story retains its Jewish cultural context, which is Jeri's heritage. Without a deep knowledge of the new culture—without being an insider—the transfer of an older story to a culture other than one's own is a form of cultural appropriation.

Cultural appropriation happens when people claim others' cultural practices for their own use without a deep understanding of their significance. When copied or borrowed inappropriately by a cultural outsider, cultural borrowings are like stolen goods. The act is not always intended as theft. Some even argue that cultural borrowing is a form of cultural exchange.[11] Regardless of intent, the risk of cultural trespass is real. For more on cultural appropriation, see Chapter Five, "Story Rapping: Ten Considerations for Honoring Rap and its Origins"

Acclaimed storyteller and former librarian Beth Horner uses the term *innocent ignorance* to describe the first time a storyteller unwittingly uses copyrighted material without obtaining permission, tells another storyteller's own story, or irresponsibly uses material from cultures other than one's own. She believes that the "innocence" in innocent ignorance ceases to apply as one delves deeper into the storytelling experience. Beth states that, as artists, it is our legal and moral responsibility to educate ourselves about legalities and ethics. We must learn to take responsibility for the ramifications of our creative actions in terms of intellectual property and cultural respect.[12]

## Folk Process and Storytwisting Process: Similar but Different

When tales are told, tales change. And when they pass from one culture into another, they can change even more. These adopted stories are often awash in cultural details that reflect the tale's new home. In this way, folktales bear the cultural stamp of those who tell them. That is the folk process.

The storytwisting process mirrors the folk process, but there are some crucial differences. When tales are adopted into a new culture, cultural adaptations are made by a multitude of people over an extended period of time. Eventually, the adopted tale, like a Wiki prototype or a modern-day, crowd-sourced product, carries many voices. This implies that there is a modicum of cultural approval. In contrast, storytwisting accelerates the adaptation process, and responsibility for adaptive content is in the hands of one, not many.

We take that responsibility seriously. In our view, storytwisting oughtn't be interpreted as blanket permission to borrow and reset any cultural stories in whatever creative direction the wind blows. This is not only disrespectful to the tales and the cultures who tell them, but to the cultures where a tale is reset. Folktales are cultural artifacts. Both stories and cultures deserve to be treated with the utmost respect. For more on this, please review Chapter One: "Ethics and Culture"

## Little Red Riding Hood in the Tropics?

One can lift Little Red Riding Hood out of her European forest and place her in a tropical one instead. But can we also cloak her in native attire common among indigenous people living in that rain forest? Even with the best of intentions, cultural outsiders can tear down, cheapen, or stereotype a people by placing a story in a new and different cultural context. Although traditional stories have been and still are passed from one culture into another, it is not cultural outsiders who refashion folktales with new cultural clothing.

It is cultural insiders.

As you will recall from the first page of Chapter One, "An EyeOpening Experience" when the Irish storyteller in our storytelling workshop created an Irish story out of a traditional Jewish folktale, he was an insider. Because he was Irish, he knew what aspects of the story needed to be adapted to tell a tale that was respectful, relevant, and enjoyable to his own people. By being an insider, he acted as a filter and followed the traditional way that stories have been transmitted for millennia.[13]

Likewise, if a version of Little Red Riding Hood's tale was told by people in an indigenous culture in the tropics, they would dress her as they see fit. Perhaps the symbol of the cloak wouldn't make the cut. (Do people wear hooded, woolen cloaks in the tropics?) The upshot here is that Little Red's tale would be altered to fit a tropical, indigenous sensibility in ways that cultural outsiders could never fully imagine. Dressing Red up in what we *think* is the right outfit scrapes a culture's surface at best and is viciously offensive at worst.

Can we acquire deep knowledge of a new culture through research? It is a fair question, since it is common and accepted practice among storytellers to research tales in order to respectfully and fairly represent the culture and the story.[14] Learning about a culture's value system, worldview, and lifestyle expands our understanding of any existing traditional story we seek to tell. But our hypothetical "Little Red in the Tropics" is not a pre-existing tale. While there are variants from Asia,[15] the widely-known, iconic fairy tale describing a girl, her grandmother, and a wolf derives from a Euro-Western context. To superimpose this story type into another culture presupposes that it can or should fit within that culture's value system. It also implies that cultural outsiders have the ability to interpret cultural nuances fairly and accurately.[16]

Stories reflect the people who tell them. The fairy tales that we know and love do not reflect all cultures, and it is insensitive to think that they might. As it stands, those tales do not always reflect the ways and values of modern American society, which is partly why it is trendy to revamp them.

## Our Recommended Approach

In our own storytelling work, when we change the cultural backdrop of a traditional story, we set it in our own cultural milieus or in a geographic location, like deserts or cities. We encourage our students to do the same. To do otherwise adds another layer of cultural interpretation that we, as cultural outsiders, cannot fairly provide. While we champion artistic vision, we also champion cultural sensitivity. Placing Little Red Riding Hood in the tropics to see how the tale plays out in a rain forest is one thing. Costuming her in a culture's practices or artifacts can be irresponsible or even exploitative. Only intimate insiders can clothe Little Red in their culture, if they choose to do so.

We have utter confidence that fellow storytellers, with ardent souls and generous hearts, will go forth into the world of story adaptation with an awareness that won't dampen the fire of their passion, but feed it with even more respect for stories and cultures.

# NOTES

1. Lewis Carroll, *Alice's Adventures in Wonderland*, full text of *Alice's Adventures in Wonderland*, August 12, 2006, accessed July 10, 2016, https://archive.org/stream/alicesadventures19033gut/19033.txt.

2. J.A. Cudden., *Dictionary of Literary Terms and Literary Theory*, revised by M.A.R. Habib. (Penguin Group: London, 2013), 650.

3. Later in this chapter, we discuss the assumptions about women's roles in Jewish culture, past and present. These issues are highlighted when we translate a traditional, Old World folktale into a modern, suburban setting. See Updating a Folktale to a Contemporary Setting: "I Need Quiet."

4. Some folktale sources include Maria Leach and Kurt Werth, "Milk Bottles," *The Thing at the Foot of the Bed: And Other Scary Tales* (New York: Philomel Books, 1959), 60-62 S.E. Schlosser, "Milk Bottles." *Spooky California: Tales of Hauntings, Strange Happenings, and Other Local Lore*, (Guilford, CT: Insiders' Guide, 2005), 2-6; R. Mary Hamilton, 2001, "The Woman in Brown," on *Live from the Culbertson Mansion: Haunting Tales*, (Frankfort: Hidden Spring). Leach's tale is based on an Alabama story reported in a New Mexico journal, Schlosser's is from California, and Hamilton's from Kentucky. A browser search finds this widespread tale told in many more places, variably titled "Milk Bottles" and "The Woman in Gray." We never saw a written version of this tale before writing ours. We culled our story from the oral versions told by storytellers, or as described in Chapter One, Note 14, where Bacchilega (2013) describes the fairy-tale web. From Bacchilega we extrapolate and say that our version of "Milk Bottles" is based on stories from the folktale web.

5. An in-depth discussion of this issue is beyond the scope of this book. In short, folktales and their ilk are stored in a non-fiction section in libraries that catalog them according to the Dewey Decimal System (398.2). That would suggest that folktales are non-fiction. But it is not always so! The lines and edges blur on this issue when picture book versions of folktales are stored in the fiction section of the children's room in a library.
   On one hand, mythology and folklore collections carry history and cultural knowledge, content that belongs in a non-fiction section of the library. On the other hand, fables of talking spiders and bullying rabbits, are, for many people, fictitious. Yet don't these fictions carry life and cultural truths? Indeed, they do ... but don't many novels and other forms of narrative art carry them as well? This issue is an interesting intellectual knot which we will leave for you to disentangle. Have fun.

6. This is one reason why we call our method of adaptation Storytwisting.

7. Picture book and story collections burst with this well-loved folktale. Some sources include Nathan Ausubel, ed. "It Could Always Be Worse," in *A Treasury of Jewish Folklore: The Stories, Traditions, Legends, Humor, Wisdom and Folk Songs of the Jewish People*, (New York: Crown Publishers, 1948), 69-70; Adèle Geras, "The Overcrowded House," in *My Grandmother's Stories: A Collection of Jewish Folktales*, (New York: Knopf Books for Young Readers, 2003), 68-75; Margot Zemach, *It Could Always Be Worse: A Yiddish Folk Tale*,(New York: Square Fish, 1990).

8. This could be cultural and it could be due to the patriarchal worldview of those who collected the stories.

9. Doris B Gold., and Lisa Stein, *From the Wise Women of Israel: Folklore and Memoirs*, (New York: Biblio Press, 1993); Barbara Rush, *The Book of Jewish Women's Tales* (Northvale: Jason Aronson, Inc., 1994); Peninnah Schram, *Jewish Stories One Generation Tells Another*, (Northvale: Jason Aronson, an Imprint of Rowman and Littlefield, 1987).

10. We once adapted the very same folktale for "I Need Quiet!" That was a long time ago and the tale was not in our active repertoire at the time when we were at the camp. Neither of us realized we were re-twisting "It Could Always Be Worse" until days later.

11. Jarune Uwujaren, "The Difference Between Cultural Exchange and Cultural Appropriation," *Everyday Feminism*, September 30, 2013, accessed May 28, 2016. http://everydayfeminism.com/2013/09/cultural-exchange-and-cultural -appropriation/

12. Beth Horner, telephone conversation with author, May 26, 2016.

13. Whether his manner of re-cloaking a Jewish tale in Irish woolens was respectful to Jewish culture is another question entirely. To the best of our recollection, his version didn't feel disrespectful to its source.

14. When cultural stories are carefully researched and respectfully presented, they are considered to be teaching tools that open minds and hearts to world cultures. See for example, Anne Goding, *Storytelling: Reflecting on Oral Narratives and Cultures*, 2nd ed. (San Diego: Cognella Publishing, 2016) and Melissa Heckler and Carol Birch, "Building Bridges with Stories," in *Storytelling Encyclopedia: Historical, Cultural, and Multiethnic Approaches to Oral Traditions Around the World*, edited by David Adams Leeming, (Pheonix. AZ: Oryx Press, 1997), 8-15. For times when it is not acceptable to be a cultural outsider telling tales, please see Chapter One, "Ethics and Culture"

15. Alan Dundes, *Little Red Riding Hood: A Casebook*. (Madison: University of Wisconsin Press, 1989), 13 and 21-63.

16. Historical fiction folktales, by contrast, are typically set at points in time when contemporary storytellers (and their listeners) were not yet alive. Unless the performer has access to a time machine, it is not feasible to be a complete insider. The only way to learn about different points in history times is through research.

*There was a large mushroom growing near her,*
*about the same height as herself; and when she*
*had looked under it, and on both sides of it,*
*and behind it, it occurred to her that she might*
*as well look and see what was on top of it.*

LEWIS CARROLL[1]

CHAPTER FOUR

# Fracture Point & Point of View

MOST CLASSIC FOLKTALES ARE TOLD IN THE THIRD PERSON with an outside narrator describing the sequence of events. But all tales don't have to be told like that. There is an old saying that suggests that if we walk a mile in another's shoes, we come to understand that person's world. While every story provides the reader or listener with a peek into another's world, the language of writing offers yet an additional approach. We can change how we think about stories and the other characters in them by shifting the point of view.

Gazing at the world through a new set of eyes or from a different angle offers a wealth of insight into stories, cultures and even ourselves. So slip on a character's shoes or hooves, grow taller or shrink, and embark on this delightful journey with us.

## Twist the Dial: From One Perspective to Another

*Once upon a time there were three little pigs who*
*set out on the road to seek their fortunes.*

So begins one of the most famous tales in the English speaking world. Told in this traditional manner, the story lets us peer into an imaginary fish bowl where three pigs live. Sometimes we are up close and personal, entering their homes or minds. Sometimes we view their lives at a respectful distance. The narrator is command central and controls everything that we see and learn about the pigs' story.

The tale's narrator establishes the point of view. In literature, the point of view is "the vantage point from which a story is presented."[2] It refers to the one(s) who tells the story. But point of view also depicts the narrator's relationship to the story. Where the narrator stands in relation to the story dramatically impacts how a story is shared with others.

*The first little pig built a house out of straw.*

This excerpt is told by someone outside of the narrative. When plot and character development is seen through the eyes of an impartial narrator who is outside the events of the story, then the point of view is said to be in the third person.[3] Traditional stories are typically told in the third person.

There are two basic styles of third-person narration: omniscient and limited. A third person narrator with far-reaching vision, known as the omniscient narrator, details what happens in the story, shares inner thoughts of main characters, and is aware of all story events and background. If, on the other hand, the narrator describes the story events but shares the thoughts and insights of only one character, then that narration is said to be limited.[4]

Third person narration implies objectivity. But if an objective outsider recounts the events that happen within the story, does the audience always receive a balanced, unbiased presentation? Not necessarily.

Most third person renditions of "The Three Little Pigs" focus the narrative spotlight on the pigs. They are the stars of the story. Both narrator and audience follow a path of events driven by the pigs' experiences. We don't know much about the wolf or what his life is like. All we know is how he intersects the piggies' storyline. Although the tale is told in the third person, it is not entirely objective because it highlights the experiences of the pigs, not the wolf. The third-person narration tells the story from the pigs' perspective.

This is to be expected. Stories are always about someone, a main character or protagonist with whom we place our sympathies. We must care about the main character for a story to work. In longer works like novels, there is leeway to explore multiple characters more deeply and expand their horizons. The length of a novel is its luxury. In folktale and fairy tale-sized works, there isn't time to delve so deeply. That is why such stories typically identify one, main sympathetic character.

*But the third little pig wasn't lazy like his siblings. He took his time.*

Even though this narrative is about three pigs, we care most about the third one. He earns our sympathy because the narrative spotlight broadens and brightens when his part of the tale is told. The story turns on his actions. Through his wit and industry, the problem is solved and evil is vanquished.

## A Different Example: From One Protagonist to Another

It is also possible to shift the narrative spotlight and change perspective. One can tell the same story in the third person without focusing on the pigs as the heroes or protagonists. If we refocus perspective instead on the wolf, then that well-known antagonist from the famous story can play a different role.

> One day, a big wolf went out in search of a meal. It was an effort to eat because he, like other wolves, had to hunt for food. Unfortunately, this wolf hadn't eaten for a long time. He was weak with hunger. When he passed a house of straw with a plump pig inside, his stomach rumbled. Relief coursed through his limbs. He smacked his lips with anticipation and cried, "Little Pig, Little Pig, let me in." Then he huffed and puffed and blew the house down. The wolf pounced on the wreckage, but the pig was gone. He escaped while the wolf blew down his house. Howling with disappointment, the wolf crawled back into the forest and curled up in his lair. Hunger enveloped him. He was desperate but not daunted. Tomorrow is another day, he resolved.

In this version of the story, we want the poor wolf to eat. By shifting the spotlight onto the wolf, the audience's sympathy is also redirected. Here, we have no commitment to the pigs because the pigs and wolf have switched functions. Now the pigs serve to intersect the wolf's storyline. He is the protagonist. When we twist the perspective from pigs to wolf and tell the tale from a different point of view, we walk alongside the wolf as his story journey unfolds.

## A Final Example: From "She Said" to "I Said"

There is one last point-of-view style to discuss. When that same story is told from *inside* the fishbowl by one of its own characters, the point of view shifts from third to first person.

> Brick houses are hard to build! When I finally finished my work, I tucked myself into my cozy home. I was too tired to eat, and that is saying something for a pig. Just as I was about to fall asleep, I heard a knock on the door.

In this case, first-person narration shows us the story through the eyes of one of its characters. We walk the story road on the third little pig's shoulders. Through his eyes and heart, we see and feel his experience. Thanks to him, we have excellent insider information—even if it is not all the information—and fresh insight into an old story.

When we change a story's perspective, we learn something. By shifting the point of view or transferring sympathy from one character to another, we twist surprises into a tale or wring out new meaning. In this chapter, we offer two stories with changed points of view. "The Troll's House" shifts both perspective and point of view. The second story, "The Big Red Beet," is what we call a personal folktale, in which we share a traditional story in the first person, as if it happened to us.

୬

## From the Villain's Perspective: "The Troll's House"

### Do the Twist

The first time we read Jon Szieska's fractured version of *The True Story of the Three Little Pigs,* we were entranced. In that picture book, the wolf (Alexander T. Wolf to be precise), gives his side of the story. He explains that the houses of straw and sticks were blown down accidentally because he had a cold and sneezed.[5] Inspired by his work, we cast about for a story to twist. Then we remembered a family anecdote about Jeri and Zack's many visits to a local park.

### Why We Did the Twist

"The Billy Goats Gruff" is a famous Norwegian folktale about three billy goats who cross a bridge to eat grass on the other side. A troll under the bridge threatens to eat each goat in turn. But the first two goats convince him to wait for a bigger, older, and fatter brother. When the third and biggest goat arrives, the troll threatens him. In response, the billy goat catches the troll on his sharp horns and hurls him into the distance. Then, they eat their grass in peace.[6] Jeri recalls:

> When Zack was small, he and I play-acted "Billy Goats and Troll," a variation on the classic folktale. Because he couldn't abide the meanness in that story, Zack worked out his feelings in play. I took the role of Troll

and sat under the slide, our stand-in for the bridge. Billy Goat Zack made a commotion during his climb up the ladder and got louder when he slid down the slide. I chanted the famous refrain, "Trip-trap trip-trap o'er my bridge, who's that walking o'er my bridge," but instead of saying "I'm going to eat you up," I invited Billy Goat Zack for tea and grass in my lair under the "bridge." After the tea party, we switched roles and did it all again. And again.

Zack was not alone in having discomfort with the traditional story. In our view, it is unspeakable that the goats beat up the troll. The goats trespassed on his bridge. Despite his warning and threats to eat them, the troll did not start the trouble. The violation of his person and property needed to be avenged. That was how he became the subject for our story.

## How We Did the Twist

With the storytwisting dial turned to point of view, we replaced the traditional protagonists, the billy goats, with the troll. Instead of caring about the goats' experience, our sympathies are with the protagonist Troll. This reversed the polarity of the tale. With a troll hero, the billy goats become the arch antagonists, or villains.

---

### Teaching Twist

*Choose a favorite folk or fairy tale. Encourage students to rewrite it from the perspective of the antagonist.*

*1. Describe the fabled behavior of the character in the traditional story.*

*2. Brainstorm alternative explanations for that behavior. Possible themes might include: (a) a misunderstanding or misperception by the protagonist; (b) an excuse that demonstrates that the behavior was not malicious; (c) mistakes, accidents, or acts of nature that caused trouble in the traditional tale; (d) a claim of innocence that includes the identity of a "true" culprit.*

*3. Choose one explanation and let the writing begin.*

---

Although many of our twisted tales are not drafted in one sitting, this was an exception. A first draft was completed at the end of one writing session. It wasn't a polished piece at that stage, but the idea, the story progression, and its quirky linguistic style were spawned. The draft went through the same vicious editing process that all our stories undergo. Text was added, word choice was improved, scenes were restructured, and the narrative edges were sanded like a fine piece of wood.

Despite all the usual revisions, the very first draft practically wrote itself. We pondered this anomaly. One of us (usually Jeri) drafts our pieces, in inspired chunks, over a period of days or longer. As we considered the free-flowing story that was written on that first day, we realized that it wasn't a human sitting at the computer that day. The troll sat there instead.

### Twisting Tip

*Make sure that your reimagined story makes sense.* When a story is lifted out of the oral tradition and re-envisioned, changes to character and plot naturally occur. Every change you make in the new tale must make sense and fit into the story you are telling. If you must shoehorn an idea into the story, then it is probably best to let that idea go. For example, in "The Troll's House," our fractured version of "The Billy Goats Gruff," we had a host of ideas about the troll's friends and cousins. While that would tell us a bunch more about the troll, it did not belong in this story. It ruined the pace of the tale and wrecked the rhythm (which is already a stretch from the traditional Norwegian folktale). In the story proper, the content sounded like forced afterthoughts, so we dropped it.

Trite as it may sound, a firm belief in a character's point of view is inspirational. Spurred on by commitment to character, writing springs to life under the fingertips. Most importantly, a storyteller with a deep understanding of character is better able to express it to others in writing and in live performance.

"The Troll's House" was created and edited by the troll himself. We wrote, rewrote, and spoke in his voice. The more we embodied him, the more his concerns about the goats made sense. The better we understood his position, the more he had to say about the story.

To deepen our understanding about this character, we also delved into his childhood. The troll's mother was the center of his universe. She read him troll fairy tales before bed and cooked wonderful meals. We made up troll recipes and named his favorite dishes. We wrote about his supper table conversations, mealtime rituals, described his home décor, and his lifelong wish for pets—he couldn't have them due to allergies.

Many of these details are not relevant to the bridge-walking incident. We didn't use them all in the story. But the process helped us, as writers and performers, connect with the character more deeply. And a few, choice details paint him as a sympathetic character for the audience.

Writing the troll's biography helped us write the fractured tale. We learned that fondness for tradition and a warm spot for his mother drove him to be a defender of his home. Not only did he fiercely protect his house, but proudly honored the warm memory of his mother. When chunks of roof fell into his soup pot, the troll despaired because they defiled it, a symbol of his precious mother. The soup, a seemingly irrelevant detail in the story, represents his feelings about what happened. He was a victim of actions that threatened his house, home and maternal memory. These points were consistent with the theme of the new story.

Our starting point was to tell this tale from the troll's perspective. By exploring his biography and writing the story from his position, a victim of trespassing, his lair under the bridge was transformed into a home. The rest of the story twisted naturally into a place. A tiny, protector of his humble abode, our troll is more hobbit than monster. He is a proud little homebody who values family and tradition. Once that image was evoked and solidified, we fine-tuned the story told from his perspective.

### STORYTWIST

#### *The Troll's House*
By Jeri Burns and Barry Marshall
Copyright 2010, 2018 The Storycrafters

Home is where the heart is. That's what I've always said. My mother and father kept my home neat. I try to do the same. I love the peace and quiet of the country. I moved here from the suburbs you know. There are no lawn-mowers, no noisy kids on skateboards, no political canvassers or door-to-door salesmen—my doctor said that peace and quiet is just what I needed for my health. Less stress, you know what I mean, right?

So there I was, living in a nice cozy place, when all of a sudden, I start hearing a noise. *Trip, trap, trip, trap.* On and on it goes. How would you like that? I mean, imagine. There you are, having a nice little nap on your soft, mossy bed, when you are disturbed—hauled out of bed—no, exploded out of your dreams by *trip, trap, trip, trap*. It puts you in a bad temper, you know?

So I look outside and what do I see? There's a billy goat walking on the roof of my house. What am I, a drum? So I ask him, "What gives?"

Now I don't know what he told you I said, see, he probably made up a story that I was going to eat him up or something. Well let me tell you, for the record, that I eat nothing with horns, got me? But I was hotter than a firecracker cooking over a campfire. Let me tell you, trip trapping on my cozy nest—he had some nerve!

So he tells me that I should wait for his brother. He said his brother was bigger than him. Now I ask you, do you think I wanted to wait for his brother? This little hairy-faced, stubble-eared, four-legged muck mover was loud enough to make sap run in dormant trees—why would I want to meet a louder version of "Obnoxious 2.0?" But before I could say anything to him, he tripped and trapped a little more on the roof of my house and ended up eating the locally grown grass over the other side of the stream.

Now I told you, I like to keep a nice, neat cozy home, just like my dear old mother used to do, rest her *stroll*. When he tripped and trapped, bits of my roof showered down and soiled my hair. I don't think I told you about my hair. It's the talk of trolldom. Most trolls have long stringy hair—you've probably seen some of those hideous examples that sit on human shelves—you know the ones, they have pink or orange hair. Well real trolls are much better looking. And I am a most handsome and unique specimen (that's what my dear mother always said, and she was right about just about everything—just like your mother!) Anyway, my hair is not stringy—it's thick enough to wrap around my shoulders and keep me warm against the chill of winter. And now, thanks to that four-legged battering ram, there were pieces of rocks and dirt that soiled my locks and my cozy little nest.

I took out my broom—I keep one over in the corner in case of emergencies—and swept the mess out of my house. Have I told you about my cozy house? It's tucked into the sunny side of a bank. Moss carpets the floor. It's remarkably dry given the rushing stream nearby, which tells you about the quality of the construction. The workers around here take pride in what they do, but don't get me started on the builders in the suburbs! The roof of my little home happens to be a bridge—a long, wooden bridge with a delicate arch. It's as solid as bedrock that bridge, and it protects my cozy nest.

Anyway, back to the story. I swept out the mess and was just starting on my supper when I hear *trip, trap, trip, trap* over my head again. It was starting to feel like Halloween over here, but without the fun and candy. I poked my head out and, well, maybe you guessed it. (Foreshadowing was a technique I used when I gave you the idea that another brother would come along. It was a hint of what was to come.) My roof did not have four shadows on it but a four-legged, straggle-haired, horned-face teeth gnasher. I said, "What gives?"

Now would you believe this? The guy gave a whole song and dance about bigger brothers being better tasting than him. Look, I've got three bigger brothers and two little ones. I wouldn't know what any of them tastes like. How in the name of grass seed would he know? Something sinister about these four-legged hairballs, I'm telling you. So before I could so much as say, "How do *you* taste?" he tripped and trapped over my house, sending clouds of mud clumps down onto my head and into my soup pot.

I was having a rough time. Not only was I forced out of my beauty sleep, but the mud clumps in my hair were a bear to get out and my soup pot was caked with muck. I was tired and hungry and I have to admit, I was getting cranky. The neighborhood was going to pot even if nothing was going into mine!

Finally, I cleared up the mess made by the second beast and made myself a cup of tea. While sipping that, I refilled my soup pot with water and tossed in a few fine herbs. You may not know this, but we trolls are famous for our fine sense of smell. And it's not what you think! The whole world thinks we smell, in a stinky-poo, unfulfilling kind of way. But I have to tell you something—people who think they know all about other people's lives don't know a noodle about it. For your information, trolls have a refined sense of smell—we can tell what plants are in bloom five miles away as their gentle scents are carried on the breeze like holiday gifts on a platter—which we are grateful to receive in our well-trained discriminating nostrils. This sense of smell makes us fantastic cooks, especially my dear, darling mother. The soup I was making that day was one of her favorites. I had just gotten the right balance of clover and cilantro, a delicate feat as any five-star troll chef will tell you, when I heard it again.

*Trip, trap, trip, trap* over the roof of my house. Only now it was so loud it nearly knocked me off my feet. My calm, kind nature was being tested, let me assure you. This was private property and these foul fools were trespassing on my roof. There's only one person who is welcome on my roof, and the only four-legged creatures who can be there with him are his pals the reindeer. Other than that, it's trespassing pure and simple.

I sipped my chamomile tea to calm my nerves. (I told you, my doctor doesn't want me to be stressed.) Then I poked my dainty head out the window, and do you know who was there? No, not Donner or Blitzen, it was the biggest of the three trespassers—his fur was more matted, his breath more sour, and his hooves beat down on my roof with all the delicacy of an avalanche crashing down onto a sheet of glass. I called, "What gives?" and before I could say another thing, that horned, helmeted hunk of hairy homeliness reached out with his horns and plucked me out of my house like a fish on a hook.

I tried to reason with him. My dear darling mother always told us to do that whenever we troll brothers fought. She reminded us that blubber was thicker than winter and that nothing violent should come between us. I tried to tell him, I really tried to tell him. I mean, there was a little footpath just down the stream a ways—it was easy to cross over to the locally grown grass there. I begged him to go that way instead of tromping over my house.

Maybe he had a lot of wax in his ears, or maybe he was as stubborn as a bad rash. All I know is that he didn't listen to a word I said. He swung me up into the air and sent me flying so hard and fast I thought I'd land in the Newark airport.

But I didn't. There I was, flying through the air, whipped about like an egg in a washing machine. It seemed a lifetime of flying, and my long luxurious hair was getting tangled. Finally, I landed in soft bed of moss in a brand new neighborhood. Lovely flowers bloomed everywhere, trees of green towered over me and fluffy meadows swayed in the breezy distance. I saw a perfect place to set up a new nest—there was a big, roomy hole nestled in a tree trunk. The neighborhood was peaceful, it was quiet. There were no rough and gruff hairy goats. No bridges. The only thing I had to make certain of was if any peddlers or wanderers liked to tromp along on the road near my new house. It's made of yellow brick, but that can't amount to much, can it?

## Twisting Tips

### Changing Perspective Storytwisting Tips

*Commit yourself completely to your character's side of the story.* You have to believe in another side to the story. As you sit down to write, put on your imaginary team colors. Are you revealing injustice? Are you bringing out the muffled voice of a silent supporting character? You have to metaphorically stand with a megaphone and proclaim your support for your character's position with a rousing team cheer! If you don't clearly know whose perspective you are rooting for, neither will your audience.

---

### *Teaching Twist*

*Exploring a character's biography is a fun process Review a number of story characters from familiar folktales.*

*1. Encourage students to choose a favorite character.*

*2. Ask them to write about the character's past.*

*3. Offer writing prompts to those who need them. Include familiar events from life, such as: (a) a family dinner; (b) what happened on one of the character's family vacations; (c) typical play dates or first romantic dates; (d) what the character did for school, and/or; (e) a character's first job.*

*4. After they draft their explorations, bring the class together to discuss their observations. Ask a series of questions to stimulate conversation: What new information did they learn about the character? How could an early life experience have impacted the character's behavior or personality in the traditional story? How might some of the character's past experiences contradict famous personality traits?*

---

*Delve deeply into your character(s) at the start of the creative process.* Discover new delights about a familiar character and use them to connect yourself and your audience to the character in a new way. Novelty attracts attention, but novelty alone won't sustain it. Convince your audience that this new side of the story is worth their time. Entice them to listen to another side of the story by offering meaningful details. Make them care about a reimagined character and champion his perspective. Cute is not compelling. Depth is.

*Analyze how a familiar character behaves in your source(s).* It is important to identify familiar character traits and behaviors before you twist the point of view. They are easy to pick out with a review of your source(s), but you must go deeper. Honestly evaluate any assumptions or biases that you or anyone else can have about that character. For a new perspective to work in a fractured piece, it is imperative to understand expectations and assumptions so you can flip one (or more) on its head and craft enlightening material that opens minds.

*Find your character's voice … literally.* Whether your story is destined for print or speech, reading aloud is not only allowed, but essential. It helps you hear the character's voice more clearly, which in turn helps you to write it more authentically. We read out loud whenever there is a natural pause in our writing flow. It engages our imagination and stimulates more writing while connecting us more fully with the character. Try reading your story in a variety of styles and tones of voice. Explore emotions and traits, like anger or petulance, sadness or whimsy. Once you settle on your character's voice, you will hear it in your head while you write. The sound of the troll's voice influenced every word he said and his personality all throughout our tale.

*Paint a sympathetic picture of your new protagonist in the story itself.* Whether we like or dislike a protagonist in a story, we need to care enough about what happens in order to follow the tale. When a story is told from a different point of view, a former antagonist may now wear the protagonist's shoes (or hooves). New details about the character's motivation or unique view of the situation will help convince an audience to care enough about the character or new take on the story to see it through to the end.

## A PERSONAL FOLKTALE: "THE BIG RED BEET"

*Personal folktale* is our designation for a specific style of storytwisting. First-person renditions of traditional folktales are told as if they happened to us.

## Do the Twist

One summer day, while working in the garden, a story called "The Enormous Turnip" came to mind. It is a beloved Russian folktale about an old man who cannot harvest an oversized turnip. Various characters offer to assist and line up behind him from biggest to smallest. Everyone one tugs on the jacket or skirt of the next one in line while he tugs the turnip greens. When the littlest one finally joins in, the turnip pops out of the ground.[7] This story is widely known and retold, so while it is not part of the European canon of fairy tales, it is close.[8]

## Why We Did the Twist

As we hacked at the roots of our stubborn weeds, we wished for a Turnip-style parade of people to help us do the onerous chore.

"Who would be in that parade?" Barry wondered.

"I don't know," Jeri said, "You and me? Zack?"

"Yeah, but that wouldn't be enough."

"Barry, it sounds like we're making up a fractured "'Turnip' story ..."

## How We Did the Twist

Before we sat down to write the folktale as if it happened to us, we substituted a beet for the turnip. This substitution enhances the new piece by twisting the story right off the bat. It also bestows wordplay opportunity because, in live performance, the story's repetitive chant is accompanied by a *beat box*. But most importantly, the turnip-to-beet substitution lends authenticity to our tale. That summer we didn't grow turnips—we grew beets.

The growth of a monstrous root vegetable is an oddly intriguing story idea. Factor in a pair of competent adults who cannot harvest it and you have a dubious premise for a true-to-life story. Because the plot-based actions of this and other traditional folktale characters do not typically resemble the behavior of modern people, personal folktales benefit from techniques that bolster believability and audience engagement.

We always include people and places from our real lives in our personal folktales. This steeps them with authenticity. By embedding the unlikely traditional story plot into the truths of our real existence, those truths bond together like bedrock and support the suspension of disbelief.

To make a storytwisted "Enormous Turnip" work, we reviewed the bones of the traditional folktale to identify the setting, character, and plot details that would remain roughly intact in the reinvented one. We determined that we needed a garden, plus people and animals of various sizes. Although the specific garden and characters came from our real lives, the traditional plot and character actions from the story would preserve the reverberant echoes of intertextuality. With our eye on the storytwisting dial, our intent was to make all of our modifications consistent with the fracture point.

---

### Teaching Twist

*The objective of this exercise is to explore first-person narration. Sift through some favorite folktales and identify ones with at least one human protagonist. Ask students to choose one and substitute themselves for the main human character. They should refrain from updating the story, altering the setting, modifying the characters, or changing what happens. Their sole objective is to tell the traditional story with all its intact trappings from an insider's viewpoint.*

*If they take on the role of Jack in the beanstalk tale for example, Jack's mother cannot be their own mother. The cow cannot be replaced with a pet turtle. Encourage the students to tell the famous story as if they were Jack. The story patterns and characters from the source tale will not change. This allows them to delve more fully into the first-person experience without worrying about story other details.*

*Encourage detailed descriptions of any feelings they experience as they go along, how they manage tasks, and what they see along with the rest of the familiar story content. What nuances are discovered about the story? How do they feel about the other characters? What do they learn about themselves?*

---

Finding a garden and characters was easy. We have a garden in our yard. Jeri, Barry, and Zack are three people. We have a cat. The summer we wrote the tale, Zack babysat our neighbors' kids, Diego and Oscar, so we had two more prospects.

One crucial detail stopped the writing train, however. Who would be the last and smallest one on the conga line of harvesters? At first, we chose Oscar, the younger boy. This was consistent with the Russian folktale, where the least powerful of all—the mouse—is the one whose assistance is the magic ingredient that manifests a successful harvest. But Oscar's place at the end of the line was troublesome for two reasons. First, toddlers are bigger than cats. The story's message was about how the smallest makes the biggest difference. If Oscar stood behind the cat, his size would blunt that message. Second, if a human stood behind a cat in line, a human would have to tug the cat. The image of a person yanking a cat's tail or tugging at her harness was not an option.

So we had a decision to make. We could delete the kitty to make Oscar the hero of the story. But the cat's involvement in the story was very exciting to our son, Zack. And, as the resident child in our house, he argued that animals in the harvesting line would boost the joviality factor for family audiences. We agreed with him and kept the cat.

The next task was to brainstorm a list of additional animals that met two conditions: (1) they were smaller than a cat, and; (2) they could be found in our yard. We identified a field mouse, squirrels, chipmunks, groundhogs, birds, or small rabbits.

The bunny was our first favorite. But before going further, we asked ourselves a question. What would the presence of a bunny do to the overall meaning of the story? A timid, tiny bunny is common prey, and that is about as powerless creatures get. That notion was consistent with the traditional story's meaning. So far, so good. But we dug deeper. Are all bunnies timid and harmless? In theory, yes, but garden bunnies who devour your kale and collards are definitely not.

We have a garden bunny who we call Bun-Bun. That name may sound affectionate, but affection is not intended. Garden bunnies like Bun-Bun are not American's most wanted pets. They are disasters in fluffy disguise. They are not sweet and they don't deliver jelly beans. Garden bunnies are plagues— okay, they are cute plagues. The point is that the dark side of "bunnydom" shone a different light on the reimagined story. Instead of cute and sweet, our smallest creature would be a reviled and despised one.

Next, we brainstormed a list of unpopular earthly creatures. From garden pests like bunnies and moles, to snakes and cockroaches, our minds rolled on. Then we asked the million-dollar question. What is more reviled than a critter that stings or bites?

That rhetorical question added depth to the traditional moral of the story. A tiny, cute creature, like a rabbit or guinea pig, would not save the day in our story. Instead, a tiny, often reviled creature would do the job. A number of possible candidates could fill that role, but snakes and insects topped our list.

We could have chosen a critter randomly from a grab bag of loathsome creatures. But we believe that personal folktales work best when truth is part of the story so we speculated about the revolting critters in our own lives. That was when we thought about our relationship with bugs. And that was a direct line to Jeri's mother. Here is Jeri again:

> My mom can't stand bugs. She taught us that they're the scourge of humankind. In all seriousness, my mother trained us to run outside if we saw a bug in the house. And if she didn't happen to run outside with us, she'd take care of it with the full force of her chemical arsenal. (Her weapons of mass destruction were easy to find. They were stored in spray cans under the kitchen sink.) Like a suburban superhero, my mom cleansed our home of bugs, one fly at a time.

Jeri's mother's bug behavior is legend in our family folklore, but there is also a universal aspect to it. Her seek-and-destroy tendency is mirrored in the world at large. As a society, we discard the things that displease us. We devalue that which disgusts us. We toss away what we think has no value. And when we discard, we lose something that might have unseen value. That motif permeates our reimagined version of "The Enormous Turnip." It is the heart of our tale. To embrace what disgusts or scares us and to find value in all things are apt story messages for today's throwaway world.

The most important takeaway is this: Without fracture, we might never have achieved this insight. Storytwisting showed us a new way to think about an old tale. It inspired us to conceive a message for our tale that is consistent with the traditional tale's message about the important contributions that even tiny creatures can offer.[9] But our tale adds an extra layer. It also reflects today's modern, throwaway, "everything-must-be-perfect-and-beautiful" focus in contemporary society.

We were delighted with this idea in theory, but pragmatism forced us to analyze it further. The insect at the end of our story's harvesting line had to be forceful enough to upset a cat. While mosquitoes are universally despised, a mosquito's bite wouldn't phase a kitty. When we turned our attention to stinging insects, that too required probing. The cat would notice a bee sting, but a bee could send the story down an alternate route because some die after losing their stingers. Although the meaning of our story—the hidden value of the most reviled—would remain, a bee's sacrifice would impart sadness, an emotion that didn't fit the tone of the fractured tale. We could have taken a moment to explain that our bee was not the stinger-losing type, but that solution felt more cumbersome than elegant.

---

### Teaching Twist

*The adaptation of traditional stories to real-life situations can be challenging when there are talking animals, giant beanstalks, or fanciful places from that do not exist in real life. This exercise explores how to tackle that: Place a fairy tale palace in a personal folktale.*

*To tell a fairy tale as if it happened to you, there must be truths from your life. Since there are no fairy tale palaces where we live in the Hudson Valley of New York, we must make a substitution. Historic mansions dot the shore of the Hudson River. Any of them can play the part of a palace. Since fairy tale queens and kings are not usually named, we will follow that precedent and refer to the people of those places as Rich Farmer, the Leader, or the Business Tycoon.*

*Identify a historic site, mansion, or upscale building near where you live. A government building can serve this function as well. Identify people who live or work at that place. Describe the power they wield, power like that of a King or Queen. Invent a title for the "king" or "queen" that is consistent with their roles in your community. Then describe the "palace" in detail. From that description, a true-to-life designation for "palace" will emerge.*

---

We went with a wasp. Its sting would distress the cat and the wasp would survive to see another day.

By using a real-life contrast between Jeri's family of origin, where insects were sprayed out of existence, and our current home, where suffering wasps are given sugar water in bottle caps during the lean, winter months, we made truth a twisting feature and wove a family story into our personal folktale. By extension, we also presented a relevant message for modern times (with a nice comeuppance for those who disrespect insects).[10]

∽

## Storytwist

### *The Big Red Beet*

A Personal Folktale Based on "The Enormous Turnip"
Copyright 2010, 2018 The Storycrafters
Told in a trio with Barry, Jeri, and their son, Zack Marshall.

**Jeri:** Do bugs bug you? They bug my mother! Let me tell you a little bit about my house when I was growing up. My Mom insisted that if a creature had six or eight legs, then it had no redeeming value. Other parents ran fire drill exercises with their kids—my Mom taught us to evacuate the house if there was a bug creeping around. Then she would whip out the can of Raid that (in my childhood eyes) was tied to her belt like the Lone Ranger, and presto, the fastest draw on Long Island, no more bug.

**Barry:** We wanted Zack's relationship with bugs to be calmer. So we were easy around insects in our house. We even showed them hospitality. One winter we fed a wasp sugar water for weeks until the spring sun was warm enough for it to go out.

**Zack:** My parents did their best, but I just don't like bugs. Especially spiders. And our cat, Stellaluna thinks their only purpose in life is breakfast, lunch, dinner, and snacks.

**Jeri:** The cat loves to chase them, especially in autumn, as if some base animal instinct tells her that the summer bounty of bugs, like garden vegetables, will soon be a thing of the past.

**Barry:** Now fall is a busy time at our house, moving wood, canning and freezing food, and getting the garden prepared for winter. While we work, Stellaluna, chases the last flies and wasps of summer all over the house. One day last fall the weather was perfect. It was such a crisp, clear day, we had to get outside and do some of the fall chores.

**Zack:** Even the cat was antsy, chasing a wasp all over the living room. She knocked down one lamp and almost tipped a glass of water.

**Jeri:** To get a bit of work done and to get away from our wild kitty, we went into the garden to clear out the worst of the summer weeds and do a bit of harvesting.

**Zack:** The neighbor's little children, Diego and Oscar, came over.

**Jeri:** You see, their parents, Paris and Meg, are serious do-it-yourselfers. That year, they renovated the upstairs of their house and removed an overgrown, dying forest in their backyard. Every day we heard the steady clank of Meg's hammer and the scream of Paris' chainsaw ... nearly all day long. Meg and Paris needed child care.

**Barry:** And we needed ear plugs.

**Zack:** Whenever I was around, I would babysit the kids. So when Diego and Oscar came over that day, we headed over to the swing set.

**Jeri:** Our garden was fenced in, so to keep the cat from messing up the living room, we brought her into the garden with us.

**Barry:** As we were clearing out one of the beds, I noticed a huge bunch of greens. As I looked closer at it, I realized that they were beet greens. Apparently we didn't harvest one of the beets from earlier in the season. Our beets were particularly big and sweet that summer. Since this bunch of greens was really big, I figured that this one last beet must be a pretty hefty. So I bent down, reached for the greens, and I heaved, and I pulled, and I yanked and I lugged and I strained and I tugged.

Then I had an idea. (Barry turns to Zack.) Hey Zack, this is a rhyme about a beet, so I think we need a beat box. (Zack begins rhythm while Barry chants.) I heaved and I pulled and I yanked and I lugged and we strained and tugged. (Accompanied by beat box rhythm.) But nothing happened. The big red beet didn't come up.

**Jeri:** Barry beckoned to me and said ...

**Barry:** That must be one big red beet. Would you give me a hand?

**Jeri:** Sure thing.... So I stood behind him and held tight to his belt

**Barry:** ... and I held on to the greens.

**Barry and Jeri:** Then we heaved, and we pulled, and we yanked and we lugged and we strained and we tugged but that big, red, bulbous beet didn't come up.

**Barry:** That must be one big red beet! We need more help.

**Jeri:** We called to Zack and asked for his help harvesting the beet.

**Zack:** I brought Diego and Oscar into the garden. They'd be safe, with the fence all around it. They picked raspberries while I stood behind my mom and held her pony-tail.

**Jeri:** I held Barry's belt

**Barry:** … and I held the greens.

**All:** Then we heaved, and we pulled, and we yanked and we lugged and we strained and we tugged but that big, red, bulbous beet didn't come up. (Zack not spoken but beat box.)

**Barry:** That must be one big red beet! We need more help.

**Zack:** Just then, Diego and Oscar came running over. Oscar said, "Help."

**Jeri:** The boys were small. We weren't sure about this.

**Zack:** But Oscar cried "Help" again, so we thought, why not?

**Barry:** They each grabbed hold of one of Zack's belt loops.

**Zack:** I held my mom's pony tail.

**Jeri:** I held Barry's belt.

**Barry:** And I held the greens.

**All:** Then we heaved, and we pulled, and we yanked and we lugged and we strained and we tugged but that big, red, bulbous beet (pause so that audience joins in for …) didn't come up!

**Barry:** That must be one big red beet! We need more help. But who? We couldn't ask Diego and Oscar's parents. They had just brought a hydraulic drill with a 200-foot bit into their front yard to install a geothermal heating unit for their house.

**Zack:** What about the cat?

**Jeri:** Barry looked at me …

**Barry:** … and Jeri looked at me. There were so many people already.

**Jeri:** How could a tiny cat do any good?

**Zack:** But mom, what harm could she do? We might as well try.

**Barry:** We shrugged … Okay.

**Zack:** So I chased Stella around the garden until I caught her and I put her front paws on the bottom of Diego and Oscar's shirts.

**Barry:** They held on to Zack's belt loops …

**Zack:** … while I held my mom's pony tail.

**Jeri:** I held Barry's belt.

**Barry:** And I held the greens.

**All:** Then we heaved, and we pulled, and we yanked and we lugged and we strained and we tugged but that big, red, bulbous beet—with audience— didn't come up!

**Barry:** That must be one big red beet! We need more help.

**Jeri:** Now we've got to tell you a little detail. When we all left the house to go outside, we didn't know that the wasp that Stella had been tormenting all morning, had flown out right behind us.

**Zack:** At that moment, it was in the garden, buzzing around Stella's tail, probably thinking about getting her back for the morning torment.

**Barry:** Diego cried, "Bug!"

**Zack:** Are you afraid? He won't bother you if you don't bother him.

**Barry:** Diego shook his head and said, "Bug help!"

**Jeri:** How can a bug help us?

**Barry:** Diego and Oscar both cried …

**Barry and Jeri:** "Bug help!"

**Jeri:** And before we could react, even Zack joined them for a chorus of …

**All:** "Bug help!"

**Jeri:** And believe it or not, no sooner did they say "Bug help!" for the third—and frankly speaking, the most magical—time, that wasp landed on Stella's back like a cowboy riding a horse.

**Barry:** But it's so little. How can something so small help?

**Zack:** Diego and Oscar told us they could see the wasp's forelegs gripping Stella's fur.

**Jeri:** Since the kids really wanted to try it, we decided to do it just for them. So the wasp gripped Stella's fur …

**Zack:** Stella held the bottom of Diego and Oscar's shirts …

**Barry:** They held on to Zack's belt loops …

**Zack:** I held my mom's pony-tail …

**Jeri:** I held Barry's belt …

**Barry:** … and I held the greens.

**All:** Then we heaved, and we pulled, and we yanked and we lugged and we strained and we tugged but that big, red, bulbous beet—with audience— didn't come up.

**Barry:** That must be one big red beet! We need more help.

**Zack:** Let's try it one more time.

**Jeri:** And one more time, the boys cried …

**All:** "Bug help!"

**Barry:** Then, just as were about to haul on that beet again, the wasp stung the cat.

**Jeri:** Stella yowled. Her claws gripped so tightly to the boys' shirts that one of her claws scratched Diego.

**Zack:** Diego screamed and pulled harder on my belt loops. I fell backwards, nearly pulling my mom's pony-tail out of her head.

**Jeri:** And I dragged Barry and his belt with me.

**Barry:** The cat fell in the green beans.

**Jeri:** Diego and Oscar flew across the garden and landed in the spinach.

**Zack:** I was caught like a baseball in the "mitt" of the collard greens.

**Jeri:** I fell into the basil (and never smelled so good) …

**Barry:** … and I landed on the squash, squashing it.

**Jeri:** And do you know what?

**All:** That big red bulbous beet came up!

**Barry:** It flew high in the air like a burgundy ball and landed, *kerplop*, in the harvesting box, which meant that our harvesting box was now a "beet box" (beat box sounds).

**Jeri:** So we gathered up the broken beans, squished squash, potatoes, spinach, basil, collards and put them in the box with the big red beet.

**Barry:** We took them all in the house and dumped them in a big soup pot and made a great, big vegetable stew.

**Jeri:** I washed Diego's scratch and put a band aid on it.

**Zack:** I went to Diego and Oscar's house to invite their parents over to eat stew and to hear the story of what happened. They had just finished installing a super-power nuclear research telescope on their roof, so they were pretty hungry.

**Jeri:** We put some of the stew in Stella's bowl …

**Barry:** … and we put some beet juice in the lid of a jar for the wasp.

**Jeri:** So my mother was wrong. There is redeeming value to all living creatures no matter how big or how small, including bugs.

**Zack:** And Stella has never chased a wasp again, to this very day.

**Barry:** And that's the story of …

**All:** … The Big Red Beet.

⥲

## TWISTING TIPS

### First-Person Storytwisting Tips

*Include personal facts in your personal folktale.* The truer and more accurate these facts are for you, the more they ring true for the audience. Truth conveys authenticity, brings imagery to life, and urges an audience to suspend disbelief and come along for the ride when things get out of whack. While you may also intertwine a personal story and folktale, it is not necessary. Personal folktales stand on their own as well.

*Tweak a few personal facts, if necessary,* to make your personal folktale work. A personal folktale is not a memoir with an expectation of truth.[10] It is a fictional piece embedded in the setting of your existence. Just because you have a shade garden doesn't mean that it can't serve as the location for a reinterpreted "Enormous Turnip" tale. Turnips and other root vegetables require sunlight. Sometimes you must tweak reality and move that garden out of the shade for your story to make sense.

*Take your time to build the foundation of your story.* Lull the audience into accepting the mayhem of a personal folktale by establishing believable context. In "The Big Red Beet" for example, we describe our enterprising and noisy neighbors, Meg and Paris. Early in the tale, the descriptions are accurate. Meg and Paris could be anyone's neighbors. They add authentic depth to our neighborhood, which in turn adds depth to our story's setting. Our final description of them, however, enters the tall tale realm and the audience accepts it. By that point in the story, the world of reality has completely collapsed into fictive fantasy as we collaborate with animals as anthropomorphized equals. Because Meg and Paris are truthfully described in the story's foundation, the audience meets bizarre exaggerations with graceful appreciation.

95

### The Necessity of the Narrator in Personal Folktales

Storytellers wear many hats: writer, performer, and cultural interpreter are some examples. One that marks a storyteller with a capital "S" is the hat of the narrator. While all stories are narrated, the narrator role is integral to live storytelling performances and deserves special attention in personal folktales.

While telling a tale, a storyteller sometimes lingers luxuriously in the narrator role, flirting with the audience by sharing knowing nods or commentary about the doings of a character. At other times, the teller embodies that character and speaks in her voice. Storytellers flip back and forth between characters and narrator, surfing from role to role. Like a movie camera, the narrator pans out for a panoramic view of the story's events or moves in for a character close-up. This graceful back and forth movement is part of what gives a story texture and makes it come alive. But where a movie's camera shots are controlled by a director, the story is in the capable hands of the narrator.

Recounting a story entirely as an outside narrator—without jumping into the shoes of a character or evoking story events through physical or vocal expression—is what Livo and Reitz describe as telling about a story, not actually telling it.[12] You see, the narrator's fluidity is a signature part of the storytelling art. As an impartial outside observer or a knowledgeable insider, the unfettered narrator flits from one point of view to another. The teller describes a story's events in one moment and lives them in the next, all the while polka-dotting the narrative with personal comments about the story events.

In performance storytelling, the narrator is not a separate, disembodied voice, but the flesh-and-blood person who tells the tale and forges a connection between the story and the listeners. The narrator is a person, not a persona. An authentic, no-frills storyteller builds audience trust, and through point of view and commentary in reaction to story events and characters, garners respect.

To tell the personal folktale as a storyteller with a capital "S," consciously integrate the narrator into personal folktales. In addition to being a character in the story, recount selected story events in your regular narrator voice, just as you would in a folktale that isn't about you. The authentic narrator is particularly vital in personal folktales.[13] Immersed in "experiences" or "memories" as a character in the story, the narrator can otherwise be swept away by the adventure.[14]

In "The Big, Red Beet," for example, we start the story informally, by discussing Jeri's mother. We speak of her from a distance and then recount an anecdote about her. While sharing it, our body language, words, or subtext sends messages from our narrator selves, like "Yeah, we know this sounds a little strange and yet it's for real." Because we start the tale as everyday people, not as characters, we introduce our authentic selves as narrators at the very beginning and expose the audience to our natural, commentary style. This connects us to our listeners. It also increases the likelihood that they will accept our story commentary and join us as we are propelled through an unlikely folktale plot. Knowing us as narrators orients listeners at the story's start and then provides a comfy home base for those moments when we bounce back and forth between our roles as folktale characters and narrators.

When we tell personal folktales, we treat ourselves just like we treat any other character in a story, moving from story narration to character portrayal and back again. Even as we vault into fast-paced, climactic moments in our personal folktales, we return to the here and now, to our narrator selves. Even something as tiny as a subtle glance or a single word clearly communicates that we are still in control as the narrators. In our experience, a clear cut narrator and commentary upgrades the personal folktale from cutesy cleverness to a viable and meaningful storytelling experience.

*Include facts from your life, but don't overdo it.* You want to make your piece a believable folktale, not a saga. Artfully expressed personal content that (1) conveys the setting; (2) helps build a picture from the tale; and (3) doesn't bog down the action is content worth keeping. It helps if audience members can picture your story with you in it, an essential first step toward making the tale believable. If they believe your story at its start, they will commit for the story ride.

---

### Twisting Tip

*Explore your characters fairly and fully.* Whether you tell a straight tale or a twisted one, it is important to study the nature of your characters. While this can be a useful writing warmup, it is much more than that. A thoughtful analysis of characters helps you develop your version of the story, paint richly nuanced and memorable characters, and avoid unintended stereotypes. As you mine your characters' attributes, be awake to your own biases and misconceptions—we all have them them—unchecked, they can pollute story magic and offend audiences.

---

*Reinterpret the actions of traditional characters carefully* in a personal folktale. In a story with archetypal, one-dimensional characters, violent actions are acceptable in the context of the tale. But when a character in the story is the flesh and blood person sitting in the room with you, acceptability drops precipitously. In "The Big Red Beet" we tussled, ironically, with the way the characters "yank" the next character in the line. Pulling a cat's tail is a violent image that we rejected. A related and delicate issue was the physical connection among humans. To grab someone else by the seat of the pants crosses a boundary. It reads strangely to any audience, but is completely inappropriate for family audiences. Physical connections between adults and children can easily be misconstrued—the adults touch no children in our tale, and the only child-adult connection is son to mother. Our solutions to this are cartoon-like. They make story sense, fit with our sensibilities about violence or extremely anti-social gestures, and work for our intended audience.

## Twist for Thought: Two Sides of Monsters and Heroes

When Jeri was growing up, her parents would often say: "There are two sides to every story and somewhere in the middle lies the truth." This wonderful aphorism reveals how bias works. Bias prejudices us to favor one thing at the expense of another.[11] In order to approach the truth of a matter, one has to look at the other side, or perhaps several other viewpoints.

This was tattooed on Jeri's soul. In graduate school, she investigated multiple sides of every issue to find that murky middle place where elusive truth dwells. It is a minor miracle she finished her Ph.D.

But she was not alone in her efforts. In their quest for knowledge or truth, academic scholars and researchers minimize bias through careful investigations to make truth as transparent as possible. Scientific investigation and Jeri's parents' old adage are both focused on finding objective truth. But storytelling is not always focused on objective truth. When a story follows one character's perspective, we learn truths about living life, such as *persevere and you will succeed*. We don't need to hear every character's perspective to learn that. Life truths can be taught through one character's perspective. But if we look at another character's perspective, we are likely to learn a different life truth. That is why we twist that old saying and say that there are two sides to every story, and somewhere in the middle lie the *truths*.

We believe that there are multiple truths in every story. One truth can't apply to all actors in a tale. For example, not every character in a story perseveres and succeeds. Other perspectives reveal additional truths. Storytellers aren't academics offering reams of data and scientific analysis. We tease out other perspectives and unfold important life truths from the fabric of a single narrative.

"The Billy Goats Gruff," like other folktales, is a biased story. From the outset, we are prejudiced against the troll. But when we twist the dial and tell the story from the troll's perspective, we discover his humanity. We also note an element of injustice that is not apparent when the story is told in the traditional manner—we learn that the troll is an obstacle for the billy goats to overcome. His bridge, or rather his life, is something to get past in order for the goats to meet their needs. The troll's existence is irrelevant except where it impedes their goal-seeking.

The story, "The Troll's House" is an allegory, a work of art that reveals something about reality. Consider this in relation to the way impoverished people are trounced upon as others power-walk to greener pastures via highways and bridges built through inner-city neighborhoods. New infrastructure carries advantaged people to life in the suburbs. The world below the highway is unseen and irrelevant to commuters who speed over those neighborhoods to the glorious, grassy suburbs far from the inner city. The people and real estate under that highway may be regarded as unworthy or of lesser value because the destruction of their environment is allowed. Sometimes those below the highways are perceived as monsters. When people are unseen or are perceived as monsters, it makes it much easier for others to dismiss them or even trample them out of existence.

### Twisting Tip

*Identify the overarching message or meaning of your story.* Every tale has a dominant theme or message. We articulate one for every straight or twisted tale we tell and store it, like a Post-it note, in our minds, in our documents, and well, on Post-it notes. Sometimes our interpretation of this message evolves in writing, as in our story about the beet. Meaning is the story's backbone. It is also important for another practical reason. Knowing the message is analogous to having a port in a brainstorm. It anchors the new story so that new content has a place to land. By stating and committing to a theme, you can determine what ideas will function well in your new piece. Test each idea by asking two questions: Does this new idea correspond to my theme? Does this new idea also carry the story forward? If the answer to both question is yes, then it is worth keeping.

No one wants to be ignored. No one likes to be discounted. If you lived in a neighborhood that was destroyed to make life more convenient for others, wouldn't you feel angry about it? Well, the troll in the well-known billy goats tales lives in such a place.

This is why his story speaks so strongly to us. We see it as a modern tale of injustice embedded in a traditional nursery tale. Injustice is an unfortunate and relevant issue for the world, yesterday and today. By getting inside the troll's mind and heart, we understand that the troll was upset for legitimate reasons. When we hear his story, we begin to see him as a whole character, not a sketch of a monster. His protestations are understandable. When we view the events of the story from his perspective, he and the goats trade places. He is the one who captures our sympathy and the billy goats are the monsters who cause trouble.

When we define those we perceive as different as monsters, it says more about us than about them. Twisting the story lens to a different point of view makes us aware of this unfortunate human tendency—it can pulverize unfair stereotypes about all kinds of traditional story characters: passive girls, witchy older women, world-crushing princes, evil pagans, and unfamiliar monsters. We discover that maybe, just maybe, there is more to these familiar characters than meets the eye.

As an allegory, this process reveals the all-too-human proclivity to malign those who are perceived as different. By extension, if investigating another character's perspective in a work of fantasy can broaden our minds and break down stereotypes, imagine what the same process can achieve in the real world?

There are two sides to every story, and somewhere in the middle lie the truths.

# NOTES

1. Lewis Carroll, *Alice's Adventures in Wonderland*, Full Text of *Alice's Adventures in Wonderland*, August 12, 2006, accessed July 10, 2016, https://archive.org/stream/alicesadventures19033gut/19033.txt.

2. The Editors of Encyclopædia Britannica. "Point of View." Encyclopedia Britannica Online, accessed May 31, 2016, http://www.britannica.com/art/point-of-view-literature-and-film.

3. Chris Baldick, *The Concise Oxford Dictionary of Literary Terms*, (Oxford University Press: Oxford, New York, 1990), 173.

4. Ibid.

5. Jon Scieszka, and Lane Smith, *The True Story of the Three Little Pigs: As Told to Jon Scieszka*, (New York: Viking Kestrel, 1989).

6. Claire Booss, ed. "The Three Billy-Goats Who Went up into the Hills to Get Fat," in *Scandinavian Folk and Fairy Taless*, (Avenel: Gramercy Books, 1984), 29-30. Stephen Carpenter and Peter Christen Asbjørnsen, *The Three Billy Goats Gruff*, (New York: HarperCollinsFestival, 1998). Janet Stevens, *The Three Billy Goats Gruff*, (San Diego, New York, London: Harcourt Jovanovich, Publishers, 1987). Rebecca Hu-Van Wright and Ying-Hwa Hu, *The Three Billy Goats Gruff*, (Cambridge: Star Bright Books, 2014). Like so many other beloved childhood stories, there are a huge number of retellings, including numerous picture book renditions with the translated text of the earliest-known (to us) collector of the story, Peter Christen Asbjørnsen and Jørgen Moe, trans. by George Webbe Dasent, (Edmonston and Douglas), 1859.

7. Vivian French and Stephen Lambert, "The Enormous Turnip," in *The Kingfisher Book of Nursery Tales*, (Boston: Kingfisher, 2003), 54-65. Elisa Davy Pearmain,"The Turnip," in *Once Upon a Time: Storytelling to Teach Character and Prevent Bullying,*. (Greensboro: Character Development Group, 2006), 46-47; Janice M. Del Negro, *Folktales Aloud: Practical Advice for Playful Storytelling*, (Chicago: ALA Editions, 2013), 19-21. Aleksey Nikolayevich Tolstoy and Niamh Sharkey, *The Gigantic Turnip*, (Brooklyn, NY: Barefoot Books, 1999).

8. A widespread folktale, the Turnip story is like a "classic" in the storytelling community and in the wider world. Like the fairy tales that everyone knows, the Turnip story has a nearly transcultural status. This was the dominant reason we chose to twist this story. A secondary reason is that Jeri has Russian ancestry.

9. When we developed our remix of "The Big, Red Beet," our actual source was the folktale web ("folktale web" is a term we adapt from Cristina Bacchilega's "fairy tale web," Bacchilega 2013). The folktale web includes our memory of this tale from

having heard and read it over the years, plus some written versions we happened to have around the house at the time we wrote it. We mistakenly thought that Tolstoy was the first collector of this tale. We were wrong. In preparing this book, we came upon what we now believe is the earliest recorded version of this story. What amazes us is that in Aleksander Afanas'ev's version (Afanas'ev, 1975, 26-27), the final creature is an insect! There are a number of insects, and they are all beetles. So after all the digging and analyzing for our own fractured and updated version, we came back around and honored the spirit of an early version of this story. Folklore works in mysterious ways, and it is one reason we believe that time and careful consideration produces a respectful approach to creation.

10. For the record, Jeri's mom now uses all-natural products in her quest for an insect-free existence. A compromise for the planet (but not the target insect).

A personal folktale is an interesting story genre. It seems like it exists in the netherworld between memoir and fiction. But when we dig below the surface we find that the personal folktale is your garden-variety fictional story.
In a pure memoir, we wouldn't advocate changing details about personal existence to make a story work better. But in a personal folktale, the rules of the game are different. This type of story fits fiction into a factual existence. Bending and flexibility—or twisting—is acceptable in a fictional piece. And though there are absolute truths in personal folktales, though based in truthful foundations, the tales themselves are utter fiction.

For a brief introduction into some of the issues of truth and memoir writing, see Tracey Seeley, "When Is Lying in Memoir Acceptable? 3 Key Issues | WritersDigest. com," WritersDigest.com. May 31, 2011, accessed May 31, 2016. http://www. writersdigest.com/editor-blogs/there-are-no-rules/guest-post/when-is-lying-in-memoir-acceptable-3-key-issues

In the world of storytelling, personal stories, which are spoken memoirs, are also expected to be true. In his book about personal storytelling, Jack Maguire consulted with numerous personal storytellers around the country. Every storyteller agreed that a personal story must reflect truth as the storyteller perceives it. Objective truth may be different. For example, when specific dialogue from many years ago is not remembered factually, but imagined as it might have been, that is an example of perceived, not objective, truth. But as you can see, the essence of truth remains. See Jack Maguire, *The Power of Personal Storytelling: Spinning Tales to Connect with Others*, (New York: Jeremy P. Tarcher/Putnam, 1998), 23-24.

11. There are additional subtleties to a definition of bias, depending on whether it is a brief definition or a more involved one. See, for example, the first and later definitions here: Merriam-Webster, accessed May 31, 2016, http://www.merriam-webster.com/dictionary/bias.

12. Norma J. Livo and Sandra A. Ritz, *Storytelling: Process and Practice*, (Littleton: Libraries Unlimited, Inc., 1986), 148-149.

13. Whenever a storyteller intones an inauthentic storyteller singsong or dons an artificial accent to share a story, a wall is built between teller and listeners. Storytellers

are not characters in a play, but real people. Once an inauthentic communication style is struck, it's a strike against effective communication with listeners.

14. It is possible, and even advisable, to allow the narrator to be present when embodying a character as well, as if you are wearing two hats at one time. While it sounds complicated, it is not difficult to manage. You can revert back to the narrator it by making a momentary aside in your natural storytelling voice, not the character's voice. In this manner, the narrator peeks out through the character, like a flickering light.

*Twinkle, twinkle, little bat*
*How I wonder what you're at*
*Up above the world so high*
*Like a tea-tray in the sky.*
LEWIS CARROLL[1]

CHAPTER FIVE

# Fracture Point & Rhyme

AUDIENCES OF ALL AGES ENJOY TALES TOLD IN RHYME. The cadence and music of rhyme lulls listeners into the flow of story. Whenever we perform a rhymed piece for groups of any age, they lean in closer. When we share a rhythmic chant, they bounce along more vigorously than when we offer non-rhythmic participatory phrases. Audiences attend more deeply when rhythm and rhyme are woven into storytelling, making the performance space sizzle with intensity.

A lifelong love of rhyme begins in the cradle. Perhaps early childhood exposure to poetry makes rhymed language a source of comfort and delight throughout our lives. Perhaps our brains are wired to appreciate them.

Babies and young children delight in the beauty of language. They sing songs, chew on words, and giggle at funny sounds. To spur on their love of language and a grasp of speech, adults drench them in nursery rhymes. We also sing to them.

Research supports the adult instinct to share rhymed language with children. Rhymed language helps young children develop awareness of sound.[2] This in turn helps them learn and remember words.[3] Sound recognition, facilitated by rhyme, predicts reading success,[4] is linked to literacy,[5] and is related to students' ability to read three years later.[6] Further research demonstrates that the benefits of early exposure to rhymed language persists into adolescence.[7] Step by step, the human brain is strengthened by sounds and rhyme.

Cognitive poetics is a new field that integrates cognitive psychology and the study of language processing in the analysis of literature. Recent research findings demonstrate that adults respond emotionally to poetry. Rhyme and meter, separately and together, affect how we perceive beauty, meaning, and emotional feeling in the artistic performance of a poem.[8] Public speaking for people of all ages is enhanced with poetic turns of phrase, rhyme, and metrical emphasis. Educator and author Janice Hamlet notes that rhythmic speech carries emotionality and imagination.[9] It is not surprising then, that rhymed stories engage audiences of all ages.

*Teaching Twist*

*Educators may be interested to know, that recent rhyme research suggests that new words and concepts may be more likely to be learned and remembered when their placement in a rhymed stanza is at the end of a rhyming line.*[10]

### Twist the Dial: From Prose to Rhyme

In this chapter we focus our efforts on three kinds of rhyming stories—story rap, balladry, and sonnets. The rap that we present is a fractured version of the beloved, widely known fable, "The Tortoise and the Hare." In contrast, source folktales for the other stories included in this chapter, "The Baker's Dozen" and "The Quail Sonnet," are not well-known. As adapted retellings, those two stories are not fractured or parodied.[11]

### Do the Twist: Story Rap

Rap, a genre of popular music and an example of spoken word poetry, is the verbal and musical expression of hip-hop culture. Rappers (who have also been called Masters of Ceremony or MCs) perform spoken, rhymed words, usually over beats or rhythms. The structure of rap has become more complex so that machine-gunned rhymes are accompanied by polyrhythmic, electronic beats. Its content varies significantly, from boasting and insults to messages about politics, social justice, sexuality and violence.[12]

We write and perform raps, but we are not rappers in the popular music sense of the word. We are not hip-hop artists. Our artistic aim is to merge old, familiar stories with a contemporary spoken word style. There are many rap genres—Gangsta, Christian, and Old School, to name a few. We call what we do "story rap."

**Why We Started Doing Story Rap**

We started writing story raps completely by accident. One fall, the Norman Rockwell Museum in Stockbridge, Massachusetts, asked us to tell stories for an art exhibit featuring the work of children's illustrators. The sponsor requested a set of stories that related to stories in the exhibit. She promised to send us the full list of titles in the coming weeks, but she indicated that the stories were mostly from the classical canon, tales like "Cinderella" and "Sleeping Beauty." Our immediate reaction was that we could easily accommodate this particular request since our repertoire already included cultural variants of some of the stories she mentioned. The program sponsor liked the idea of including cultural variants, but wanted at least one immediately recognizable version of a story in our overall program. We were confident that we could develop a performed telling of one of the stories in the exhibit, so we agreed to take the booking.

A number of weeks later, the program sponsor sent us the list of book titles. To our dismay, there was not one story on the list that we wanted to learn. In fact, we actively disliked many of them. With the actual performance now only two weeks away, we were in a bind.

A guiding principle among most storytellers is to love the stories we tell. Telling tales without a true connection poses challenges to the artist, the story, and the audience. First of all, there are very few artists willing to spend hours and hours shaping a distasteful piece and then performing it again and again. How much justice can the artist do to a story that they don't like? Lastly, and most importantly, it is challenging to engage an audience of listeners when the performer isn't committed to the tale. Our bind was clear: How could we develop a performance piece, as we were contracted to do, and still retain our artistic integrity?

Desperation, the mother of invention, came to the rescue. We decided to try to write a rap version of one story. Rap can be edgy. It can send positive or negative messages. Whatever the tone and meaning, raps are wrapped in the thrill of rhythm, rhyme, and creative language.

The decision to write a rap version of a fairy tale made sense for us. We already accompanied some of our stories with drumming. From the perspective of professional development, grafting spoken rhyme to rhythmic drumming was an exciting, artistic challenge. As to our integrity, rap's edgy attitude gave us poetic license to tweak parts of any story that offended us.

---

### History of Rap Music: A Thumbnail Sketch

Modern rap developed in the 1970's. Rap arose as one element of hip-hop culture, along with break dancing and graffiti art. Born in the streets of the Bronx, it is an artistic protest movement.[13] Today, the music continues as it began, as the artistic expression of an oppressed minority. However, it is also a mainstay of popular culture around the world.

The roots of rap are far older than the 1970's. They can be traced back to the heart of traditional culture in West Africa, to verbal play and the rhymed and musical stories of griots, the traditional storytellers of the region.[14] In addition to rhyme and rhythm, other oral conventions of the African diaspora are incorporated into modern rap.

Playing the Dozens is a traditional verbal contest in African-American culture. Often incorporating rhyme, the Dozens slings insults at opponents, at their families, at their partners, and more. The content is highly variable. It can be vicious or playful, misogynistic, sexual, or political.[15]

The Caribbean has related oral styles. Jamaican toasts, where DJs chant over rhythms, emigrated to the Bronx around the time rap was born. The artist Kool J Herc, originally from Jamaica, is often credited with bringing this significant contribution to American rap.[16]

Extempo is a Calypsonian tradition of the spoken word that has been an active part of Trinidadian culture since the early 20th Century.[17] Artists spontaneously compose verses on various topics, such as current events, politics, and culture. Competitions, or Extempo Wars, add another layer of challenge because performers must insult other competitors and fit their content to a theme at the same time.[18]

Although rap technically arose from hip-hop culture, it is also an outgrowth of traditional storytelling and oral styles carried across oceans and throughout history.

---

Thanks to rap style, we transformed "Rumpelstiltskin," a fairy tale that we found revolting, into a story we love to tell. For more on this, please see Chapter Seven, "Fracture Point: Character"

## How We Write Story Raps

Every time we write a story rap, we begin by choosing whether to twist the dial from prose to rhyme alone, or to twist multiple story elements at once. In Chapter Seven, we offer "Little Red Riding Dude Rap," which has multiple twists. Because it is more complicated to twist multiple story elements at one time, for this chapter, we discuss twisting the dial to rhyme (and rap) only.

We have written over twenty raps. While specific writing issues for each rap are unique, we have distilled the overall creative process into several phases:

1. Review
2. Outline
3. Literary Sketching

4. Drafting Text
5. Modified Freestyle
6. Read-A-Louds

## Review[19]

First, we carefully review the tale that we plan to rap. If we work with a Grimm's or Andersen fairy tale, we consult various translations. When working with a myth or folktale, we seek several variants of the selected story. This process has a twofold purpose: (1) to reacquaint us with a source story; and (2) to identify images and plot points that are consistent and divergent across most versions.

## Outline

Our outline includes the bones of the story, (see Chapter Two, "Storytwisting Strategies") iconic phraseology, names, key setting details, characters, and motifs that are in all versions. Next, we highlight what are likely to be the widely familiar components. In "The Tortoise and the Hare," for instance, some familiar aspects include:

- A hare who makes fun of a tortoise for being slow.
- A challenge to race.
- A tortoise who moves along slowly and steadily.
- A hare who takes his time, naps, or takes breaks.
- A tortoise who presses on and wins the race.

The outline may contain more or less content than the rap ultimately will. Editorial decisions about cuts and changes are made later.

## Literary Sketching: An Expanded Form of Brainstorming

Just as a painter draws rough sketches of subjects before embarking on a big work, we conduct word experiments and develop written sketches of characters or story events. Combined, these writing activities are what we call *literary sketches.* Because every rap is unique, there is no sketching template that works each time. Varying in form and content, a literary sketch can include playful word explorations, free associations, thematic brainstorming, and nuanced scene development. It can also explore innovative ways to identify characters and name synonyms for chief motifs. The literary sketch may include anything from a cohesive picture of a character to a set of random words or ideas that can be set aside for later use, like dried herbs on a spice rack.

Literary sketching is our favorite step. Often, we approach the sketch in a frenzied burst of creativity. Other times, we build up our notes a little at a time over the space of weeks or months.

But it also happens that neither approach bears fruit. In that case, we let the rap go dormant for months at a time, like a caterpillar in a chrysalis. We wish we could report that the story turns into a butterfly during that time. It doesn't. We are the ones who undergo the metamorphosis. Time away from the story gives us fresh insight and breaks through writer's block. Somehow, that period of dormancy allows the imagination to take wing, so that sketching can begin anew. While this metamorphosis process applies to any writing, we find it particularly useful for raps and wordplay stories.

Sketches are important because they help us explore story images and language style at the same time. We notice patterns in characters, observe hidden ironies, find opportunities for snark, consider political correctness, build in edgy darkness, and so much more.

For example, in "The Tortoise and the Hare Rap," the literary sketch included all of the possible ways that our Hare could be slowed down in his famous race. Here are a few of them:

- Stopping to nap
- Visiting a friend
- Getting food
- Daydreaming
- Going to the bathroom.

Then we looked at the themes represented by these ideas. Eating, going to the bathroom, and possibly napping, reflect the concept of need. What if eating was combined with visiting a friend? That sounded more like a desire.

But then we noticed daydreaming and that suggested distraction.

From there, we changed thematic tacks and wondered if, instead of a conscious choice to meet a need or desire, the hare is hampered by distractions? That led us to write a separate list that included:

- A carnival
- Party
- Playground
- Roadside signs
- A television in a house
- Electronic distraction

Bingo. The moment we wrote *electronic distraction,* we selected the distractions of today's world as the theme to drive the rest of the sketching process.

The next step in the sketching process is to identify rhymes for each and every one of these words or concepts. We make lists that include rhymed phrases, inventive ways to rhyme words, and we develop characterizations shaded with modern attitude. We repeat this process for all story elements, and for other parts of the story, like the insults that Hare slings at Tortoise, the ways that Tortoise lives his life that are the objects of Hare's scorn, and so on.

Marina Warner describes the language of fairy tales as *symbolic Esperanto.*[20] In rap, the universal language is raw, rhythmic rhyme.

## Drafting Text

It is tempting to say that we draft a rap after the sketches are done. But we never totally complete our sketches before starting to write a draft of the actual rap text. Drafting is but another layer of the rap writing process. It doesn't halt the sketching phase, but invigorates it. We draft and sketch concurrently, just as if two highway routes were converging and we were driving on both highways at once. One process merges with the other, making the creative process more vigorous.

## Modified Freestyle

Freestyle rapping is improvised lyrical and rhythmic composition. While it is true that we do much of our writing at a computer, in large part, our raps are composed away from the machine. We don't freestyle our raps start to finish, but emulate freestyle technique. Once we begin the writing process, story images and random phrases course through our brains like ear worms. Everyday activities are infused with strains of rhythm, rhyme, and linguistic experimentation. Some of our best work is born in line at the supermarket or in the shower. We rhyme random phrases while washing dishes and adjust rhythms as we stack firewood. We have rap battles in the car, tossing phrases back and forth in a rhythmic ping-pong match of wits. We record the good stuff on whatever device is handy.

*Teaching Twist*

*Identify a list of favorite childhood folktales that your students know and write a class rap version of the story.*

Our modified freestyle works for composing story raps in the same way freestyle works for rappers. It allows creativity to flourish. As it turns out, recent research has documented an interesting effect that freestyle rapping has on brain activity. Using functional MRIs, scientists have monitored brain activity while rappers freestyled. According to the study, a rapper's brain activity is altered during freestyle. The self-monitoring and self-censoring sections of the brain dial down while centers of emotion, integration and language become more active. The result of this altered brain activity during freestyle is an increase in creativity.[21]

Rappers know that freestyle works. We know that modified freestyle works for composing story raps. Thanks to science, we now know why.

## Read-A-Loud

Every writing or editing session begins with a read-through. In part, it is a writing warmup. But it also reacquaints us with the style, tone, and feel of the reinvented story so that new material is consistent with existing content.

Once there is rap text in a computer document, Jeri checks and rechecks the oral nature of the words, ensuring that they sound more like natural speech than words from a piece of written literature. She speaks every line and every rewrite many times. Speak, rewrite, repeat. By reading it out loud, she tastes the text on her tongue and listens to its music—what looks good on the screen doesn't always work in the mouth or on the ear. Then, both of us read each rap aloud and comb through it again and again. One reads and the other listens. This crucial step puts us in the shoes of future audiences.

As we read a rap aloud, we ask ourselves a number of questions.

- Is it easy to say and listen to?
- Are the words natural to speech and oral in nature—as opposed to literary?
- Does the rhythm and text flow comfortably?
- Do consonants add sonic interest without creating distraction?
- Does the sound evoke a mood that is consistent with character or dramatic moments in the tale?

If the answer is "no" to any of the questions, then we revise the words or rhythm of our rap until the rhymes resonate, the mood makes its mark, and cadence cruises.

Read-a-louds chisel away awkwardness in rhythmic passages. They might involve a complete rewrite of an entire stanza or the substitution of a one-syllable synonym for a two-syllable word.

But smooth rhythm is not always the goal. Because rap is built on rhythmic complexity, we want unexpected triplets, off beats, and rhythmic surprises. Breaks in established rhythmic patterns catch the attention of listeners. They amplify meaning or draw focus to important moments in the story.

Rap is an oral art. Like storytelling, it requires translation from print. Regular read-a-louds detect rhythmic problems. They also red-flag literary language that can saturate any story written at a computer. Verbal emphasis, rhythmic accompaniment, and articulation of words create polyrhythms that

---

### Story Rapping: Ten Considerations for Honoring Rap and its Origins

Modern rap was developed by minority people in oppressed communities. And here we are, a white rural-dwelling couple, writing raps. Does it necessarily follow that when we write and perform story raps, we are engaging in cultural appropriation? Is it generally a form of disrespectful cultural borrowing when storytellers rap? We raise this issue because we have heard pieces across many disciplines that are presented as raps. While they rhyme, they don't all have rap's edge. Even when it is not intentional, cultural appropriation can happen.

Defining cultural appropriation is complicated. It includes disrespectful cultural borrowing and a dominant culture's exploitation of a marginalized people's cultural products. Unfortunately, there are no easy, unified answers about cultural appropriation,[22] and that is why we've done much reading and soul searching. Ethical scrutiny carried us into the heart of our own profession, where we find a longstanding tradition for storytellers of all ethnicities to pay homage to other cultures by sharing cultural stories in a respectful manner (See Chapter One: Ethics and Culture). Our raps are created in that same spirit.

Rap is a spoken-word tradition. As spoken-word artists, we strive to evoke the art of rap, honor those who created it, and parlay "ye olde" storytelling content into a modern, globalized communication style.

Born of research and deep thinking, here are ten considerations we carry whenever we rap.

1.   It is important to give credit where credit is due. Before sharing any of our raps, we provide a brief overview about where and why rap evolved. In this way we honor the art form and pay tribute to the African-American communities where this style developed.

2.   While modern rap's roots are in urban, minority communities, it is now a worldwide musical phenomenon. The art form has crossed borders, economic classes, and racial divides to become a popular music style. One might say that it is transcultural.[23] Because rap is a huge part of shared popular culture, it is an effective way to relate to modern audiences.

3.   We have researched rap history and culture and have learned about the social and economic conditions that give rise to modern rap. We keep that in heart and mind whenever we write or perform them.

4.   Rhymed storytelling with musical accompaniment was not invented in modern times. While modern rap's roots can be traced to West Africa, other cultures also tell–and told–rhymed tales, including Celtic, Slavic and Indian cultures, to name a few. While not all are traditions produce raps in the contemporary sense, rhymed storytelling with musical accompaniment is not unique to rap.[24]

5.   Rap has many styles and genres, story rap is one entry on a long list of them.

6.   We are honest about our backgrounds. We know who we are and who we are not, and we are clear about that with listeners. Sometimes, we introduce raps by saying, "Next up, the Jew from Long Island and the WASP from New Jersey are going to rap–a truly multicultural experience."

7.   Over the years, we have asked many members of numerous communities of color if we are wrong to rap and if our work is in any way offensive. And over the years we have received nothing but solid, enthusiastic support.

8.   Our story raps do not masquerade as hip-hop and we don't claim to be rappers. We don't dress in costume or take on personas when we rap. We are Barry and Jeri, storytellers from the Hudson Valley, sharing a tale, rap style.

9.   To reflect the musical style, we accompany ourselves on hand drum.

10.   With its roots in social protest, rap is an excellent and apt genre for stories that address social issues and upset the fairy tale apple cart, which is just what our raps tend to do.

Rap is a rich part of popular culture and a socially important artistic force that excites people all over the world–including us. We strive to make our approach to story rap a positive act of cultural appreciation intended to enrich lives and deepen cultural understanding through the arts.[25] In our efforts to be respectful, we also evaluate each rhymed piece through the lens of the ten considerations described above. Some rhyming pieces are not raps. Instead of calling them raps, we call them rhymed stories in the bardic tradition.

In the end it is up to you to determine your comfort with rapping. Whether you write raps yourself or encourage students to do so, we urge you to deepen your understanding of rap history and style so that you approach it in a fair and respectful manner.

animate text in ways that print cannot recreate. Read-a-louds are indispensable with story rap to ensure that the final piece retains linguistic power and raw style.

**STORYTWIST**

### *The Tortoise and Hare Rap*

By Jeri Burns and Barry Marshall
Copyright 2001, 2018 The Storycrafters

A long time ago in a faraway place
Two famous animals decided to race
One was the Tortoise, he was the green one
The other was the Hare, he was the mean one

One day, Tortoise walked from the east to the west
Hare said, "Are you moving or did you stop to rest?"
Tortoise liked to make egg soufflés from scratch
Hare would say, "Will you be done before the eggs hatch?"

Tortoise liked to take things easy and slow
Hare was always on the go, go, go
Tortoise admired views, smelled the flowers
He would read, paint and meditate for hours
Tortoise baked his bread and he made his clothes
Hare had no time for activities like those
His life was in the fast lane, on the jump no doubt
He used a laundry service, went to the gym and ate out
But in between meetings, Hare always found a minute
To diss the shell and the Tortoise that was in it

Hare's insults were sharp—he was always attackin'
"You're a slug, you're a sloth, you're the Sultan of Slackin'
You are slower than a snail stuck in slime
Yo, you're the king of wasting time
I mean, you're a fortress of torpid Tortoise!
Are you alive or in rigor mortis?"

Though Tortoise's shell was thick, Hare was on his case
"I've had enough, Hare, it's time for a race!"
So a date for the great, race was set
"That's a day," Hare said, "Tortoise will regret!"

On your mark, get ready, get set, and go!
Hare zipped away, Tortoise went with the flow

Hare turned around, he was ahead alright
So he sang a little song that is not so polite:

"Na, na, na, na, na, na, na, na, na, na, na
"How do you expect to get any place?
Moving as you do, at Tortoise pace"

Still at the starting line, Tortoise wasn't speedy
Hare said, "I can work with this solid lead"
He slowed to a jog, "If this don't beat all,"
Pulled out his cell phone and made a conference call

While he caught up on some texts he went off the cement
Hare had a little accident
He bumped into a tree and felt a bit ill
Then Tortoise caught up, "This is no time to chill!"
Hare picked up speed and whipped out of sight
Then he sang that little song which is not so polite
"Na, na, na, na, na, na, na, na, na, na, na
I will leave you in the dust without a trace
You'll go home in disgrace, at Tortoise pace!"

Hare looked back, Tortoise lagged behind
"Time to unwind and go online!"
He pulled out a handheld computer apparatus
Then surfed and Tweeted and posted his status
He was blogging 'bout the race when he heard a cough
Tortoise passed right by, Hare didn't log off
He went hip hip-hopping at a frightening speed
In no time at all he was back in the lead
Hare was moving so fast he nearly took flight
Then he sang that little song that was not so polite

"Na, na, na, na, na, na, na, na, na, na, na
You're wasting my time- you call this a race?
You'll go home in disgrace at Tortoise pace!"

Hare passed a house and noticed that inside
There was a television on; his eyes opened wide
He was locked in place in a couch-potato stance
Stuck in a screen-addicted trance

He was still as a statue, eyes on the screen
Mouth hung to his knees, it was an ugly scene
He would have sprouted roots, but then he heard commotion
As the spectators hooted and cheered with emotion

Hare looked up and was shocked to see
Tortoise near the finish line, "This can't happen to me!"
Hare ran in a flash, but was yesterday's news
Tortoise won gold medals and was giving interviews

Hare's ears flopped down, then he had a cosmic shift
He said, "I guess I'm not too swift."
Hare took Tortoise out for some bouillabaisse
Then walked Tortoise home at Tortoise pace

After the race, Hare and Tortoise understood
That many different paces make our world good
So the next time someone says—You're too slow!
Or too young or too old, too high or too low!"
Tell 'em, "Let others go at their own pace
So that everyone can win in the human race!"

## Twisting Tips: Rap

*Listen to a lot of rap.* Even if you are familiar with the style, careful listening helps you write a better rap. In addition to rhymed language, raps have complex rhythmic qualities that are interconnected with the words. There is linguistic convention and rhyming style. In addition to end rhymes—at the end of lines—rap uses other poetic literary devices, such as internal rhymes and

### Teaching Twist

*As an alternative to writing raps of familiar childhood stories, encourage students to write raps on topics that are being studied in class. Nonfiction content, like biography or a historical event, can be expressed in rap style. For a bigger project, divide an event that you are studying, like the Civil Rights Movement, into modules that equal the number of students in your class. Assign a module to each student to research and write. When all the modules are completed, piece them together for a comprehensive class rap on that topic.*

assonance. Furthermore, rap is more than rhythm and rhyme. Rap is a form of social protest. It is cut with a blade of rebellion. Confrontation and attitude are its artistic signature. By listening to rap, you can emulate and honor rap's stylistic conventions in your own work.

*Talk to teens.* Pick up the latest jargon. But don't craft your entire rap in teen jargon. A brushstroke here or there is all you need to speak directly to teens and college students, which is important. Too much jargon alienates listeners who are unfamiliar with it. Furthermore, jargon is trendy. Whether or not it is overused, your text could sound outdated in a year or two.

---

### Teaching Twist

*Because rap is a contemporary musical vernacular, young people don't need a rap primer in the same way as adults. To give them a taste of rap's edgy side, all you need to do is allow them to use every day slang in their rap writing. By bringing slang and rap into the classroom, students may feel a touch rebellious, and that attitude and edginess is totally appropriate for writing rap.*

---

*Write slang and jargon into the unrhymed parts of lines.* Make your future life simpler by keeping slang text out of end rhymes in case you need to remove outdated jargon and modify the text later.

*Include modern references and informal language.* Rap is current and contemporary. Story rap is also flavored with modernity. "The Tortoise and Hare Rap" incorporates informal phrases like "I'll leave you in the dust" and "the Hare was on his case" as well as modern references to Internet culture—"he surfed, he Tweeted, posted his status." The juxtaposition of an old story with modern, informal language, adds humor, genre authenticity, and implied commentary.

*Utilize dictionaries of slang, excellent resources for writing raps.* You can check precise meanings of phrases or enjoy a good browse. One site that is particularly useful is www.urbandictionary.com. A Wiki-style website, it offers definitions of slang terminology. Because it is a Wiki, you will need to double-check information drawn from it. We also consult www.onlineslangdictionary.com because it has a (limited) thesaurus function.

*Include unexpected rhythmic combinations.* Rhythmic flexibility is a characteristic of rap. Strict adherence to a single rhythmic pattern is not necessary. Rap does not have Dr. Seuss predictability. Polyrhythms and rhythmic alterations are expected and desired, at least to some degree.

❧

## PROSE FOLKTALE SET AS A BALLAD: "THE BAKER'S DOZEN"

Many storytellers in the Capital District of New York State tell a version of a beloved, Albany-based folktale. We thought it would be nice for local audiences to hear that tale told in quite another way.

In brief, the tale tells of an old woman customer who asks a baker for a dozen cookies and insists that thirteen makes a dozen. The baker only gives her twelve. She tells him he will regret it. Then his business suffers. When she visits again, he still refuses to give her an extra cookie. Consequently, the business suffers more. When the bakery is on the verge of collapse, the baker prays for help. In answer to his prayer, St. Nicholas visits and reminds him about generosity. When the baker sees the old woman next, he gives her the thirteenth cookie and his business returns to normal.[26]

Our vision for this story was influenced by the colonial history of New York State and the folkloric roots of the tale. "The Baker's Dozen" is a traditional Dutch tale set in Albany during Dutch colonial rule. At the time, Albany was called Beverwyck. But the Dutch were not the only European colonists in New York. Eventually, the English wrested control from them. To mirror colonial history, we braided together two folkloric threads for this Albany-based story. Because ballads are a British musical storytelling genre,[27] our version of this Dutch-influenced colonial folktale is stylized in the English ballad tradition.[28]

### Do the Twist

Traditional ballads are sung stories that figure among the earliest forms of folklore. Those written by the prolific composer "Anonymous" are passed orally. Ballads by modern composers have literary roots. Some ballads recount legendary and historical events, some are romances, and others make comments on current events.[29] With original or borrowed melodies,[30] ballads are plot-driven stories that are lean on details and tell about the supernatural, tragedy, adventure, love, and more.

Ballads are composed of four-line stanzas, or quatrains, that rhyme. Quatrains in a typical English ballad abide by an A-B-C-B rhyme scheme (explanation follows.) Sometimes the rhyme scheme is A-B-A-B.[31] Ballads have refrains of varying lengths. Some have no refrain at all.

We researched the ballad style by listening to the music and reading collections. But mostly, our knowledge of ballad was borne of firsthand experience. Barry lived in rural England. He was steeped in the tradition and noted the characteristics of ballads he heard, including one particular trait. The refrain—or chorus—sometimes shifts to mirror the content of each preceding verse. The morphing text of our refrain reflects this English ballad trait.

In addition to rhymes and refrains, ballads are creatures of meter. The words of a ballad create rhythm in the way syllables are stressed. In general, the syllables alternate between being stressed and unstressed.

Furthermore, each line in a ballad stanza or quatrain has a predetermined number of stressed and unstressed syllable pairs. Our ballad is typical of many others where the line lengths vary from four stress lines to three stress lines.[32] In poetic terms, each stressed pair in a line is referred to as a *foot*. As noted in the table, "Ballad Stanza: Meter and Rhyme Scheme" a sample stanza from our ballad has alternating four and three foot lines.[33]

### Ballad Stanza: Meter and Rhyme Scheme

| QUATRAIN WITH STRESSES<br>Bold-face type indicates stressed syllable | NUMBER OF FEET | RHYME SCHEME |
|---|---|---|
| **Long** a-**go** in **Bev**-er-**wyck** | Four | A |
| there **lived** a **gen**-tle **man** | Three | B |
| He **was** the **fin**-est **ba**-ker **and** his | Four | C |
| **fame** spread **through** the **land** | Three | B |

The rhyme scheme of ballads is based on end rhymes—with rhymes landing on the last syllable(s) of the line. In an A-B-C-B rhyme scheme, B words rhyme. Usually, end rhymes are perfect rhymes, like band, land, and even understand. However, imperfect rhymes can also be used, as in the table example—"gentleman" and "land."[34]

Before we wrote our ballad, we reviewed several prose versions of "The Baker's Dozen," sketched out the story line, and crafted our interpretation of the story's meaning. Next, we penned the text of a few sample stanzas and the refrain. Then we composed the music.

## The Power of Singing

Anyone can sense the power of music, and science stands right behind that statement. The human capacity for singing is universal, beginning in babyhood when we make our first sing-song sounds. Whether it is an evolutionary adaptation or an evolutionary accident, music is part of our lives.[35] And for good reason. Music has the power to evoke emotions, foster connections between people, and bring happiness.[36] Music scientists maintain that music contributes to emotional health,[37] and studies of people singing in groups show that it improves wellbeing,[38] has therapeutic properties,[39] reduces anxiety,[40] develops trust among group members,[41] and so much more. Research also shows that listening to songs live[42] and singing in groups are positive experiences for emotional and physical health.[43] For these reasons alone, storytelling performances that incorporate sung stories with choruses that listeners sing can be valuable for audiences.

We don't have to be trained singers with fancy voices to bring the positive effects of music to people and raise everyone's voice in the chorus of a song. Ballads are not operatic arias. They are informal and native to storytelling because they are sung stories. Their melodies are easy to learn and are particularly resonant when linked to the mood and content of the story.

Technically speaking, ballads can be spoken instead of sung. Even so, the melody tells part of the story. Music is key in balladry because the genre is thin on descriptive detail. A melodic mood puts emotional meat on the bones of the narrative—just enough to paint a picture or draw a character.

There is no need for additional musical accompaniment in ballads. It is emblematic of the style to sing ballads a capella. That is why all of our ballads— traditional and original—are sung unaccompanied.

## How We Did It and How You Can Too

A ghost story ballad is chilling when set to a haunting melody. Comic ballads chortle when sung to a jocular melody. Paired in the telling, text and tune work in tandem to illuminate a tale.

The music for "The Baker's Dozen" was composed in an English ballad song style. We listened to many examples, and emulated the style by writing

# The Baker's Dozen

music composed by
Jeri Burns & Barry Marshall

lyrics written by
Jeri Burns & Barry Marshall

Long a-go in Bev-er-wyck there lived a gen-tle-

man he was the fin-est bak-er and his

fame spread through the land, he made the sweet-est

tast-y treats and buns and rolls ga-lore and

an-y-one who tast-ed one____ al-ways asked for

more more more mid-dle-ee-id-le-mid-le

more

original melodic and harmonic content. Explaining the technicalities of musical composition is beyond the scope of this book, but we can share usable ideas for how you can musicalize a ballad.

Begin by drafting two or three stanzas of your ballad, but no more. It helps, too, if you compose the language of your refrain. This can save hours of rewrites if your pre-written melody does not fit the text that is written later.

Let's say you discover or invent a musical phrase that captures the mood of your story but does not fit the syllabic stresses in your text. You will find it more difficult to sing if you must stress words in ways that are unnatural. If it is strange to sing, listeners will notice. Here is an example.

Sing the following text to the melody of "Twinkle, Twinkle, Little Star."

**Jane**, *a* **young** *wo-***man** *from* **Kent**

*Her* **ef-***forts* **were** *ve-***ry** *well* **meant**

As you can see, the stresses fall nicely on some of the words, like Jane, young and Kent. But they are wrong for the second syllable of the words "woman" and "very." For the sake of this illustration, let us suppose that the "Twinkle" melody is the best one for your ballad about Jane from Kent because it fits the mood of your story. If that is the case, then you have to rewrite your text so that the syllable stresses land properly in spoken English. Matching each syllabic stress to musical emphasis make ballads easier to sing and more enjoyable to listen to.

---

### Twisting Tip

*Maintain a number of thesaurus options for all of your writing.* Start with the one in your word processing program, but don't stop there. Thesauruses are as unique as snowflakes; always consult several—the more lists you have, the broader your word choice pool.

---

One reason we recommend writing a small part of your text before developing a melody is to avoid the rewrite described above. The other reason is because the melody helps write the rest of the words. Where a list of rhymes sparks ideas for how to complete a rhyming stanza, musical phrases also stimulate the imagination. Melodic phrasing and musical rhythms influence the choice of words. Lyrics can be written to fit rhythm and melody. Furthermore, musical mood of your melody can influence the narrative tone and text. In sum, melody, musical phrasing, and rhythm can influence the language of your story.

In "The Baker's Dozen," our refrain repeats one word intermixed with nonsense words. Initially, the plan was to keep the nonsense syllables the same in each chorus, but replace the main word in every successive refrain. We did not plan to use the same end rhyme—more, floor, store, etc.—for the entire ballad. But Barry had a shower epiphany:

> I was singing through the ballad in the shower, working on a new stanza. When I came to the refrain, "more, more, more, middle-di-eidle-deidle more," instead of singing the end rhyme "more" I accidentally sang "floor" instead. So I followed that slip of my tongue through its conclusion and sang "floor, floor, floor, fliddle-di-eidle fleidle floor." It was fun to sing.

We both loved this idea. It turned the refrain into a bit of a tongue twister joke. Before going with it, we wrote out a list of words that rhymed with "more" to see if was feasible to do as a running thread throughout the ballad. It was.

The music of the ballad affects the way the story is told. Each verse is like a mini-story, reflecting how plot works. The first two lines, declarative in nature, set up the moment. The third line depicts the climax and the fourth line brings it back down. The actual melody follows the contour of these mini-plots. Each verse—or stanza—rises on the third line and falls on the fourth.

## Developing a Ballad Melody: Two Approaches

Ballads are not lush, harmonic masterpieces. Like the narrative, a ballad's music is spare. There is no fancy theme and variation or melodic development, no bells and whistles.[44] The melody repeats with each verse so that the rhythmic and melodic pattern lulls listeners into the story and allows them to focus on the text. Simplicity and repetition also make it easier to develop a melody.

*Borrow a public domain melody, it's harder than it sounds.* There are two ways to develop a ballad melody. The first is to re-purpose an existing one. Traditional ballad melodies in the public domain can be borrowed for your tale, just as they were at the height of the European ballad tradition.[45] It is up to you to determine if your borrowed melody is in the public domain. If it is not, you can ask for permission or pay for the rights from copyright holders.

Borrowing a tune seems easier than writing one, but wrapping words around a pre-written tune is not as easy as wrapping leftovers in foil. Expect to adjust the music or your text. Furthermore, it takes time and patience to find tunes and verify their copyright status. It is a research expedition. Approach this process like a visit to a thrift store. Try various melodies on your words like clothing items. Mix styles. Be open. Your ears and inner story heart may be tickled by something unexpected. You also might find a sure-fire melody that fits the mood of the story perfectly. But like some new clothes, it may need to be hemmed or let out. If you use a public domain tune, you can freely alter melody, phrasing, or rhythm to fit your ballad. If you use a tune that is not in the public domain, you must get permission from the copyright holders to use and/or alter the tune for your use. Furthermore, you may have to pay for the rights.

*Compose a melody, it's easier than it sounds.* The second route to a melody is to write your own. You can compose a simple melody by listening to the contours of your natural *prosody* (vocal intonation and rhythm) as you read the verse aloud. As long as you avoid monotone in your reading, your voice naturally rises and falls with the text. Re-read the text again and exaggerate the tonality of your voice. Then, hum a tune that follows those contours. When your voice tones trail down, your melodic line will go down. When the pitch of your voice rises, so will your tune. If your piece follows ballad meter, your ballad rhythm is already set.

Composing a simple melody may sound daunting, but the job is not as difficult as you might imagine. Look at "The Baker's Dozen" music in "How We Did It and How You Can Too" As you can see, every quatrain uses the same melody. The second line of every verse echoes most of the melody of the first line. And the third line starts by echoing the first two lines. There is not much to compose. The challenge lies in finding a melodic contour that fits all the verses of your ballad.

✧

## STORYTWIST

### *The Baker's Dozen*

By Jeri Burns and Barry Marshall
Copyright 1996, 2018 The Storycrafters

Long ago in Beverwyck there lived a gentle man
He was the finest baker and his fame spread through the land
He made the sweetest tasty treats and buns and rolls galore
And anyone who tasted one always asked for more

'Twas over on Broadway he had his bak'ry shop
His customers would look around and their eyes would pop
There were cakes and pies and breads and buns galore
And anyone who tasted one always asked for more

Of all the treats and pastries baked by this man
'Twas the fame of his cookies that spread throughout the land
And so one winter's eve he heard the bell on the door
In walked an old woman tapping her cane upon the floor.

"A dozen cookies please in the shape of Old St. Nick."
He wrapped them in a sack, with motion deft and quick.
But the woman didn't turn to walk toward the door.
"Thirteen makes a dozen sir, so please give me one more."

"Such a silly thing you say, that I've never heard.
Twelve makes a dozen, on that you have my word.
Here are your cookies, thanks for coming to my store,
I've given you a dozen, and I'll not give you one more."

She looked at him with glaring eye and said, "Oh yes you will!"
She took her bag of cookies, and then she paid her bill
Out she walked into the night and as she shut the door she said,
"You're going to be sorry that you didn't give me more."

He told the tale to his wife, she was a wise old dear
"Husband why not give her more, 'tis the giving time of year?"
"Oh wife what kind of businessman would give away the store?
I've given her a dozen and I'll not give her one more."

Next day as he was kneading bread he heard her tapping cane
She stood at the counter and she asked him once again
He waved a finger in her face, "I've told you once before,
I've given you a dozen and I'll not give you one more."

That day in the bakery all went awry
Ev'ry loaf of bread fell flat, he burned up ev'ry pie
Buns were hard as rocks, cookies crumbled by the score
He thought to himself, "I've never had a day like this before."

He sold next to nothing, on that awful day.
"I need a good night sleep, this bad luck will go away."
But as he rose to leave that old hag was at the door,
"I've done with you, now go away, I'll not give you one more."

The next day was no better, in fact it was much worse
The store was filled with rats, this surely was a curse.
His brand new brick oven collapsed upon the floor
And not a single customer passed inside his door.

That night he sat amidst the wreck of his business grand
He cried, "I was the finest baker ever in this land!
Oh good St. Nick what shall I do I'm going to lose my store?"
And then he heard a tapping of a cane upon the floor.

Well he looked up, and there before him St. Nicholas stood,
A bishop's hat upon his head, in hand a crook of wood.
His beard of white so long that it dragged upon the floor.
The baker cried in wonder, "St. Nicholas at my door."

Then St. Nicholas spoke to him as sure as he did live.
"'Tis in the spirit of the season that we freely give."
Then in the wink of an eye where Nick had stood before
Was the older woman, tapping her cane upon the floor.

The baker found a single cookie sitting on the shelf
It bore the likeness of St. Nicholas himself.
He gave the cookie to the hag standing in the door
"You asked me for a dozen, I hope you'll take one more."

Out she walked into the night the cookie in her hand.
Once again he was the finest baker in the land.
After that whenever someone came into his store
And asked him for a dozen, he always gave one more.

So 'tis said both far and near that ever since that day
Twelve plus one makes a baker's dozen, that's the way.
So when you're at the bak'ry and count twelve be sure to
Stop right there and tell this tale and they'll give you one more.

☙

## TWISTING TIPS: BALLADS

*Study ballad lyrics to learn stock phrases and terminology.* Whether they are traditional or literary ballads, soak up their language, rhythm, and style. Identify stock turns of phrase. A term such as "nut brown hair" shows up in many traditional ballads. Fitting the ballad rhythm perfectly, it is a gentle, iconic description. It evokes the feel of traditional balladry and demonstrates the leanness of ballad descriptions. "Nut brown hair" is as descriptive as you get about a trollop's tresses or a mare's mane. No need to feel uncreative about borrowing stock phrases from public domain ballads—it is a characteristic of ballad style.[46]

*Make use of stock ballad phrases to promote rhythmic fidelity.* The linguistic palette of "The Baker's Dozen" is peppered with words like 'tis and 'twas. This serves double duty. Quaint touches like these decorate a narrative with verbal accessories that match the time period, like doilies. They also allow a two-syllable phrase like "it is" to squeeze into the metrical pattern without altering the rhythm of the ballad. Stock phrases, like "nut brown hair," also fit ballad rhythm.

*Use words that sing.* Lyrics work best when the words roll off the tongue. Singers are challenged when they have to enunciate too many consonants in quick succession or when long, sustained notes involve awkward vowels—like the short letter "i." Performer discomfort can make the song harder to understand.

*Use contractions to smooth over awkward mouth mechanics in sung ballads.* In "The Baker's Dozen," we use the little-used phrase, "I'll not" in lieu of "I won't." To our knowledge, "I'll not" is not a stock ballad phrase. While its quaint style happens to fit the mood of the tale, it also improves mouth mechanics—it is much easier to sing "I'll not" than "I won't." Try it yourself. Say each phrase out loud. The oral shift to make the "w" sound is more awkward. These issues are worthy of consideration in any spoken work, but when sung, awkwardness is more pronounced. Such considerations are particularly important in wordy sections of ballads.

*Sing through your ballad to determine what is hard for you to sing.* With additional practice, the trouble may cease. But if, after a reasonable rehearsal period, you still find the piece hard to sing, revise those tricky passages. If the ballad is hard for you to sing, it will be hard for listeners to hear.

*Incorporate dialogue in rhymed stories.* This idea is a standard recommendation for literary works in general, but in plot-driven balladry it is essential. Dialogue provides character description and propels the narrative forward.

### "THE QUAIL SONNET"
### DO THE TWIST: AN ADAPTED RETELLING IN SONNET FORM

## Why We Did the Twist

"The Quail Sonnet" is our tribute to the great Pete Seeger, an activist, musician, and storyteller. His environmental and social justice efforts were accomplished, in part, by rallying people together through song. Our sonnet is based on an Indian Jataka tale that tells how a flock of quail, caught in a hunter's trap, flap their wings in unison to escape.[47] Our adapted retelling is a faithful rendition of the traditional story told in a sonnet, a type of poem. We wrote it the year Pete died, to share in memorials at the festival that supports the Hudson River Clearwater Sloop, Inc., the environmental education and advocacy organization that he founded.

## The Skinny on Sonnets

We began this process by reviewing classic sonnet form. Sonnets are fourteen-line poems about "a single sentiment, with a clarification or 'turn' of thought in its concluding lines."[48] Like sung ballads, a sonnet's syllables have alternate stress patterns. The characteristic metrical sonnet pattern is *iambic pentameter,* with five unstressed/stressed pairs—or feet—on each line.[49]

### *Sonnet: Meter Rhyme Scheme*

| QUATRAIN WITH STRESSES<br>Bold-face type indicates stressed syllable | NUMBER OF FEET | RHYME SCHEME |
|---|---|---|
| A **hun**-ter **in** the **wood** stood **near a tree** | Five | A |
| A **lea**-fy **har**-bor **in** the **dark**-ened **night** | Five | B |
| A-**round** a **branch** his **net** hung **si**-lent-**ly** | Five | A |
| And **down** be-**low** his **bait** caught **mor**-ning **light** | Five | B |

Sonnets have a variety of structures, but the best-known are the English and the Italian sonnets. English sonnets are divided into three quatrains and one couplet. Each quatrain furthers a thought and the final couplet states the theme of the sonnet. The Italian sonnet is divided into an octave (eight lines) and a sestet (six lines).[50]

A distinguishing feature of the sonnet is called the *turn* or, in Italian, the *volta*. The volta is the moment in the sonnet when the sentiment turns back on itself or changes direction. It is often preceded by the words "but," "yet," or "and yet."[51] In Italian sonnets, the *turn* occurs around the ninth line. Although it can vary in English sonnets, it often occurs at the ninth line as well.

## How We Did the Twist

Our first decision in writing our adapted retelling was to select the sonnet form that was the best fit for our story. We started with a review of several versions of the source story. The tale itself and our interpretation of it helped us choose the sonnet form. We identified three separate scenes which would easily fit the three quatrains of the English-style sonnet. The source stories also had two characters who could each tell their part of the tale using the Italian-style sonnet. One character's view, the hunter, could be reflected first in the octave, the lead quail could be reflected in the sestet. While this two-character view works for many tales with character pairs, it didn't match the structure of the folktale or our interpretation of its meaning.

> ### Teaching Twist
>
> *Aesop's fables are short narratives that easily fit into sonnet form. To familiarize students with the meter, rhyme scheme, and "turn," have them select and write an original sonnet based on a familiar fable.*

Holding the quail tale up to the English sonnet for a closer look, we noted that the message, moral, or clarification of the story could be stated in the final rhyming couplet typical of the English sonnet, especially if we formatted the story like a fable. Also, in framing the story, we saw how we could place the sonnet's "turn" at the start of the third quatrain, on the ninth line. The structure of the English sonnet matched our tale perfectly.

Our next decision was to choose between the Spenserian and Shakespearean sonnet, both of which are English sonnets. Their rhyming patterns differ, with the Spenserian A-B-A-B B-C-B-C C-D-C-D E-E and the

Shakespearean A-B-A-B C-D-C-D E-F-E-F G-G. It wasn't immediately apparent which was best, so we let the writing process decide for us. Since both sonnets have the same rhyme scheme in the first quatrain of the story, we wrote that first. When we started writing the next quatrain, the Shakespearean style spoke up first and won the bid.

Let us now turn to how a sonnet's turn or volta can be adapted for storytwisting. As discussed, the volta represents a change of direction about sonnet's sentiment or thematic thought. Stories also have pivotal, turning moments. For example, a storytwisted turn may represent the moment when a tale turns from depicting the problem to illustrating the solution or lack of one. The volta can also reflect a turning from one character's perspective to that of another, or could depict a single character's experience of the story event in before-and-after fashion.

As always, we identified our interpretation of the tale's message at the start of the process and set it aside for later use, like a Post-it note (see Chapter Two, "Meaning"). Then we divided our story into three scenes or sections that correspond to three parts of basic plot structure: rising action, climax, resolution. For more on plot, see Chapter Eight, "Fracture Point: Plot to Mashup" In our working shorthand, we use different words to denote these ideas: the setup, the trouble, and the *fallout*. The term, fallout is broader than resolution. It captures a diverse range of possible story endings, because tales can resolve happily, with unfortunate consequences, or be open-ended without a definitive resolution.

---

### Teaching Twist

*Review "The Boy Who Cried Wolf" and "The Princess and the Pea" with your students. For each story, identify content for the setup (rising action), the trouble (conflict or climax) and the fallout (resolution).*

---

Next, we matched each story scene to the structure of a sonnet. The first scene is the story's set up—rising action. The next quatrain depicts the trouble—climax. The final quatrain, where the turn occurs, recounts the fallout—resolution. With the story's message in mind, we drafted each quatrain according to sonnet form. Our last step was to compose the final couplet.

## STORYTWIST

### *The Quail Sonnet*

By Jeri Burns and Barry Marshall
Copyright 2016, 2018 The Storycrafters

A hunter in the wood stood near a tree
A leafy harbor in the darkened night
Around a branch his net hung silently
And down below his bait caught morning light

A flock of quail peck-pecked that grain-fed snare
When net descended like an open jaw
They flapped and thrashed and cried out in despair
The hunter had them in his woven claw

Then one bird flapped his wings and voiced his call
The others joined with him in their reply
No longer out for self but out for all
They flapped in sync and rose up to the sky

We change the world and fly off to the sun
When hearts and wings and voices sing as one

## TWISTING TIPS: RHYMED STORIES

*Explore rhyming dictionaries* for rap, ballad, sonnet, and other rhymed pieces. They are indispensable aids. Each dictionary varies in user friendliness—some are more intuitive than others. Try several online or hard copy versions to identify styles that work best for you.

*Do rhyme-strengthening exercises.* References help with rhyming, but natural, intuitive rhyming is very satisfying and speeds up the writing process. Like calisthenics, it gets easier over time. Start simply: Challenge yourself to rhyme the next word you hear spoken. Next time, think up two rhymes for a word, then three rhymes, and so on.

*Play interactive rhyming games in daily life.* In-person conversations and digital chats, like texting, are opportunities to stretch your rhyming muscles.

Spontaneously compose couplets to answer questions or improvise quatrains that describe your last meal. Do it again, but with smoother rhythm. Engage in rhyming battles with a friend or family member (our son, Zack, plays regularly with us).

*Write a rap or ballad in any order.* If you have an idea for a scene toward the end of the story, go ahead and write it. That material will inspire other portions of the piece. Every rhymed story follows its own creative path. Enjoy the journey.

*Compose the chorus or refrain of a rap or ballad early in the process.* The text of the chorus can artfully influence word choices in the rest of the piece so that they echo the chorus, emphasize its thematic meaning, or create wordplay. Knowing the refrain early is helpful because it can affect the composition of verses leading up to the it.

*Curate unexpected rhymes.* There is no denying it, some rhymes are trite. How many love songs rhyme the words "of," "above," and "love?" It is much more delightful when rhymes are fresh and surprising. For example, in "The Tortoise and Hare Rap," we have an unexpected pair of end rhymes: "speedy" and "lead, he."

## Twisting Tip

*Expect writing problems to be solved away from the computer.* Such "aha" moments often come unbidden. Perfect word pairs, vivid imagery, rhymed lines and solutions to rhythmic problems are born in their own time. Inspiration doesn't comply with writing schedules. When an idea hits, record it immediately.

*There are also times for expected rhymes.* It is fun when the audience ends the rhymed line for you. Not only does it invite audience participation, but gives you a chance to take a breath, if needed. Like any other performance technique (or salt), use sparingly.

*Embrace the limits of poetic form.* Although it seems counterintuitive, the limits of poetic form do not handcuff creativity. They inspire inventiveness! Rhyme scheme and meter help writers sharpen ideas to a fine point. The artistic challenge is to elegantly fit the formula without sounding formulaic.

*Scrutinize every word in your rhymed tales.* If words are important in prose tales, they count even more in ballads and sonnets because rhyme curtails language options. Furthermore, metrical requirements impose word choice limits to fit syllables and stresses into rhythmic patterns. The array of words that meet such requirements is limiting. In contrast, rap offers greater rhythmic freedom because it is stylistic to leap out of the meter to emphasize content.

*Craft your chorus or refrain with intention.* Sometimes, the refrain is meant to amplify the overall message of your story. Because it repeats, the message digs in. Sometimes the refrain is meant to give the audience a listening break and the story's message is a punch at the end of the piece—as in "The Tortoise and Hare Rap". Both approaches work if you can articulate reasons for making a choice.

*Stress your syllables properly.* Words uttered out of rhythm or with unexpected emphasis can break a story's spell. Distracted by a rhythmic bauble, listeners wonder what went wrong instead of listening to the tale.

*Include unexpectedly stressed words or changes in rhythm with intentionality.* Sometimes you want an audience to notice something particular about the tale. A change in rhythm can steer focus to an important, dramatic moment in the story. An improperly stressed syllable can be used purposefully in wordplay or to develop a character. Although ballad and folk rhyme styles are more forgiving about this than sonnets and other literary poetry, we don't recommend it if the main reason is *Wow, I couldn't find a good rhyme for that, so maybe they won't notice if I do this instead.* Intentionality makes it artful!

For example, in "The Baker's Dozen" ballad we wrote, "**Was** the **old**-er **wom**-an, **tap**-ping her **cane** u-**pon** the **floor**." The regular ballad pattern of two syllables for each stress or beat is apparent except for the phrase "tapping her cane" where there are three syllables for one beat. Though subtle, this rhythmic anomaly, or triplet as it is called in musical terms, draws attention to the tapping cane. The extra syllables evoke the sound of a tapping cane. Because the triplet rhythm accompanies her entrance to the bake shop at the start of the ballad and at the end, the sound and object are also associated with her character. Finally, the triplet invites audience attention precisely at the dramatic moment when the hag and St. Nick are exposed as one being.

*Minimize fancy or flowery language in rhymed stories.* Avoid the tendency to over-decorate your text like a cake with cloyingly sweet frosting flowers that mar the flavor of the moist chocolate cake underneath. Meaning (and flavor) is lost in floral fanciness. Let the chocolate cake speak for itself.

## Twist for Thought: Every Word Counts

Language choice is an artistic writing decision that can affect the meaning, tone, and pacing of a tale. It can also influence how characters are perceived. That is why wordsmiths carefully select words to represent and accentuate emotional or narrative content. Words are so powerful that *even one* can underscore or undermine thematic, cultural, historical, and moral meaning.

To shed light on the thought process behind the selection of one word in a rhymed story, take a little journey with us to the analytic-intuitive recesses of artistic minds.

Near the end of the ballad, "The Baker's Dozen," the character of St. Nick appears in the bakery. Right before he appears, the Baker cries,

Oh good St. Nick what shall I do I'm going to lose my store?
And then he heard the tapping of a cane upon the floor.

Well he looked up and there before him St. Nicholas stood.
A bishop's hat upon his head, in hand a crook of wood.

Many words could be used to describe the object in St. Nicholas' hand. Why did we choose the word "crook?"

As you will recall from reading the full ballad, the old woman taps her cane whenever she visits the bakery. In this excerpt, a visitor enters the shop and the baker hears tapping. Voila! With one tiny descriptive word, the baker and the audience suspect that the old woman has returned.

To increase these suspicions, we add a touch of misdirection. In the second line, we name the tapping object a "cane," a word already associated with the hag. This misdirection builds up to the surprise when the baker and the audience discover St. Nick at the door.

## Thoughts Before Selecting the Word "Crook"

Next came the decision about what to name the object in St. Nicholas' hand. To continue to call it a "cane" would telegraph that St. Nick and the hag were the same person. This would work in a retelling for audiences who are in on the secret. By knowing in advance that St. Nick was the hag, they could experience delicious anticipation as they waited for the baker to find out. In such a version of the story, which we will refer to as Story A, it makes sense to build anticipation with literary techniques such as repetition, parallelism, and foreshadowing—by referring to the object as a cane all the way through.

But we had to determine what made sense for our version, Story B. We asked ourselves some questions. Does calling the object a "cane" reflect the underlying meaning of our version of the story? Is it consistent with images we want to convey at this point in the plot?

For us, the answer to both questions was no. In our retelling of "The Baker's Dozen," the hag/St. Nick duality is a plot twist. Deceiving the baker and audience about this mysterious character mirrors the shape-shifting, spiritual sage/crone archetype who teaches the baker about generosity. It also adds zing to moment when the judgmental baker recognizes his differential treatment of the hag and the bishop. Thanks to this plot twist, not only does the baker learn his lesson, but audiences are surprised along with him when they discover that St. Nick and the hag are one.

Either approach to this moment in the story is valid. In Story A, the audience hovers outside the story, watching and waiting for the baker to get his comeuppance. In our version, Story B, the audience experiences the surprise right along with the baker. This second version was consistent with how we interpreted the tale and the message we wanted to convey, that it is folly to judge the messenger. To heighten the drama, we decided that St. Nick must seem like a separate and distinct entity from the old woman.

## How We Selected the Word "Crook"

The next step was to select a word to describe his walking stick. As the historical St. Nicholas was often depicted with a staff in hand, "staff" seemed a reasonable lexical replacement for cane. Before settling on that word, we looked up the word "staff" in a thesaurus in case another possibility might emerge. That is when we discovered "crook."

Not only does "crook" connote an old-style crutch, but it offers a bit of *assonance*—rhymed vowel sounds—when paired with the word "wood," as in "crook of wood." The poetic device was perfect for this rhymed story. As a subtle extra touch, the word "crook" is associated with shepherds, a common trade in days gone by. Because a "crook of wood" is evocative of the era of the story's setting and pulls attention away from the old woman's cane, it made sense to insert it in a story that takes place long ago.

Every word counts, especially in a rhymed piece. The fewer words used to tell a story, the more important each word becomes. Words can count for many things simultaneously. They can underline meaning, set the tone, or add to the cultural or historical backdrop of a story. Each word, layered one upon another, adds up to establish tone, setting, mood, meaning, and character. Each word makes the story more powerful. For these reasons, word choice deserves careful consideration.

Browse thesauruses and dictionaries, play word association games, or enjoy some free-styling. Build up a cache of interesting words to mull over. Then, choose the right word for your tale, a gem that sparkles in a setting of your creation.

# NOTES

1. Lewis Carroll, *Alice's Adventures in Wonderland*, full text of *Alice's Adventures in Wonderland*, August 12, 2006, accessed July 10, 2016, https://archive.org/stream /alicesadventures19033gut/19033.txt

2. Morag Maclean, Peter Bryant and Lynette Bradley, "Rhymes, Nursery Rhymes, and Reading in Early Childhood," *Merrill-Palmer Quarterly 33(1987): 255-281.*

3. Kirsten Read, "Clues Cue the Smooze: Rhyme, Pausing, and Prediction Help Children Lean New Words from Storybooks," *Frontiers in Psychology.* 5 (2014), accessed April 14, 2016. doi: 10.3389/fpsyg.2014.00149

4. Mary E. Reynolds, Kristie Callihan, and Erin Browning. "Effect of Instruction on the Development of Rhyming Skills in Young Children. *Contemporary Issues in Communication Science and Disorders* 30 (Spring 2003): 41-46.

5. Maclean et al., "Rhymes, Nursery Rhymes," 255-281; Carl J. Dunst., Diana Meter, and Deborah W. Hamby. "Relationship Between Young Children's Nursery Rhyme Experiences and Knowledge and Phonological and Print-Related Abilities." Accessed June 3, 2016. http://earlyliteracylearning.org/cellreviews/cellreviews_v4_n1.pdf.

6. P.E. Bryant, L. Bradley, M. Maclean, and J. Crossland. "Nursery Rhymes, Phonological Skills and Reading." *Journal of Child Language* 16, no. 02 (1989): 407. https://www.cambridge.org/core/journals/journal-of-child-language/article/nursery -rhymes-phonological-skills-and-reading/53EE25F1E011C8090E659A8FABBB2 09E

7. G. W. Macdonald and A. Cornwall. "The Relationship Between Phonological Awareness and Reading and Spelling Achievement Eleven Years Later." *Journal of Learning Disabilities* 28, no. 8 (1995): 523-27. http://journals.sagepub.com/doi/ abs/10.1177/002221949502800807.

8. Christian Obermeier, Winfried Menninghaus, Martin Von Koppenfels, Tim Raettig, Maren Schmidt-Kassow, Sascha Otterbein, and Sonja A. Kotz, "Aesthetic and Emotional Effects of Meter and Rhyme in Poetry," *Frontiers in Psychology* 4 (2013), accessed June 3, 2016, https://www.ncbi.nlm.nih.gov/pmc/articles/PMC3560350/.

9. Janice D. Hamlet "The Reason Why We Sing: Understanding Traditional African-American Worship," in *Our Voices: Essays in Culture, Ethnicity and Communication.* Fifth Edition, edited by Alberto Gonzalez et al.,(New York: Oxford University Press, 2012), 112-117.

10. Kirsten Read, "Clues Cue the Smooze," 2014.

11. As a local, non-indigenous legend, we would be willing to parody or fracture "The Baker's Dozen" if it were generally familiar to audiences. On the other hand, we would not parody or fracture the Quail story because it is not a tale from our cultural background or locality.

12. Soren Baker, *The History of Rap and Hip-Hop*, (Detroit: Gale, Cengage Learning, 2012); Cookie Lommel, *The History of Rap Music*. (Philadelphia: Chelsea House Publishers, 2001).

13. Lommel, *Rap Music*, 2001; Baker, *Rap and Hip-Hop*, 2012.

14. Lommel, *Rap Music*, 10-14; Elijah Wald, "African Roots," in *Talking 'Bout Your Mama: The Dozens, Snaps, and the Deep Roots of Rap*, (New York: Oxford University Press, 2014), 135-151.

15. See generally, Wald, *Talking 'Bout*, 2014.

16. Lommel, *Rap Music*, 21-22.

17. Marva Newton, telephone conversation with the author, June 7, 2016.

18. Wald, *Talking 'Bout*, 148-149.

19. This ancient fable is found in countless publications, such as Aesop, Arthur Rackham, and Vernon Jones V. S.(trans.), "The Hare and the Tortoise," in *Aesop's Fables*. (New York: Avenel Books, 1975), 92-95; Frances Barnes-Murphy, Aesop, and Rowan Barnes-Murphy, "The Tortoise and the Hare," *The Fables of Aesop*, (New York: Lothrop, Lee & Shepard Books, 1994), 14; Heather Forest, Story Arts | Aesop's ABC | The Tortoise and The Hare, accessed June 06, 2016, https://www.storyarts. org/library/aesops/stories/tortoise.html.

20. Marina Warner, *Once Upon a Time: A Short History of Fairy Tale*. (Oxford: Oxford University Press, 2014).

21. Siyuan Liu, Ho Ming Chow, Yisheng Xu, Michael G. Erkkinen, Katherine E. Swett, Michael W. Eagle, Daniel A. Rizik-Baer, and Allen R. Braun, "Neural Correlates of Lyrical Improvisation: An FMRI Study of Freestyle Rap," *Scientific Reports* 2 (2012), accessed June 3, 2016, doi:10.1038/srep00834.
    For a report on this study, see Daniel Cressey, Daniel. "Brain Scans of Rappers Shed Light on Creativity." Nature.com. November 15, 2012, accessed June 03, 2016, http:// www.nature.com/news/brain-scans-of-rappers-shed-light-on-creativity-1.11835.

22. Cultural appropriation is a contentious issue. Not only that, it is a bear to define since there are complex layers and elements and disagreement about its permutations. Some argue that any act of cultural "borrowing" is a form of appropriation. Others suggest that there are categories of appropriation. Richard Rogers, for example, discusses four: cultural exchange, cultural dominance, cultural exploitation, and transculturation. Cultural exchange, like trading, happens among people of equal status. Cultural dominance occurs when a majority culture imposes its culture on a minority group. Cultural exploitation is when cultural products are taken without permission, benefiting the "borrower" without consideration of the cultural source. Rogers' final category, transculturation, is a new conceptualization that doesn't

negate the other three, but attempts to move beyond them. Transculturation refers to cultural products that evolve through multi-cultural connections and globalization. See Richard A. Rogers, "From Cultural Exchange to Transculturation: A Review and Reconceptualization of Cultural Appropriation," *Communication Theory* 16, no. 4 (2006): 474-503. doi:10.1111/j.1468-2885.2006.00277.x. This idea is consistent with Donald Haase's view that fairy tales have moved beyond the bounds of culture to be transcultural.

For a structural view of cultural appropriation—focused more corporate actions rather than those of individuals, see Adam Elliot-Cooper, "Moving Beyond 'Igloo Australia'," *Media Diversified* (blog), July 17, 2015, accessed June 5, 2015, https://mediadiversified.org/2015/07/17/beyond-iggy-azalea/.

23. Donald Haase, "Decolonizing Fairy-Tale Studies," (*Marvels & Tales* 24, no.1, 2010): 31, accessed May 20, 2016, http://digitalcommons.wayne.edu/marvels/vol24/iss1/1. Haase describes fairy tales as transcultural products because they cross many borders; his justification for the transcultural nature of fairy tales may apply to rap music as well.

24. Anne Pellowski, "Bardic Storytelling," in *The World of Storytelling: A Practical Guide to the Origins, Development and Applications of Storytelling.* Expanded and Revised Edition.(Bronx: H.W. Wilson Company, 1990), 21-43. Pellowski indicates African bardic traditions are accompanied by drumming (Pellowski 39) and other bardic storytelling traditions are accompanied by stringed instruments.

25. The formulation of this list was inspired, in part, by Jenni Avins, "The Do's and Don't's of Cultural Appropriation," The Atlantic, October 20, 2015, accessed June 03, 2016. http://www.theatlantic.com/entertainment/archive/2015/10/the-dos-and-donts-of-cultural-appropriation/411292/.

26. Heather Forest, and Susan Gaber, *The Baker's Dozen: A Colonial American Tale.* (San Diego: Harcourt Brace Jovanovich, 1988), Aaron Shepard, and Wendy Edelson, *The Baker's Dozen: A Saint Nicholas Tale,* (New York: Atheneum Books for Young Readers, 1995). Charles F. Skinner. "The Baker's Dozen." *Myths and Legends in Our Own Land.* Philadelphia and London, 1896. Accessed 5/21/16. http://sacred-texts.com/ame/lol/lol009.htm

27. David Pickering, *A Dictionary of Folklore,* (New York: Facts on File, 1999), 22.

28. It is common knowledge that the United States was already inhabited when Europeans came. The Albany area was home to the Mahican people, and bordered on the edge of Iroquois territory. Our story's focus on European settlers is not a dismissal of this important part of history. But the tale is not, to the best of our knowledge, connected to any Native nation.

29. Chris Baldick, *The Concise Oxford Dictionary of Literary Terms,* (Oxford University Press: Oxford, New York, 1990), 21.
J. A. Cudden, *Dictionary of Literary Terms and Literary Theory.* Revised by M.A.R. Habib. (Penguin Group: London, 2013) 64-66.
David Adams Leeming, ed. *Storytelling Encyclopedia: Historical, Cultural, and Multiethnic Approaches to Oral Traditions Around the World.* (Pheonix: Oryx Press, 1997), 72-3; Pickering, *A Dictionary of Folklore,* 1999, 22-3.

30. "Traditional and Ethnic—The Library of Congress Celebrates the Songs of America," The Library of Congress, accessed January 30, 2016, https://www.loc.gov/collection/songs-of-america/articles-and-essays/musical-styles/traditional-and-ethnic/.

31. Cudden, *Dictionary*, 2013,66.

32. Baldick, *The Concise Oxford*, 1990, 22.

33. These are also called trimeter and tetrameter respectively. See, for example, Cudden, *Dictionary*, 2013, 739 and 716-717.

34. Jack Lynch, "Ballad Stanza," Lynch, Literary Terms, accessed January 30, 2016. https://andromeda.rutgers.edu/~jlynch/Terms/ballad-stanza.html.

35. Daniel J. Levitin, *This Is Your Brain on Music: The Science of a Human Obsession*, (New York: Plume/Penguin, 2007).

36. Catherine Y. Wan, Theodor Rüber, Anja Hohmann, and Gottfried Schlaug, "The Therapeutic Effects of Singing in Neurological Disorders," *Music Perception* 27, no. 4 (2010): 287-95, http://mp.ucpress.edu/content/27/4/287.

37. Levitin, *This is Your Brain*, 2007.

38. Gunter Kreutz et al., "Effects of Choir Singing or Listening on Secretory Immunoglobulin A, Cortisol, and Emotional State," *Journal of Behavioral Medicine* 27, no. 6 (2004): 623-35, doi:10.1007/s10865-004-0006-9; Stephen Clift and Ian Morrison, "Group Singing Fosters Mental Health and Wellbeing: Findings from the East Kent "singing for Health" Network Project," *Mental Health Social Inclusion Mental Health and Social Inclusion* 15, no. 2 (2011): 88-99, doi:10.1108/20428301111140930.

39. Betty A. Bailey and Jane W. Davidson, "Amateur Group Singing as a Therapeutic Instrument," *Nordic Journal of Music Therapy* 12, no. 1 (2003): 18-32, doi:10.1080/08098130309478070.

40. A. M. Sanal, and S. Gorsev, "Psychological and Physiological Effects of Singing in a Choir," *Psychology of Music* 42, no. 3 (2013): 420-29, doi:10.1177/0305735613477181.

41. A. Anshel, and D. A. Kipper, "The Influence of Group Singing on Trust and Cooperation," *Journal of Music Therapy* 25, no. 3 (1988): 145-55, doi:10.1093/jmt/25.3.145.

42. Lucanne Magill Bailey, "The Effects of Live Music versus Tape-Recorded Music on Hospitalized Cancer Patients," *Music Therapy* 3, no. 1 (1983): 17-28, https://academic.oup.com/musictherapy/article/3/1/17/2756890/The-Effects-of-Live-Music-versus-Tape-Recorded.

43. Kreutz et al., "Effects of Choir Singing or Listening on Secretory Immunoglobulin A, Cortisol, and Emotional State," 631-632.

44. Some ballads have a little more variation when they have sections, called bridges, where music and sometimes rhythm changes.

45. "Traditional Ballads—The Library of Congress Celebrates the Songs of America," The Library of Congress, accessed June 05, 2016, https://www.loc.gov/collections/songs-of-america/articles-and-essays/musical-styles/traditional-and-ethnic/traditional-ballads/.

46. Leeming, *Storytelling Encyclopedia,* 1997, 72.

47. Robert Chalmers, "The Jataka, Volume I: Book I.--Ekanipāta: No. 33. Sammodamāna-Jātaka." The Jataka, Volume I: Book I.--Ekanipāta: No. 33. Sammodamāna-Jātaka, January 2006, accessed June 06, 2016, http://www.sacred-texts.com/bud/j1/j1036.htm, Originally published: Cambridge: Cambridge University Press, 1895.; Norma Livo, "The Escape of the Pigeons," *Bringing Out Their Best: Values Education and Character Development through Traditional Tales,* Westport: Libraries Unlimited, 2003), 173-174; Rafe Martin, "The Wise Quail," *The Hungry Tigress: Buddhist Legends and Jataka Tales.* (Cambridge: Yellow Moon Press, 1999), 71-74; Elisa Davy Pearmain, "The Flock of Quail," *Once Upon a Time: Storytelling to Teach Character and Prevent Bullying,* (Greensboro: Character Development Group, 2006), 54.

48. "Sonnet—Glossary Terms—Poetry Foundation," Poetry Foundation, accessed January 23, 2016, http://www.poetryfoundation.org/resources/learning/glossary-terms/detail/sonnet.

49. Cudden, *Dictionary,* 2013, 668.

50. "Sonnet," http://www.poetryfoundation.org/resources/learning/glossary-terms/detail/sonnet.

51. *Encyclopædia Britannica Online,* s. v. "volta", accessed June 06, 2016, http://www.britannica.com/art/volta-poetry.

*No wise fish would go anywhere*
*without a porpoise.*

LEWIS CARROLL[1]

CHAPTER SIX

# Fracture Point & Wordplay

WORDPLAY IS A BELOVED PART OF LINGUISTIC EXPRESSION. It abounds in comedy, literature and music. One might even say that Shakespeare's works are plays of and plays on words. Poetry, rap, and children's literature embrace word-play. Persuasive and rhetorical writing benefit from it too. There are so many wordplay styles that they merit individual, intriguing names, like *antanaclasis*.[2] Ironically, names for particular wordplay devices sound like plays on words themselves.

Popular culture and social media love wordplay. George Takei, of *Star Trek* fame, with a Facebook following bigger than the population of the state of Georgia, regularly shares posts that involve plays on words. Wordplay games trend on Twitter. In early 2016, #MakeASongFrench engaged thousands of Twitter followers in an online "wordplay parlay-*vous*." A couple of our contributions included "My Bonne Nuit Lies Over the Ocean" and "Seine in the Clowns."

According to the *Oxford English Dictionary*, wordplay is defined exactly as it sounds: Playing with words through witticisms, ambiguous meanings, and delightful puns.[3] Clever, linguistic manipulation of letters and words lends levity to literature or causes it to drip with *double entendre*. Whether wordplay is employed strictly for humorous effect or is woven with deeper thoughts and commentary, it conjures a feeling of duality as one phrase or word is recast as another. This aspect alone delights readers and listeners of all ages.

## Twist the Dial: From Words to Wordplay, or Wordtwisting

Subtle uses of wordplay in stories can portray character. Imagine a woman in her kitchen, preparing supper for her sister with whom she does not get along. They are having supper to discuss moving their father into an assisted living facility. The woman watches the clock, chops carrots, glances at the clock again. Her shoulders tense. She finishes the carrots and starts on the onions when she cuts her finger. While washing her injury, the woman notices that her oven is set to the wrong temperature. She checks the meat to find that it's undercooked. Drying her finger in a towel, she readjusts the oven temperature with her taut, free hand when the doorbell rings. She mutters to herself about the looming dinnertime conversation, referring to it as dinnertime "consternation."

Her verbal flub may be smirk-worthy, but it also communicates her stressed state of mind. Consider a variation on this same theme: A different stressed woman twists those same words to convey a barbed message to an argumentative relative at their dinnertime "conflagration."

In both cases, wordplay is tinged with humor—we expect one word and get another. It also has a literary effect because it reveals the character's mood. The main difference between the two examples is that in the second, wordplay pokes a sarcastic, doubled-edged finger into the imagery.

These vignettes illustrate how wordplay can be integrated into writing and storytelling. As a literary device, lexical creativity adds narrative flair. But wordplay can be more than literary flourish. It is possible to tell an entire story through wordplay.

Although there are many styles of wordplay, like the *malapropisms* in the examples above,[4] in this chapter we focus our efforts on three types of wordplay stories. We twist the dial from tales told in standard English to stories that are spiked with spoonerisms or pervaded with puns—and maybe even littered with a little alliteration. We also include a bonus story in a wordplay style of our own invention: the *spinneroosm*. The chapter concludes with a discussion about memorization techniques for wordplay and rhymed stories.

**Wordtwisted Tales: Spoonerism Stories**

Spoonerisms are delightful verbal utterances that reverse the first sounds of different words to create new and unexpected phrases. These delicious "tips of the slongue" read nicely but work better when spoken aloud. From sheer, aural nonsense to sexual innuendo to humorous combinations of real words, spoonerisms are linked to a Nineteenth Century Oxford don named W.A. Spooner who famously swapped his letters and referred to Her Majesty, the dear old queen, as a "queer old dean."[5] Spooner was somewhat attached to this linguistic anomaly, uttering spoonerisms with sufficient regularity that this distinct verbal reversal was named after him.

Like any wordplay device, isolated spoonerisms add spice to stories, speeches, or other public speaking opportunities. But when they are the dominant language of a narrative, they seep across the categorical border from literary device to literary style. Shel Silverstein's posthumously published poetry collection, *Runny Babbit*, is composed with spoonerisms.[6] In addition to poetry, Spooner's spoken sputtering infiltrated the telling of stories. One of the most famous stories in the world, "Cinderella," has been parodied through spoonerisms time and again. The folklorist Alan Dundes and his co-author Carl Pagter offer three spooneristic variants of the tale, "Prinderella and the Handsome Cince." Dundes and Pagter also identify an additional variant, "Rindercella," associated with Archie Campbell, the actor from an old time television show called *Hee Haw*.[7]

"BEEPING SLEAUTY"
A SPOONERIZED VERSION OF "SLEEPING BEAUTY."

**Do the Twist**

The first time we heard a spoonerized story, it was a version of "Cinderella."[8] The audience howled with laughter from start to finish. So did we. From then on, we heard it so frequently that whenever we came upon a storyteller, we expected Prinderella and her Handsome Cince to be there too. The tale had gone viral.[9]

## Why We Did the Twist

With a passion for linguistic challenges, it was natural that this story inspired us to tackle a spoonerized tale. Instead of learning "Prinderella," already an audience favorite, we wrote our own. We selected "Sleeping Beauty" as our first go-round for two reasons. First, we liked the sound of the phrase *Beeping Sleauty*. Second, the story filled a vacancy in our "Sleeping Beauty"-free repertoire.

## How We Did the Twist

The process of writing a spoonerized story is slow and pleasantly painstaking. We begin by brainstorming phrases and images from the story. Next, we reverse letters in each phrase in as many combinations as possible. "Beeping Sleauty" instantly rewarded us with fun ideas and delightful phrases that could be included in a grown-up version of the tale.

For our foundational piece, we decided to use the Brothers Grimm's text, the one that includes familiar, iconic parts of the tale that most adults and children know.[10] Charles Perrault's story, like its Italian literary predecessor by Giambattista Basile, enters darker realms of human behavior, the "Lord of the Flies" version, if you will.

Next, came the choice of a title. In the Grimm's story, she is called Brier (or Briar) Rose.[11] For our title, we turned to Perrault, and Sleeping Beauty.[11]

After a careful review of the Grimms' Briar Rose, we listed phrases, images, character names, and iconic language from the source story, all in standard English. We also identified themes, concepts, and story actions of import. Then, one by one, we brainstormed some spooneristic stand-ins for each item listed. Below is our brainstorm list for the concept *enchanted sleep*:

### ENCHANTED SLEEP

| | |
|---|---|
| • slagical meep | • toma-cose (comatose) |
| • slenchanted eep | • sleamless dreep or seamdress leep (the latter is fun, full of real words, but hard to say elegantly) |
| • slong leep | • seamless dreep (a variation on the above, a bit of a cheat) |
| • nong lap | • sleep deep (we ended up using this in a different Spoonerized story) |
| • sleep dumber | • ast fasleep for a very tong lime |

We ultimately chose the phrase "sleep dumber" because it evokes the emotional moment of the story. The reversal of letters turns the word "deep" into "sleep" and accentuates the meaning of the image. While "seamless dreep" attracts us for its humor, the spoken nature of the phrase "sleep dumber" is less likely to interrupt the magic of the moment because it is easier to understand. And instead of ending hard on a "p" sound, the "r" in the word "dumber" trails off gently, hinting at the mystery of enchantment. Although spoonerized tales are comedic works, we minimize comedy for comedy's sake in favor of comedy for story's sake.

### Teaching Twist

*Set ground rules for student wordplay stories. While it is engaging when words touch off-limit topics and bathroom humor, witticism wilts when the same joke type occurs again and again. If you set a predetermined number of "naughty" wordplays per story, students can revel in rebellion and brainstorm all the potty puns they desire. At the same time, they must craft and select the best ones for their final piece.*

In all of our spoonerized writings, the brainstorm list represents the origins of the new tale. Once we have numerous items to work with, we start the draft. As new ideas burst forth during the writing process, we add them to the list. Like other twisted tales, however, spoonerisms aren't written in one sitting, but rather in "stits and farts."

As you can see, spoonerized wordplay is a personal "engraved invitation" for veiled cursing, middle school humor, and sexual innuendo. Fun and naughtiness are intertwined because we are suddenly "allowed" to utter unexpected, risqué, or socially unacceptable words and phrases. In the context of a spoonerized story, nearly anything is acceptable because it is not what it seems.

It is tempting to stocking-stuff numerous saucy phrases into one story, but we must advise restraint. Here is a case where less is more. An overabundance of fun phrases steals focus from the story and puts too much attention onto its component parts—the words. If we concentrate solely upon the individual bricks that built a castle, we don't see a finished architectural marvel but only the parts that made it. Too many out-of-context phrases makes words float free from the narrative and threaten to transform it from a story with meaning to a nonsensical, lexical free-for-all.

Rebelliousness through wordplay requires balance in other ways too.

Ribald and scatological humor must be spoken out loud, so you must evaluate your comfort when uttering it. You should also evaluate your audience's willingness to hear it. In the case of "Beeping Sleauty," we have two versions of the tale. One rendition is geared for family audiences, and one is for grownups and older teens, in which we replace gentle phrases with tangier ones. See "Appendix A" for a family-friendly version of the tale.

**Please note:** We follow the spoonerism style of spelling—direct swapping of starting letters—as much as we can for consistency. But there are times when standard spelling rules and needed vowel sounds don't make an even exchange, so we have to change the way the word is spelled for the wordplay device to work in written form.

---

### Teaching Twist

*Writing a full-fledged spoonerized story is a complicated project. You can start small and practice with Mother Goose nursery rhymes. They are manageable in size and offer a myriad of word pairs to choose from and explore. Overzealous students will try to spoonerize every pair of words. Not only is it unnecessary, it can be too much. Experiment and analyze the results together, as a class. Remind students that spoonerisms work wonderfully with non-consecutive pairs of words.*

*Hack and Hill went up the Jill*
*to wetch a pail of fater,*
*Hack dell fown and croke his brown*
*and Hill came umbling tafter..*

*Encourage multiple attempts with every nursery rhyme to stimulate a general writing habit that includes experimentation, evaluation, rewrites, and editing.*

---

## Target Audience for Spoonerized Stories

This brings us to questions about the audience for spoonerized stories. First of all, must audience members know the pre-existing story in order to appreciate a spoonerized one? When we wrote "Beeping Sleauty," our son Zack was a toddler. We recorded it when he was a preschooler, so he heard various renditions and rehearsals of the fractured tale, without ever hearing a straight version. Although he was exposed to many different stories as a little guy, the content of the original version of this tale was not right for him in his earliest years.

Fast forward to when Zack was a kindergartener and we attended a puppet show at a nearby school. The puppets and set were magical. Silence filled the room when the sparkling, briar hedge slowly rose up over the puppet stage to the strains of lyre music. The raising of the scrim took a solid minute or so, and the audience was still and stunned by the beauty and theatricality. As the magical briar hedge neared the top of the castle, our son suddenly squealed , "Mommy, Mommy, that's the thedge of horns!" Zack had never heard the story in standard English until that day. He had gleaned the entire thing through spoonerisms. So although a spoonerized story is the funniest for people who know the source tale, even if they don't, it connects them to the narrative and inspires joy in linguistic silliness.

Is it reasonable to conclude then, that spoonerized stories are good bets for audiences of children? Shel Silverstein's *Runny Babbit*, a collection of spoonerized poems, is a "billy sook" for children. It is recommended for ages four to eight.[12] We tell our spoonerized tales to family audiences regularly. One of our greatest spoonerism fans is a seven-year old boy, who quotes our spoonerisms and makes up his own in conversations with his family on a daily basis.

Despite this, we don't tell spoonerized stories to audiences composed entirely of young children. Although our preschooler learned the traditional story through (or in spite of) the spoonerisms, it was over a period of time, hearing our repetitious renditions and rehearsals. A one-time performance of a spoonerized story can't provide that to listeners. Instead, we share these tales with children of all ages in intergenerational, family audiences. Younger children are less likely to become frustrated and tune out when parents help them understand, and they sink into the silliness of the language more easily when adults and older children laugh along.[13]

Although people of all ages enjoy spoonerized stories in their own ways, in our experience, college students and adults like them best of all.

## Wordplay Writing Methods: Many Strands Make Tight Work

Wordplay stories rebel against form and meaning. It is one reason we—and audiences—love them. The process of creating wordplays is rebellious too because standard writing procedures do not always apply.

*Create a writing rhythm by sitting in an uncluttered space at the same time every day and write, whether you feel like it or not.* This declaration is a distillation of sage advice that writers often share with one another. It is believed that a

---

### *Wordplay Stories: Based on Intact Tales*

Familiarity with a source tale ignites the writing process and boosts listener enjoyment. A narrative blueprint, the source tale lays out the salient points, iconic events, words, and parts of the story that listeners are likely to expect. The more connected the old and new stories are, the more we can twist the daylights out of familiar phrases and images to foster amusement for our audiences (while allowing undercurrents of social criticism to slyly seep through the cracks). A careful review of a foundational story is our first step in writing wordplay tales.

A faithful portrayal of a familiar tale helps an audience understand the newfangled language more readily. Recognition of characters and story events allows them to predict and remember, which fosters their grasp of the unusual language. Furthermore, they catch the nuances of each play on words when they recognize the source image.

Before writing a spoonerized story, identify the iconic moments of the source tale. The audience will expect them to occur in the storytwisted piece, even if mentioned only in passing. To leave these moments out will leave your audience wondering. Express iconic moments in either standard English prose or wordplay. Accordion your narrative as you see fit, but be sure to mention them. Such references act as signposts on the journey through a winding, wordtwisted tale. They also form the backbone of humor and criticism.

Narrative fidelity to a source story is important because wordplay obscures the familiar aspects of stories more than other twists of the storytwisting dial. Wordplay stories are at their best when the audience doesn't have to work very hard to understand them. Familiarity with the narrative makes the listening easier. The less they have to work, the more fun they have, as the popular aphorism states: "All plork and no way makes Back a dull Joy."

We don't mean to suggest that you must never deviate from a traditional piece. We can and do. But when we deviate, we marry meaning to intention—any change in our remix matches the new tale's themes and motifs.

In one sense, our wordplay stories are like straight retellings peppered with wordtwists. But only in one sense. Each individual wordtwist and the parodic tone of the story combine to invest wordplay stories with satire and social criticism. Straight as wizards' wands in terms of plot structure and character, these tales are still as storytwisted as they come.

---

regular writing rhythm primes the brain like regular nutrition feeds the body. Nourished by healthful habits, words and ideas sprout. We benefitted from that writing wisdom while writing this book.

A desk-based regular writing rhythm has utility for wordplay stories. We review and edit what we have written, scour word lists to generate new ideas for puns, and hop between reference websites. Through the careful manipulation of letters and words, sentence fragments are recombined to birth juicy spoonerisms and wordplays of familiar phrases, what we call *phraseplays*. These activities are morning coffee for the writing center of the brain. Any and all of our writing benefits from these exercises. For more about phraseplays, keep reading! They are discussed in further depth later in this chapter.

In spite of the benefits of a regular writing schedule, when it comes to crafting individual plays on words, hours at the desk may produce more frustration than usable content. Be willing to let your brain write wordplay stories at the computer during designated times, but also be willing to let your brain chew on wordplay ideas in the course of daily life. Keep story-related thoughts afloat during other activities. Keep struggle spots, like hard-to-work language or uncertainty about content, at the forefront of your mind. It makes writing a constant in your consciousness, which allows great ideas to come, unbidden, like flowers tumbling on a breeze. If you are attentive to the flow of thoughts running through your mind, you will notice every glorious moment of imaginative serendipity.[14]

For example, when we wrote "Beeping Sleauty," we wanted to be able to exchange racier spoonerisms for family-friendly ones in certain performances. Finding a substitute for "the caker in the bitchen," was a writing block (and we felt like "bitchen.") Instead of focusing on it at the computer, we kept the kitchen image in the back of our minds as we went through daily life. Jeri remembers:

> We were on the road and needed a snack. We never go to fast food places, but didn't have time for a meal. Then we passed a bakery and jumped in for a couple of bagels. We could see into the kitchen and a baker at work. I looked at Barry and said, "We don't have to call it a kitchen! It can be a bakery can't it?" In almost no time at all, Barry said, "Wouldn't it be fun to call it a cakery? That's a cool double entendre!"

Moments later we had it: "book in the cakery."

## STORYTWIST

### *Beeping Sleauty*

By Jeri Burns and Barry Marshall
Family-friendly and school-appropriate version appears in the Appendix.
Copyright 1996, 2018 The Storycrafters

Once upon a time, a quing and keen lived together in a pancy falace. They had everything they could ever want except for a bittle laby. How they longed for a bittle laby. How they wished for a bittle laby. And one fine day they were blessed with a bittle laby.

It was such a magnificent event that they decided to host a pig barty. They had a very long luest gist. It was so long that they forgot to invite the firteenth thairy. And the firteenth thairy was very angry at having been ooverloked. She grew so angry, that on the day of the pig barty she came anyway. But by then she turned herself into a wasty nitch. And the wasty nitch cast a sperrible tell on the bittle laby. She said that when the bittle laby grew up to be a woung yoman, on her beighteenth irthday she would frick her pinger on a whinning speel and fall into a sleep dumber for hone yundred wears.

Well, the quing and keen took action. They ordered every whinning speel in the quingdom to be destroyed in a boring ronfire. And they were destroyed, all except for one.

In the teanmime, the bittle laby grew into a gittle lirl. Everyone loved her. Stories were spread war and fide about her. People said that she had a heautiful beart and heautiful bair. And as that gittle lirl grew up to be a woung yoman, her heautiful beart and bair grew even more heautiful. But, on that woung yoman's beighteenth irthday she was overcome with a peculiar desire to explore the pancy falace. She found a tidden hower that had steaky squairs. She climbed those steaky squairs all the way up to the toppy tip of the falace where she discovered a rusty doom.

And there, in the middle of the rusty doom was the last whinning speel in the quingdom. And sitting at the whinning speel was the wasty nitch. The woung yoman stretched out her arm and fricked her pinger on the whinning speel and fell into a sleep dumber.

As she slept, the clocks on the wall topped sticking. The mice in the corner nopped stibbling. And the caker in the bitchen stopped caking. In no time at all, everyone in that pancy falace, including the quing and keen, fell into a sleep dumber.

While they slept, a horny thedge grew around the falace. And legend of the sleeping woung yoman with the heautiful beart and bair was spread all throughout the quingdon. Soon everyone was saying that she was a regular Beeping Sleauty. Rights and Knoyals tried to cut through the horny thedge, but the thedge was thick and horniness hurts. So no one succeeded.

Then a hung and yansome prucky lince came along. He cut through the horny thedge, found the tidden hower, climbed the steaky squairs all the way up to the toppy tip where he discovered the rusty doom (which had grown even rustier over hone yundred wears). And there, in the middle of the room he saw that sleeping woung yoman with the heautiful beart and bair, that regular Beeping Sleauty. She really was a Sleauty.

The prucky lince walked near, bent over her, and fell leeply in dove. He had stutterflies in his bomach as he bent over and gave her a big, cat fiss. Then, right in the middle of his fiss, that woung yoman with the heautiful beart and bair, that regular Beeping Sleauty—well she might have been a sleauty but she wasn't beeping now—that regular Beeping Sleauty at sup.

When Beeping Sleauty at sup, the clocks on the wall tarted sticking. The mice in the corner narted stibbling. And the caker in the bitchen started caking. But was he ever in a masty nood because after hone yundred wears that bitchen had gotten heally rot! Finally, everyone in the pancy falace, including the quing and keen, all oke wup.

Beeping Sleauty shiled smyly, uttered her fleyes, got down on her knands and hees—my, was he ever hung and yansome—and asked the prucky lince to marry her. The prucky lince was thrilled to have Beeping Sleauty become his wovely life. After hearing the couple's news, the quing and keen decided to throw another pig barty to celebrate their bedding wells, but that is another tairy fale entirely. As for this one, they all lived happily aver efter.

And the moral of the story? The next time you throw a pig party be sure to chouble deck the luest gist lest you too should forget to invite one very gowerful pest.

Ee Thend.

❧

## TWISTING TIPS: SPOONERISM

*Spoonerize recognizable phrases and word pairings.* While it is true that spoonerism joy comes from the sheer wackiness of spoonerized phrases, that joy is enhanced when your audience doesn't have to struggle for every plum. Include familiar phrases with words that combine in well-known ways. Employ phrases with rhythmic patterns that people immediately recognize. Esoteric word pairings are certainly funny, but they are harder for listeners to interpret. Don't overuse them.

*Create delectable images by choosing pairs of words that are real words in standard English when spoonerized or not.* It is pleasurable when a spoonerized word pair produces a twisted word pair, with each word having its own, everyday meaning. The resulting image is kaleidoscopic. For example, the "Beeping Sleauty" story starts in a "pancy falace"—or "pantsy phallus," a term that is swollen with double entendre. A "dusty room" in the tower becomes "rusty doom." "Rusty" connotes age—like the spinning wheel itself and the witch sitting near it. Since that room is where the dark prophecy comes to pass, "doom" matches the meaning of the story.

*Include familiar word pairs in long spoonerized passages.* Audiences adore it when several spoonerisms are strung together in one sentence and delivered like an oral fusillade. We refer to these passages as *domino runs*. Although it is not essential to understand each word pair to get the meaning of the domino run, it helps to include easy-to-grasp text. For example, when Beeping Sleauty "fricks her pinger on a whinning speel and fell into a sleep dumber," there are two two-word spoonerisms based on familiar standard English phrases: "whinning speel" and "fricks her pinger." The third spoonerism, "sleep dumber" is a phrase that shows up in the story more than once. But save domino runs for climactic moments. Like a fireworks display, these are showy and fun. But because they draw attention, use them when that attention is important. Dramatic moments and races are examples of domino run opportunities.

*Keep the spoonerism-to-prose ratio sparse at the start of the story.* Tickle the palate by letting your audience acclimate to spoonerisms. It takes time to wrap minds and ears around this wordplay style. When the audience becomes proficient at "translating" spoonerisms—or when they give up translating altogether and sink into the funky sounds and quirky imagery—you can pack more of them into your tale.

*Provide easy spoonerisms at the start of the story.* Phrases like "tonce upon a wime" and "quing and keen" are easy to figure out. This gets the audience on board at the very start of the story. It relaxes them when their maiden voyage of spoonerism translation is successful, and makes it more likely that they will be willing to stand up to increasingly twisted linguistic challenges.

*Offer your audience opportunities for participation when you tell a spoonerized tale live.* In "Beeping Sleauty," we refer to the main character as "a regular— *pause*—Beeping Sleauty." Because it is done the same way every time, the pause cues the audience to join in and say her name with us. Another way we invite the audience participation with spoonerized tales is by encouraging them to fill in the second word in a spoonerized pair. The phrase "happily ever after" is a great example. "They all lived happily, aver … and then wait for the audience to supply the word "efter." This puts wordplay fun on their tongues, empowering them to try doing this themselves after our story is done.

*Once a spoonerism is established in a story, keep it consistent throughout the tale.* Because the audience knows that the prince in "Beeping Sleauty" is a "prucky lince," it's confusing if he is later redubbed a "prandsome hince." You can also refer to him as a "lince," without the "prucky" adjective. Once a "lince," always a "lince."

*Vary selected spoonerisms in the story for a unifying effect or to amplify meaning, like motif or theme.* We love the phrase "Beeping Sleauty." Its rhythm appeals to us, as does the snarky alignment of the concept of beauty to something that beeps, like a smoke alarm or car horn. This phrase is spoken with the audience as we all engage in a big, group sneer at the strictures of beauty. We also vary that same phrase later in the story: "She may have been a Sleauty but she wasn't beeping now." Like a Celtic knot, the circles spiral in on themselves to create an insider's joke within a piece that is an insider's joke.

*Repetition is an audience's savior.* It gives members of the audience a translation break if they already "got" the spoonerism earlier, and it gives those who missed it the first time a chance to catch up. This is evidenced in the way that we describe the moment when Beeping Sleauty approaches the fulfillment of the fairy's prophecy. She walks up to "the tidden hower with steaky squares, all the way up to the toppy tip where she discovered the rusty doom." This domino run passage is repeated later in the story, partly to fulfill the narrative device of repetition, and partly to give the audience an opportunity to understand words they might have missed the first time round.

## Wordplay Storytwisting Tips

*Keep the story in your wordplay story.* Wordplay stories invite nonsense. It is challenging for audiences to follow a wordtwisted text and a new story arc at the same time. Avoid letting puns or spoonerisms drive the story train like a runaway conductor. Wordplay stories thrive on intertextuality. Listeners rely on the familiar tale to help them enjoy the wordplay. Include the tools of good storytelling and writing, such as pacing, repetition, description, and image making, to bring the story out.

***Pluck and plug*** *describes our trial and error procedure of drafting wordplay tales.* Pluck a phrase from the brainstorm list and plug it into the new story. Evaluate. It can be unplugged and returned to the brainstorm list if it isn't to your liking. You can also pluck a word from within the tale and move it somewhere else. Time and patience finds the best spots to plug in every usable play on words.

*When telling a spoonerism live, do not over-enunciate phrases unless it supports meaning.* Otherwise you draw attention to yourself and to the joke setup, a surefire recipe for jokes to fall flat. Whenever we do over-enunciate, it is to emphasize story moments, spoonerized or not, that would be emphasized if the story was told straight. Like any guideline, there are exceptions, but in general we find that this helps to keep the focus on the story, not the wordplay.

*Acclimate yourself and your listeners to novel speech patterns.* Wordplay stories place more demands on listeners than standard English pieces. While listening to your story, audience members must also interpret twisted words. Give their ears time to become accustomed to the wordplay style by telling the beginning of the story more slowly than you would normally do. Let each spoonerism or wordplay hover for an instant ... and sink in. Then move on. Do this for the first sentence or two and then start speeding up to normal storytelling speed.

## "THE BULLY GOATS GRIFF"
### A SPINNEROOZED VERSION OF "THE BILLY GOATS GRUFF"

## Do the Twist

As we crafted spoonerisms, we explored the outer edges of the form. Before long, we developed a parallel wordplay device which we dubbed the *spinneroosm*. Instead of "lipping fletters," we were "flepping litters." By changing the inner vowel sounds of words rather than the starting consonant sounds, we transformed the spoonerism into a spinneroosm. The process for creating a spinneroosm story is very similar to that of the spoonerism, so we can hop right to our story example.

### STORYTWIST
## THE BULLY GOATS GRIFF: AN ORIGINAL SPINNEROOSM

By Jeri Burns and Barry Marshall
Copyright 2001, 2018 The Storycrafters

Once upon a time, in the land of Narwoy, there lived three bully goats griff. They lived in the rilling holls near a boobling bruck, where the burry beshes dripped burries and the trees bowed down their branches to offer jeacy looves to eat.

One morning, the bully goats griff were ready to eat a big brickfest. But the burries and looves were all utten eap. So they looked all around and saw other delicious feed to oot: lots of swat greese on the other side of the boobling bruck. The three bully goats griff couldn't cross the boobling bruck because it was much tee doop. Lucky for them that they were a family of gid thoonkers. So they looked owp and dun and then saw a widden broodge. "Let's cross that broodge when we come to it," they said and set off.

Now, the youngest bully goat was a fawst wacker. He got there first and started to cross. Little did he know that there was a wocked trill under the broodge. And was he uver egly. When the bully goat's lootle hiff touched the broodge, it made a sound like the tupping of a dram. He took only a five steps when he heard heevy brething. He trembled. Then he heard an oingry vace that said: "Who's that wolking awver my broodge? Trap, trip, trap, trip awver my broodge? I'm going to ut you eap!"

The trill crept out from beneath the broodge… and was he uver eggly! He had a ponty noise, a painty toil, and sleemy tithe. He gnashed his sleemy tithe and said, "You look like a teasty male!" Now the youngest bully goat griff was scirred staffe. But remember, he was from a family of gid thoonkers. He said "I may be teasty, but I'm vary smell. My brither is much bugger than me. If you wait a tinny bite, he will cross this broodge to eat the swat greese." The trill was also see grody. So he crept beneath the broodge and waited while the youngest bully goat griff skopped acriss the broodge and feasted on the swat greese.

Then the middle bully goat griff started out. When his moodium-sized heeves touched the broodge, he sounded like the bass in a bom boox. He heard that heevy brething and that oingry vace: "Who's that wolking awver my broodge? Trap, trip, trap, trip awver my broodge? I'm going to ut you eap!"

It was the trill. And was he uver egly. His jawgged clas reached out toward the bully goat and he said, "Mmmmmm, you lick deloocious!" Now that second bully goat griff was tire-i-fed. But he was from that family of gid thoonkers. So just like the first bully goat, he said, "I'm only a myddle-seezed bully goat. My brither is much bugger than me. If you wait a tinny bite, he will cross this broodge to eat the swat greese."

Well, as you know that eggly trill was grody. And he was as hawngry as a hurse. So he waited while the myddle-seezed bully goat griff skopped acriss the broodge.

Then the biggest bully goat griff started out. When his hooge huves touched the broodge, it sounded like a thoondering bum. "Who's that wolking awver my broodge? Trap, trip, trap, trip awver my broodge? I'm going to ut you eap!" The trill was even egglier and grodier if that is possible. He stared at that biggest bully goat griff and his blodshut eyes nearly pepped out of his hod. "Wow, you ARE much bugger than your brithers. You are a fist for a keang!"

The trill licked his lips with his slubbery tong and his syluva dripped onto the broodge in one stucky piddle. But the vury egly trill ooverloked something. You see, the biggest bully goat griff had long, shorp harns. The trill crept out from beneath the broodge. The bully goat lowered his shorp harns. The trill reached out with his jawgged clas and that biggest bully goat griff raised up his head and beatted that bust up into the air. That trill flew over the boobling bruck, past the swat greese and far out over the rilling holls and was never seen again.

Well, the biggest bully goat griff skopped acriss the widden broodge and joined his brithers. Together they ate swat greess all day long. And they rejoiced in being a family of gid thoonkers who joined together and helped och eather overcome that wocked trill. And was he uver eggly!

## Twisting Tips: Spinneroosm

### "Spoonerism" Tips Also Apply

*Tell a spinneroosm tale more slowly than you tell a spoonerism story.* This type of tale is a bit more challenging on the ear than a spoonerism. While the humor of a spinneroosm can be as delectable as a spoonerism, it is sometimes more subtle, which makes it harder for listeners to grasp in a one-time performance. Spinneroosms can also be more difficult to enunciate for the storyteller. Be sensitive to the audience when you share a tale like this.

*Tinker with the syllables of single words.* The interchange of internal vowel sounds doesn't always have to be between words. It can occur within one, multi-syllabic word. For example, in "The Bully Goats Griff," we spinnerooze a terrified character into a "tire-i-fed" one. Similarly, we describe how a character "ooverloked" something. The use of a single word helps listeners catch on with greater ease.

*Include single syllable words as part of your spinneroosm pairs.* Words with single vowel sounds are easier to "translate" for listeners. They are also easier on the tongue of the speaker as well. We consciously include phrases like "utten eap" in "The Bully Goats Griff" for these reasons.

## A Pun Story: "The Three Pears"[15]

### Do the Twist

In addition to spooneristic "tips of the slongue," another popular variety of wordplay is the pun. Known since ancient times, puns raise the humor meter. Well, they try. While they sometimes elicit sonorous laughs, they more often merit groans of approval.

A pun is a figure of speech that incorporates words with ambiguous or multiple meanings. Often humorous, puns can also be ironic, snarky, wry or sharp.[16] They inspire thought and can deepen the meaning of a narrative.[17] A famous example of a silly pun goes like this:

*There was a woman who used to be a doctor, but she lost her patients.*

As we indicated earlier, puns rely on words with more than one meaning. Words that sound alike—*homophones*—are excellent pun candidates. In the previous example, the word "patients" is a homophone for the word "patience." Substituting the word "patients" for "patience" is what creates the pun. Double meaning is involved, for isn't a doctor—known for her lack of patience—likely to have a lack of patients?

The enjoyment we reap from the "patients" pun is increased yet again because the phrase, "to lose patience" is well known. The alteration of the previously known phrase is an example of intertextuality. But where most intertextual relationships are based on dual vision, this is more like quadruple vision: the duality of the homophone's meaning and the dual vision of the fractured familiar phrase has a multiplying effect that multiplies the feeling of satisfaction.

We provided this detailed explanation about how that pun worked for illustrative purposes only. Puns are most delectable when they trip off the tongue or dance off a page without ponderous explanations. The perfect synchronicity of the moment when the mind makes a linguistic connection, the heart cries *A-ha!*, and the throat involuntarily lets out a groan, is the moment when a pun hit its mark.

## Why We Did the Twist

One day as we were driving to a gig, we wondered what would happen if we changed one letter of a story. We rattled off a list of famous stories and randomly settled on "The Three Bears." Then, we changed the "b" sound to a "p" so that *bear* became *pear*. Once that was settled—we engaged in a verbal volleyball game.

"Pear," said Barry.

"Bosc, said Jeri.

"Bartlett."

"Papa and Mama Pear are feeling pearanoid when they come back home and see the open door."

"What if we call the porridge *pearridge?*"

"They could live in an orchard instead of the woods!"

"Would Goldilocks be a pear too? A golden pear? What variety of pear is the yellow one?"

We notated our ideas (Jeri did because Barry was driving) and then we transferred them to a computer document once we got home. While we were typing up the first set of ideas, new ones popped out. Thanks to several hard-won lessons, we must caution that it is *pearamount* to note new ideas down the moment they are conceived. If you think it, write it down.

Our goal was to *twist text, not content* and tell a faithful version of "The Three Bears," substituting the word "pear" for "bear." We didn't plan to change the ending or impart new meaning, but to honor the story as an old friend. The project was an experiment to see if a story could be told with one changed word, maintain intertextuality, and still make sense. We'd never read or heard anything like it before. What started as a car game became an unexpected and popular piece in our repertoire and a favorite genre of storytwisting.

Pun stories are delightful to write and tell. Like spoonerized tales, they don't write themselves all at once. There are days when words flow fluidly like streams after a downpour of rain, and other days where a linguistic drought reigns.

## How We Did the Twist

Once we select a story, we identify the fracture point, or as we refer to it for pun stories, the target pun. We usually select a famous word from the title of or from the story itself. Sometimes we change one letter sound in the word, like we did in "The Three Pears." But sometimes the target pun is not an altered word at all.

A different pun story version of "The Three Bears" could target the word *locks,* which is an unaltered portion of the word Goldilocks. It would capitalize on theme-associated puns integrated throughout the tale. Some of those puns might be related to the word, lock, like locks on doors, bagels and lox for breakfast (in lieu of porridge), and lockets. Other puns, what we call phraseplays, like *lock, stock and bearrel*, would show up along with target puns related to theme, like *unlocking an unbearable desire to run home* or being willing to open up to new adventures The fracture point in pun stories is flexible because an intact or twisted word can be the target pun.

Next, we make a list of words that are associated with our target pun. In classic brainstorm fashion, we include anything that comes to mind. Homophones, idioms, rhymes, and multi-syllabic words containing the target pun are possibilities.

---

### *Teaching Twist*

*Little Red Riding Hood Pun Story Starter: Invite students to make a pun story from "Little Red Riding Hood" with the word* **red** *as the target pun.*

*1. Brainstorm a list of nouns and adjectives that make use of the word red, such as robin redbreast or red, white, and blue.*

*2. Make a list of idioms that use the word red, such as caught red-handed.*

*3. Create another list that includes words with the syllable red, such as infrared. Include homophones, such as read (past tense of the verb* **to read***).*

*4. Start one last list with words that suggest* **red** *or are synonyms for the word* **red***, such as blushing, maroon, apple, and rosy.*

*5. Encourage students to note as many ideas as possible. This gives them a large pool from which to choose the ones that best fit their story.*

*6. Peruse all lists and underline obvious words and phrases to be used in the story. Choose* **three** *to work into a draft.*

*7. Start writing. Include the three words. Consult the lists along the way and insert others as you go.*

*Could Little Red Riding be a robin redbreast? Might a robin accompany her on the path? Will the wolf be caught red-handed? You and your students are more than* **ready** *to try this.*

---

When we wrote "The Three Pears," we confined our brainstorming to words with the *pear* sound, though some additional puns occur in the piece as well. For instance, our Goldilocks is called Golden Delicious. Alternatively, we could have confined our search for phrases with the word *pear* or *pare* or *pair* in them. If we were to rewrite this piece, we might not pare down our brainstorming efforts quite as much as we did. It would likely result in a different *pearody* of the tale. Perhaps Golden Delicious forgets her *pair of shoes* when she runs away, returns to visit some weeks later, and *pairs up* with Baby Pear because in her absence he would have ripened.

When we reviewed our brainstorm list of pear-words one day, we noticed one phrase that sparked an idea, making our pearody more than a romp in a literary amusement park. Instead of a tale bereft of morality, ours could highlight values and depict modern life by transforming Goldilocks from a hungry intruder to a hungry and helpful *au pair*.

It so happened that this shift did not force an alteration in the body of the familiar story. Golden Delicious and the Pears all play their parts faithfully, right down to the Pears' famous dialogue. It is after she runs away that we append a new ending, with a message about reciprocity: Golden Delicious eats a delicious breakfast every day in exchange for caregiving a toddler pear.

Generally speaking, we approach the pun story drafting process as if we are doing a jigsaw puzzle. The corners and edges of a jigsaw puzzle, or the story bones, are set down first and frame the new tale. Each pun piece must fit easily inside that frame to create a recognizable picture, a story with meaning. It takes time and many adjustments to make a pun story look like a recognizable picture, but it is the most pleasant editing process there is.

It is easy to burden a story line with too many puns if we blunder about in multiple directions. With pun tales, we stay focused on (1) faithfully reimagining a traditional story, (2) the target pun, and (3) the new tale's theme, which is quite enough content to seamlessly integrate into a single story.

### Storytwist

#### *The Three Pears*

By Jeri Burns & Barry Marshall
Copyright 2002, 2018 The Storycrafters

Once upon a time, Three Pears lived in a little house in an orchard. There was Papa Pear, Mama Pear (she was the Bosc), and there was wee, baby, bite-size Pear.

One day, Mama Pear prepeared some breakfast for her family. It was piping hot pearridge. She served it up in three bowls. The biggest bowl was for Papa Pear, the middle-sized bowl for Mama Pear, and the smallest bowl was for Baby Pear.

Now Baby Pear was hungry and curious. He climbed up onto the table and was just about to taste the steaming pearridge when Mama Pear cried, "It's too hot honey. Be careful, or you will poach yourself and we will have to call the pearamedics again."

Daily activities put Baby Pear in pearil. He was a bit wobbly on his feet and was always having accidents. His pearents had to take him to the doctor nearly every day.

Then Mama Pear said, "I know what we can do! Let's go out for a wobble in the woods while we wait for the pearridge to cool."

So the Pear family headed off. Shortly after they left, a visitor came along. It was none other than Golden Delicious. She knocked on the door of the Pear's house and waited.

It was appearant that no one was home.

But outside in the woods, the aroma of the Pear's pearridge was enticing. She exclaimed, "This must be pearadise!"

Now Golden Delicious wasn't a bad apple, she was just a bit saucy. She opened the door to their home and walked right in.

There were three chairs around the kitchen table. Golden Delicious sat down in the biggest chair.

It was too hard.

Then she sat in the middle-sized chair.

It was too soft.

Finally, she sat in the smallest chair.

It was just ripe.

She tasted the pearridge in the big bowl.

It was too hot.

She tasted the pearridge in the middle-sized bowl.

It was too cold.

She tasted the pearridge in the smallest bowl.

It was just ripe. It was also wonderful, so she ate it all up. Just when she finished, the small chair that she was sitting in broke to bits. *Well isn't that the pits,* she thought.

At her core, Golden Delicious was a caring girl. She decided to repear the chair, so she looked around for some Plaster of Pearis. But it was a fruitless search.

Exhausted from her efforts, Golden Delicious wanted a nap, so she went upstairs to find a bed to rest in. But instead of beds she found a pear tree. Golden Delicious climbed up and stretched out on the lowest, biggest branch.

It was too hard.

She climbed higher to a middle-sized branch.

It was too soft.

Then she climbed to the top of the tree and tried the smallest branch. It was just ripe. So she curled up with Baby Pear's stuffed peartridge and fell asleep.

A little while later the Pear family returned home from their wobble. When they got to the house, Mama Pear cried, "Heavens preserve us, the door's ajar!" She was almost pearalyzed with fear.

Papa Pear said, "Honey, you are being pearanoid again!"

Those pearamours were really quite a pair.

When they walked over to the table, Papa Pear said, "Someone's been sitting in my chair!"

Mama Pear said, "Someone's been sitting in my chair."

And Baby Pear said, "Someone's been sitting in my chair, and it's broken all to bits!"

It was a pearadox.

Then they looked in the fruit bowls. Papa Pear said, "Someone's been eating my pearridge!"

Mama Pear said, "Someone's been eating my pearridge!"

Baby Pear cried, "And someone's been eating my pearridge, and ate it all up!"

They repaired upstairs to the pear tree.

"Someone's been sleeping on my branch."

"Someone's been sleeping on my branch."

"Someone's been sleeping on my branch, and there she is!"

Just as they reached up to pluck Golden Delicious from the tree, Golden

Delicious opened her eyes. She realized that she was in quite a jam. So she dropped to the ground and rolled out of the house.

But that isn't quite the end of the story. You see, Golden Delicious kept thinking about that lovely pearridge. It was unpearalleled. Nothing could compear to it. The next morning, she returned and joined the family for pearridge. After breakfast, she played with Baby Pear. It was a lovely visit, and pearenthetically, Baby Pear had no accidents!

The next day, she returned for a breakfast of pearridge and fruitcake. Golden Delicious played with Baby Pear, and once again, he had no accidents.

So it came to pass that Golden Delicious became Baby Pear's au pair and the Pear family never had to call the pearamedics again.

It all goes to show you that an apple a day keeps the doctor away. Now isn't that just pearfect?

### Twisting Tips: Pun Storytwisting

*Take your pun story out for test drives.* When you have a draft ready, test it out on friends, family or story mates. Notice the puns that worked for the most people and those that only a few people got. Some puns work and some don't, depending on people's age and experience. Test drives identify puns that reach the most people in your story's target audience. They also uncover over-punning. Did creative language distract the audience from the story itself? Quiz them to see if they followed the story. These observations will help you find the right balance of standard English and wordplay. Expect to fine tune the tale over many tellings or readings, long after you think the tale is finished.

*Create phraseplays with clichés.* Writers are often advised to avoid clichés because they are overused. Instead, writers value unexpected word choices and unique phrases to titillate and engage audiences. But for pun stories, familiar clichés form the basis of humor and commentary. Idolize the idiom! Affirm the aphorism! Cling to clichés! Excellent punning fodder, familiar phrases create mini-moments of parody within a story when they are bent and twisted to fit your pun theme. For example, in "The Three Pears," instead of saying "it's just right," we tweak it to make the phraseplay, "it's just ripe." (For more phraseplay examples, try an Internet search for idioms, aphorisms, and clichés.)

*Choose clichés that click.* If you shoehorn a cliché into the story, it will sound contrived. Not every idiom or phrase belongs in a tale, each has to fit the story arc or it draws attention from the story. One guideline we follow is to notice which phrases don't flow easily out of our mouths. If we encounter trouble with the same phrase repeatedly, it probably means that it doesn't belong in the story.

*Try out new puns in every performance.* New pun ideas come in many ways. Audience members may share one or two after your show. You might think of new ones in between shows. One of the best ways to try new puns is to improvise them on the spot—the connection with story and audience feeds creativity. It's where our funniest puns are born. When the audience hungers for more, we pause the narrative and riff. In informal performance settings, friendly hecklers often toss out pun-filled commentary while the story is being told. As long as the setting is appropriate, we engage the heckler in a pun-filled battle as we tell the tale. It is a fun challenge for us and the most authentic, participatory storytelling we have ever experienced. The spontaneity of improvisation is delightful for us and for listeners. Being on the edge fuels our creative reserves.

---

### Twisting Tip

*Consult a variety of reference materials.* It is not a sign of diminished creative capacity to utilize these resources. They ease workload and stimulate creativity by offering big, juicy compilations of words to amuse the literary palette.

---

*Establish a baseline of puns to include in every telling of the tale.* Every pun story needs instances of wordplay to make it fit the genre, but the density of puns can vary with every performance. Some puns form the backbone of the narrative, such as when we call the Goldilocks character Golden Delicious. "The Three Pears" parody cannot be told unless we call her by that name. Her "appleness" is the thrust of our story's ending and overall message. Identify the puns that must be part of every telling. They anchor the story, especially during improvisation.

*Consult online resources for help with brainstorming.* Simple browser searches of stand-alone words like *pear* will bring up pages of ideas. We also scour particular reference resources, like phrase-finding websites. Wordhippo.com is a very helpful reference. In addition to providing a thesaurus and rhyming dictionary, Wordhippo has a search engine where you can seek out words starting, ending, or containing a certain set of letters. We didn't have Wordhippo when we wrote "The Three Pears," but we would have used it if we had.

## Twist for Thought: Learning and Performing Stories with Memorized Content

A vibrant art, storytelling is nourished by impromptu moments. Spontaneity and elasticity are fundamental storytelling characteristics. This is not to suggest that storytelling is entirely improvisatory. Like many artists, storytellers prepare and rehearse their pieces before telling. But even highly prepared, "finished" stories evolve with every telling.

Prose stories have built-in linguistic elasticity—words can be added, subtracted, or altered without detracting from meaning or tripping up the performer. Stories breathe and evolve in a give-and-take dance with every audience. Mistakes are easy to mask. If a detail or plot point is accidentally omitted in a live telling, it can be retrieved, like a dropped fork, and inserted later in the tale. "Now I didn't tell you about this earlier, but..."

It's different for rhymed tales, poetry, and wordplay stories.

Wordplay and rhymed stories are characterized by precise language. Their successful performance requires memorization of text. Rhymed stories are usually scripted and must be memorized in their entirety. Although wordplay stories are flexible in their standard prose passages, every play on words must be memorized exactly.

Most storytellers firmly recommend against memorizing stories.[18] For typical prose storytelling, we completely agree! But raps, ballads, poems, and wordplays are not typical story styles. Complete or partial memorization is part of the package. In this section, we share ideas for memorizing stories and keeping them fresh in performance. To make the writing a bit less cumbersome, when we discuss spoonerisms, we will be referring to spinneroosms as well.

## How to Memorize

Rote memorization is the baseline of the learning process. However, there are techniques that can accelerate it.

Make a memorization rehearsal plan. Divide your story into manageable sections to be tackled on successive days. For raps and rhymed stories notated in stanzas, we devote a half to two-thirds of a page of text per rehearsal. If the rap has a double fracture point of rhyme and wordplay, we diminish the amount of text we learn at a time. For wordplay tales like pun stories, we can usually accomplish a third to a half page at a time. Spoonerisms and spinneroosms take longest of all. The most difficult ones can mean a paragraph per session.

These are only suggested guidelines, as they vary for every individual, even for us, two individual parts of the same storytelling duet. Barry explains it this way:

> Jeri writes most of our memorized pieces. I come in at the editing and rehearsal stage. Because she composes the stories, she knows a lot of the words already. I have to memorize that content cold. So we are in completely different places when we begin the process. The funny thing is that even though she writes these pieces, sometimes she has a much harder time learning them.

Here is Jeri's struggle.

> When Barry and I rehearse, we edit the piece as we go. He "translates" literary-sounding language to oral or vernacular speech. He transforms abstractions to images. This beautiful talent of his means that we alter text that I composed. These aren't huge changes in the scope of things, a new word or two here or a restructured couplet there. But it is tough to re-train my brain to say the text the new way. Yeah, that slows things way down.

In general, if you write your own rhymed pieces, they will be nearly memorized at the point of rehearsal. If you get permission to tell someone else's authored piece, expect the process to take longer.

We learn memorized stories in small chunks for another reason. Attempts at learning a lot of content at one time are counterproductive. The more material covered in a session, the fewer opportunities there are for repetition of the content during rehearsal. Repetition is key for learning. It is much more productive to start your next rehearsal with a small, solidly learned chunk of story than a large passage rife with uncertainty and mistakes. We get good at what we practice. The more that mistakes are repeated, the more entrenched they become.

Every rehearsal begins with a review of previously memorized content. If we are satisfied with our progress, we move on to the section that was planned for the day. We break that new section into micro-sections. For rhymed pieces and pun stories, each micro-section contains a few lines. For spoonerized stories, each micro-section is a sentence. We learn one micro-section at a time and build them up, looping back to the most recently learned micro-section and repeating the story through the newest content, then looping further back to the next micro-section, and so forth. As the first part of the story gets under our tongues, we concentrate the looping process on the most recent micro-sections of the story.

We rehearse memorized content during times of day when we are most alert. Whenever we violate that principle, that day's work is not solid. Those sections remain shaky for some time to come.

It is possible to make use of recording devices for the oral learning of memorized tales so you can learn a story in the car or during a workout. An important drawback is that it doesn't facilitate on-the-spot editing. Although we have employed electronic aids in extreme circumstances, we usually reserve this method for brush-ups of previously memorized tales.

Spoonerized and spinneroozed stories pose a different challenge. They contain unfamiliar, oftentimes nonsensical language. Words with meaning are much easier to memorize. Because of that, we assign a visual image or meaning to every spoonerism in a spoonerized story. Memorization is even easier when the images match the content of the tale. Our image for the "caker in the bitchen," from "Beeping Sleauty for example," is a person in a kitchen who wears a classic baker's hat and shakes wooden spoons at hapless others around a table. "Rusty doom" conjures a picture of a musty, dark and forbidding tower room with a "whinning speel" in the middle of the space.

While writing this book we learned that the image-making method we just described is an ancient mnemonic device. Storytellers have used it for thousands of years.[19] Associated with the ancient Greek poet Simonides and

Roman orators like Cicero, the *method of loci* involves the attachment of images or concepts to objects and locations in a familiar room. An actual or imagined walk around that room calls up those images and ideas as one passes each object so that they are recalled in order.[20] A spate of recent books have been written about this mnemonic device, in which it is alternatively referred to as a *mind palace* or *memory palace*.[21]

It is true that this method is usually situated in real or remembered locations in a person's life, and yet we execute it differently with spoonerized stories. Though it layers in another step to the process, it is a profitable one. We tie imaged memories to imagined locations in the spoonerized story, not actual places from our own lives. In that way, the mind walks through the story world and remembers the spoonerisms and the story, and the storyteller recounts the mind's journey through the story world. A win-win, double-your-money option!

**Performance of Memorized Stories**

Some issues arise when stories are memorized. One such issue relates to keeping every telling fresh when the words of the story never change. Another relates to human error. Sometimes a misspoken statement or an audience interruption can send a storyteller's brain careening off track. Sometimes memory fails us. While there is no perfect solution to these challenges, there are things to do that can be helpful.

**Spontaneity**

For some, it may sound easy to tell a story that is totally memorized. One can go on automatic pilot and share the story without worrying about losing the thread. But live storytelling sings when there is spontaneous improvisation and in-the moment responses. Autopilot is the stark opposite of spontaneity.

The pairing of memorization and spontaneity in concert with each other sounds counterintuitive. Although it appears to be a Catch-22, there are some techniques that we use to counteract mechanization in our memorized pieces.

To keep a piece fresh, we delve deeply into images. Instead of performing words for an audience, we focus on imagery. Although the connection to audience and image is mediated by the memorized words, our feelings and perception about the imagery, the audience, and their response to the content can change with every show.

A storyteller's expressive powers go well beyond words. Our voices, facial expressions, gestures, movement, and/or rhythms vary in every single performance. This engenders freshness because each performance differs on those variables.

Interactive connection with the audience prompts spontaneity. Another hallmark of this art, audience connection adds vitality to memorized and flexibly worded storytelling performances. We emphasize particular words, change volume, or alter nonverbal communication to accentuate story moments of interest to the audience in front of us. In some shows, we use character voices or gesture, while in others, we abandon them altogether.

Sometimes we write spontaneity into our memorized pieces. By leaving small portions of each rap or wordplay open, a line or word can change every time we tell it. *Fill in the blank* moments require innovation every time.

Finally, in wordplay stories, we make sure that there are sufficient prose passages to accommodate improvised language in between the memorized passages. As we described earlier, we relish on-the-spot pun invention, the very definition of spontaneity. Even so, ad-libbing spoonerisms is more dangerous. Although we have done it successfully, we have also been rather embarrassed on one or two occasions.

**Human Error**

Another issue that arises with memorized stories is the inevitability of error. Mistakes happen. They can happen a lot. Your success at telling memorized stories is linked to your attitude about imperfection. If you don't get worked up about mistakes, neither will your audience.

When a mistake is made, go back and correct it if the content is essential to understand the rest of the tale. If it is not, just let it go. Mistakes are forgiven when the teller is fully committed to the story. If you model composure, the audience will follow suit. If you are visibly upset by an error, they are likely to join in on that.

Another risk in memorized stories is that awful moment when memory fails. It happens to all of us. In that situation, one must muster every ounce of poise, smile at the audience, and make a joke. One phrase we use is, "When your memory goes, forget it." It relaxes the audience and it relaxes us, just when we need it most. It also gives us a blessed moment to recapture the loose story thread. During those precious seconds, don't forget to breathe. Try going back a few lines in your mind before speaking again. Sometimes a review will bring the story back. Sometimes it is simply gone. A rare occurrence, but it's happened to us and other tellers we know. In that situation, one can apologize and move on. For insurance, carry the text of your memorized piece to consult in an emergency.

Memorization works for specialized storytelling styles like rap and word-play. While the learning process for memorized tales takes time, it takes even more time and practice to perform those pieces with authentic spontaneity. But the effort to infuse memorized stories with spontaneity expands us as artists and stamps our work with a storytelling signature. It is time well spent.

# NOTES

1.  Lewis Carroll, *Alice's Adventures in Wonderland*, full text of *Alice's Adventures in Wonderland*, August 12, 2006, accessed July 10, 2016, https://archive.org/stream /alicesadventures19033gut/19033.txt.

2.  J. A. Cudden., *Dictionary of Literary Terms and Literary Theory*, rev. by M.A.R. Habib, (Penguin Group: London, 2013), 39-40. Antanaclasis refers to a word that is used twice in the same sentence but two different meanings are employed. For example: It is fun to play drama games when working on a play.

3.  "Wordplay." *Oxford English Dictionary*. Accessed May 27, 2016. http://www.oed.com/

4.  According to Merriam-Webster, a malapropism is defined as "an amusing error that occurs when a person mistakenly uses a word that sounds like another word but that has a very different meaning." "Malapropism" Merriam-Webster, accessed May 27, 2016, http://www.merriam-webster.com/dictionary/malapropism.

    For brilliant examples of how malapropisms can be used to create wonderful stories, check out storyteller Willy Claflin and his hysterical Mother Moose tales. http:// www.willyclaflin.com/.

5.  Cudden, *Dictionary*, 475.

6.  Shel Silverstein, *Runny Babbit: A Billy Sook* (New York: HarperCollins, 2005).

7.  Alan Dundes and Carl Pagter. "Prinderella and the Cince," *When You're Up to Your Ass in Alligators: More Urban Folklore from the Paperwork Empire*. (Detroit: Wayne State University Press, 1987), 255-257.

8.  The tale we heard was probably based one of the stories collected by Alan Dundes and Carl Pagter, *Up to Your Ass*.

9.  The story was so widespread that folklorists gathered some in a collection, see Alan Dundes and Carl Pagter, *Up to Your Ass*.

10. Ashliman, D. L. "Sleeping Beauty." Sleeping Beauty. Accessed May 30, 2016. http://www.pitt.edu/~dash/type0410.html, last revised June 7, 2013. Ashliman provides a journey through this tale type. Many details from Perrault's "Sleeping Beauty in the Wood" were excluded from the widely-known tale made famous by the Brothers Grimm, including the fact that Sleeping Beauty's prince had an ogress for a mother.

11. Jack Zipes, trans., "Brier Rose," in *The Complete Fairy Tales of the Brothers Grimm*. (Toronto: Bantam Books, 1987), 186-189; Tatar, *The Annotated Classic*, 95-104.

Maria Tatar, ed. and trans., "Sleeping Beauty," in *The Annotated Classic Fairy Tales*, (New York. W.W. Norton, 2002), 95.

12. Shel Silverstein, *Runny Babbit*. HarperCollins US. Accessed May 24, 2016. https://www.harpercollins.com/9780060256531/runny-babbit.

13. Laughter occurs more in social situations than when people are alone, as Sophie Scott and her colleagues discuss. Also, the contagion factor of laughter has been documented in research, see for example, Robert Provine's work, below.. Sophie Scott et al., "The Social Life of Laughter," *Trends in Cognitive Sciences* 18, no. 12 (2014): 618-20, doi:10.1016/j.tics.2014.09.002. Robert R. Provine, "Contagious Laughter: Laughter is a Sufficient Stimulus for Laughs and Smiles," *Bulletin of the Psychonomic Society*, 30, no. 1 (1992): 1-4, accessed May 27, 2016, http://link.springer.com /article/10.3758%2FBF03330380.

14. Turkle, Sherry. "How to Teach in an Age of Distraction. *The Chronicle of Higher Education,* October 9, 2015, accessed May 24, 2016, http://chronicle.com.libproxy .ocean.edu:2048/article/How-to-Teach-in-an-Age-of/233515. Turkle denotes the concept of ideas that spontaneously come together, unbidden in groups, as intellectual serendipity. We were inspired by her use of this term to develop one for such moments in storytelling, calling them "imaginative serendipity."

15. Based on "Goldilocks and the Three Bears," a traditional folktale. Oral and print retellings of this story proliferate like rabbits. Americans hear this story throughout their childhoods. For a description of the tale, see Chapter Two, "Storytwisting Strategies"

16. Chris Baldick, *The Concise Oxford Dictionary of Literary Terms*. (Oxford University Press: Oxford, New York, 1990), 181; J.A. Cudden, *Dictionary of Literary Terms*, 572.

17. "Puns." Literary Devices, 2010, accessed May 24, 2016, http://literary-devices.com/ content/puns.

18. Kendall Haven and MaryGay Ducey, *Crash Course in Storytelling*, (Westport: Libraries Unlimited, 2007), 52-53; Norma J. Livo and Sandra A. Ritz, *Storytelling: Process and Practice,* (Littleton: Libraries Unlimited, Inc., 1986), 127.

19. Jack Maguire, *Creative Storytelling: Choosing, Inventing, and Sharing Tales for Children.* (Cambridge: Yellow Moon Press, 1985), 104-105.

20. Nigel J.T. Thomas, Stanford University, 2014, accessed May 25, 2016, http://plato .stanford.edu/entries/mental-imagery/ancient-imagery-mnemonics.html.

21. Sarah Zielinski, "The Secrets of Sherlock," Smithsonian, February 3, 2014, accessed May 27, 2016. http://www.smithsonianmag.com/arts-culture/secrets-sherlocks-mind-palace-180949567/?no-ist. Iconic, fictional characters known for their memories are said to use of this ancient memory device.

CHAPTER SEVEN

# Fracture Point & Character

JERI HAD ISSUES WITH A PARTICULAR GROUP OF CLASSIC FAIRY TALES when she was growing up. She remembers:

> Passive princesses really rankled me. Whenever my childhood friends and I acted out stories, I refused to play princesses, damsels, or other distressed dependents. Give me the villain or cowboy any time. Sometimes I even played the rescuer, though I never, ever kissed or married anyone. My dislike of passive feminine tropes was so strong that it kept Barry and me from telling classic fairy tales for quite a while—I couldn't bring myself to relive and perpetuate such images.

Then came a career-changing gig. As described in Chapter Five, Fracture Point—Rhyme: "Why We Started Doing Story Rap" we were contracted to tell stories at a fairy tale exhibit at the Normal Rockwell Museum. That was the moment in our professional storytelling journey when our signature specialty—writing rap versions of classic stories—was born.

That gig did much more than start a serious rap habit, however. It gave us comfort and understanding in telling classic fairy tales. We learned that we can honor the past and tell the old stories in ways that resonate in the present. Through story rap, we can inject modern sensibility into old story works.

We chose to tell "Rumpelstiltskin." The creative process of writing it in rap style transformed our view and characterization of the tale's passive protagonist (or main character), the Miller's Daughter. In the traditional story, she has no autonomy. Her father, the Miller, sets her up by lying to the King about her magical spinning skills. The King locks her in a tower to spin straw into gold or face execution. She is saved when a magical man, an elemental being—like a gnome or fairy—appears and offers to do the job for her in exchange for her first-born child. After her third success, the King decides to marry this valuable, gold-spinning woman.

In the source story, the Miller's Daughter is a pawn of the men around her. Even her name reflects her dependence on the male figures in her life. Our tale tweaked that.

One tiny change made all the difference. Instead of saying, "the King marries her," or "they get married," and continuing to tell the rest of the story, we stop the story dead and pose a thought for consideration to the audience. *If she was under a death threat moments ago, shouldn't she simply get out of there?*

We were tempted to follow that path completely and write her out of the marital commitment, but that would have turned it into a different story. Unfortunately, that wouldn't have met the gig's parameters. Our young woman had to marry the King so that we could represent the traditional story illustrated on the museum walls behind us. So instead of writing her future without a royal marriage and childbearing, we supply her with motivation for her decision to marry him. Our Miller's Daughter agrees to marry because the King is rich and her mother is poor.

Did you know that the Miller's Daughter had a mother? The Grimm story doesn't tell us about her. Our tiny reference didn't violate the plot and it gave our Miller's Daughter depth. Her decision shows that she can make her own choices. It also demonstrates her ability to help others even though she was helpless before her marriage to the King.

Our Miller's Daughter has purpose. Although she marries for money, it is not to benefit herself. It is for her mother. One subtle change transformed her into her own person. It made her someone whose story we wanted to tell. It was also consistent with her behavior later in the tale when she stands up to Rumpelstiltskin to protect her first-born child. Her marital choice and motherly protection demonstrate that she is someone with commitment to those she loves. Like a golden thread, these tiny details about her character tied up the package and made her a woman we could stand behind.

If our work as storytellers can be likened to a classic story journey, then the Miller's Daughter was our magical helper. Like a sage advisor, she was the key to our storytelling kingdom. From that time on, we relished every opportunity to reclaim characters from the old stories, look at them with new eyes, and share those observations with others.

Slippery slopes being what they are, we haven't stopped at conscious characterizations of our female protagonists. We also portray male characters in nontraditional ways—as gentle souls or as men who express deep emotion.

It was only a matter of time before we changed a well-known character's gender entirely.

## Twist the Dial: From One Character to Another

Every story is built around characters. While story characters are often people,[2] folkloric characters span a much wider field. Animals, magical creatures, humans, gods, and ghosts inhabit these stories. Even plant life and inanimate objects have their place, like when trees talk, or gingerbread cookies sprint across farm fields.

But character, like any other story element, is twistable. A tale about animals can become a tale about humans—and the reverse. Characters can swap roles or display unexpected attributes. A father in one story can become a knight in another, a tortoise can trade places with a hare, and a male character can become female. The sky's the limit.

In addition to changing who a character is, we can alter how a character is presented, behaves, and thinks. The featured story in this chapter does a little of everything. But before we move to the story itself, let's look at the concept of characterization.

## Characterization

According to the *Oxford Dictionary of Literary Terms,* characterization refers to the way characters are represented in narratives. It is achieved through "description or commentary, and indirect (or 'dramatic') methods inviting readers to infer qualities from characters' actions, speech, or appearance."[3] In addition to strengthening our understanding of a character, characterization gives us insight into the meaning of a story.

When we understand how and why story characters do what they do, we connect to the character and the story. Take Cinderella. In popularly known versions of the tale, Cinderella wants to go to a ball or festival. We learn this directly from the narrator and because the plot of the tale turns on her efforts to get to the event.

The other way we learn this is through characterization. In her speech and thoughts, Cinderella repeatedly expresses her desire to go to the ball. She demonstrates this wish in her actions when she tries to fulfill "impossible" tasks set for her by her wicked stepmother. Additional strokes of characterization come through descriptive language, such as Cinderella's triumphant entrance into the ball. Description, commentary, and inferences about what she does, says, or looks like are consistent throughout the story. In combination, they characterize her sincere desire to attend the ball.

But this characterization communicates more than that. It also tells us about Cinderella's personality. It shows us that she is determined. Like a salmon driven to swim upstream to spawn, her heart and body are focused on only one goal despite the forces that conspire against her. Similarly, we learn about her kindly nature. Although she can't go to the ball, she assists her step sisters with their preening and preparations. Bit by bit, these pieces paint a picture of a kind and determined young woman with a dream, a dream she is willing to fight for.

We can twist a character's presentation, as we did by empowering the Miller's Daughter. But it is also possible to twist stories around a character's familiar traits.

For instance, what happens when our expectations about a character are not met? Instead of big and bad, what if our wolf is nice and nurturing? What if he is a deaf wolf or a wolf pup? New images and messages arise in stories when expectations are shaken up. Alternatively, the Big, Bad Wolf can remain big and bad. But he can also be recast as a nasty, entitled prince who devours working peoples' land and homes to build a new palace. We can carry this idea into another story and instead of a wolf, a nasty prince could lead a red-caped young woman astray, suggesting other connotations. We don't usually think of wolves as princes, so the image of a dark, powerful prince in this wolf role is ironic indeed.[4] In the classical folktale canon, it is generally believed that the Wolf is evil because of his vicious attacks on pigs, innocent children, and bedridden grandmothers. He is the villain. Similarly, we expect tricksters to be self-serving and heroes to be persistent. We have these expectations, partly because we know the characters and their stories. But this also occurs because they are stock story characters or archetypal figures.

An archetype can be defined as a "persuasive idea, image, or symbol that forms part of the collective unconscious"[5] or as recurring patterns that reflect human nature in life and literature.[6] Carl Jung was instrumental in placing this idea into psychology and literature. He identified characters who recur time and again, like The Trickster and The Mother.[7] Joseph Campbell carried this work into the realm of mythology[8] and others applied it to the study of the fairy tale.[9] Recognizable story patterns, like Cinderella's rags to riches theme, and characters with universal traits, like villains such as a big, bad wolf, are two examples of literary archetypes.

When we twist tales, we shatter archetypal expectations and provide fresh and surprising interpretations. We can also deepen our understanding of them as well.

Literary characters are often described in terms of their complexity. Ever since E. M. Forster described characters in his 1927 book *Aspects of a Novel*,[10] characters have been described as *round* or *flat*. Characters that are round are multilayered. They have a variety of traits that can be contradictory. Flat characters are two-dimensional and without depth, usually possessing one or two predictable traits. Round characters are dynamic. They are the ones who change in some way over the course of a story. Flat characters are static. They do not change.[11]

If we play with characterization in our reimagined tales, we can flatten out round characters or round out flat ones. Static characters can be beefed up, reinvigorated and they can become dynamic. Such changes teach us something about the characters themselves and expose a new side to the story. When we changed the character of Little Red Riding Hood to a boy—as you will see—that character deepened while the wolf's character became rounder too, illuminating new story territory.

Twisted stories tingle when familiar characters deviate from our expectations. Such deviations offer a grab bag of opportunities for surprise, comedy, social commentary, intellectual stimulation or poignancy. This is one prime reason people are attracted to fractured retellings of old, favorite tales.

### A Brief Word About Character Change as a Consequence of Storytwisting

The literary element of character can serve as the point of fracture for a story, but even when it is not the twisting target, character is often affected by twists to other parts of the tale. For example, when we twisted "The Billy Goats Gruff" and told the tale from the troll's perspective, (see Chapter Four: "The Troll's House") we learned about the troll. The tale debunked his legendary characterization as a mean and nasty bridge dweller by revealing him as a harmless homebody with pride in his homemaking skills. It also changed the characterization of the Billy Goats, traditionally cast as innocents threatened by an evil monster under the bridge. In our tale, the goats are monsters who embody their "Gruff" moniker. Twisting the dial to one fracture point

---

### *Teaching Twist*

*Character role reversals are a fun way to play with stories. Suppose your students reverse "The Billy Goats Gruff and the Troll" and write "The Three Trolls Gruff—or Tough—and the Billy Goat."*

*1. Review the traditional folktale.*

*2. Provide the setup. The first of three trolls tries to cross over a grassy field to get back home to its lair under the bridge. But the troll encounters a goat nibbling the grass in that field.*

*3. Review the famous refrain, "Trip, trap, trip, trap over my bridge, who's that walking on my bridge?" In this role reversal tale, there is no bridge over the grassy field, so the refrain needs to be altered. Provide students with a refrain of your devising, develop one with the entire class, or encourage them to draft their own.*

*4. Consider this: In the traditional tale, the goats plead with the troll to wait for a bigger, fatter brother. The new story may need a different plea.*

*Including the setup, the plea, and the refrain in a creative outline before writing serves triple duty. It channels the wilds of the imagination, manages the scope of the project, and preserves reverberant echoes, or intertextuality, with the source tale.*

---

sometimes requires other story elements to twist so that plot and meaning makes sense in the remix.

## A Gender-Swapped Tale: "Little Red Riding Dude" Rap

### Do the Twist

In every retelling that we have ever seen or heard, the main character in "Little Red Riding Hood" is a girl. Even the various stories that are typically considered to be the folkloric roots of this classic tale have female protagonists.[12] The steady feminine impulse across time and cultures coupled with our rebellious nature interacted. We had to write a piece featuring a male protagonist.

We twisted the story dial and selected "character" as the point of fracture for our reimagined "Little Red Riding Hood." Our new story would feature a boy in the title role. It was an exciting prospect. But first we had to solve a practical conundrum, a boy in a riding hood? To make sure that the key phrase, *riding hood*, would make sense in a gender transformed tale, our writing process began with research.

The Little Red Riding Hood that everyone knows and loves wears a hooded cape called a riding hood. Traditionally, riding hoods were worn by women and girls as jackets and for riding, presumably on horses or in carriages.[13]. At first we played with the idea of a male protagonist wearing a red, hooded sweatshirt and referring to him as "Little Red Riding Hoodie." We rejected that idea because hoodies are simply hoodies, not *riding* hoodies. Furthermore, a two-syllable word like *hoodie* is more challenging to rhyme than *hood*. Since our piece was to be a rap, the rhyming potential of words, particularly those that repeat throughout the piece, is of prime consideration. Even so, we kept the red hoodie in the story, but used it differently.

At this juncture, we suspended our riding hood research and decision-making pursuit and focused instead on the word hood. What might a twisted "Riding Hood" title look like if we tweaked the word hood? In answer, we listed other hood words and phrases, such as neighborhood, hoodlum, boyhood, hoodwinked. Nothing hit.

As you may imagine, the creative process is a bit like playing pool. Once a ball gets rolling, it hits a wall and pings in another direction. Because we expect this in the writing process, we don't get frustrated, but continue pinging until the right idea lands.

Focusing again on the word, hood, we explored a variant title. We hovered for a moment over "The Little Red that Could." With a nod to a favorite children's book, we could twist themes from two stories into one blended tale. But "The Little Engine That Could" is not a folktale, so we left that idea and pushed on, like that optimistic, hardworking little engine.

Since the word, *could*, didn't work, we explored other rhyming words. We conducted an alphabetical walk through word lists in search of a decent match. Scanning the possibilities, we selected "D" for dude. That was when we heard a *thwap* as our metaphorical pool ball landed in the pocket.

The name "Little Red Riding Dude" worked on two levels. It incorporated a play on words, always a plus in twisted stories, and the near rhyme of dude, and hood, appealed to us. Our next step was to tackle the first conundrum, teasing out why our lad was a riding dude.

### Twisting Tip

*Conduct research with questions, not anticipated conclusions.* Open-mindedness is an invitation to possibility, but it does not mean that "everything goes." An open mind engages consideration of angles that might otherwise not be considered. Just as the process of brainstorming opens literary doorways, open-minded research also reveals exciting avenues to explore. It was through research that we stumbled on the idea to include skateboarding slang in our "Little Red Riding Dude" story.

This problem was a bit gnarly. We could have cut the word, riding, altogether, but that would have required some kind of explanation. The solution came unexpectedly from across our street.

At the time we were writing this piece, we had some very active teenage neighbors. In wintertime, they sledded down their steep hillside lawn right onto the street. In warm weather, they skateboarded down the road. One summer day as they skateboarded by, we wondered if they ever skateboarded down the sloping lawn. That tiny question tumbled into others. Could they skateboard through our yard? Across a farm field? Into a forest? Once we thought about the forest, we connected the idea to our developing story. Little Red Riding Dude would ride his board to Granny's. Riding wouldn't relate to his clothing, but to his *activity*. Boom.

---

### Teaching Twist

*Students can learn about characterization by responding to a set of prompts about a favorite fairy tale character. This process will involve recall about the story and some imagination.*

*1. According to the story, what does the character want?*

*2. What part of the story or plot tells you this?*

*3. Give three examples from the story or your imagination of statements or thoughts that support the character's motivation or wish.*

*4. Name two character actions that support this motivation.*

*5. What do other characters say or do to confirm this motivation?*

*6. What three descriptive words or phrases could describe this character when a goal is achieved or failed.*

---

Dude is a word associated with surfing. We learned that skateboarding language and culture are also rooted in surfing. It was perfect! Skateboard riding conveniently solved the riding conundrum. But the overlay of a skateboarding component onto "Little Red Riding Hood" had to make narrative sense. We took a deeper look.

All we had was a skateboarder in the forest on the way to Granny's. It was an interesting premise, but it presented an important question to disentangle. If we were to remain faithful to the traditional story and accentuate intertextuality, Red had to leave the path. But his departure had to make sense. Deeper research into the world of skateboarders identified a culturally and narratively sound answer. In skateboard culture, there is a tendency among boarders to innovate daring tricks, attempt skills in new locations, and challenge rivals to show off their tricks in contests. Could that impulse draw him off the path?

As excited as we were about skating into this new territory, we put on the brakes and looked at the storytwisting dial. Our point of fracture was character. We changed the story protagonist from a girl to a boy. That was our twisting intent. Was this skateboarding element serving that primary purpose? Would it overtwist the story?

Careful and honest consideration is imperative at this stage. We cannot tell you how often we dump exciting content because it does not support the fracture point. In this situation we believed that skateboarding culture wasn't thrust onto the story, but it was in service of it. By suffusing the tale with touches of skateboarder culture, we were able to kill three problems with one skateboard. First, riding a skateboard and calling a boarder a dude is consistent. Second, boarders challenge each other to competitive contests to show off new tricks. It made sense to exploit that cultural truth in our twisted tale because it added legitimacy to our presentation of that culture. Finally, skateboarding culture helped us puzzle out yet another narrative trouble spot. Instead of collecting a bouquet of flowers to divert Little Red from his errand, our Little Red is distracted by the competitive nature within himself and/or as a member of skateboard culture.

For a brief time, we considered transplanting the action out of a forest entirely to place it in an urban or suburban "forest." But the tale already—and ironically—diverged from the its usual path and strayed into unexpected places. We didn't want to divorce the new piece further from its roots. And even if we had been able to twirl the context of our twisted piece into a non-forest setting and still make it resonate, there was another key sticking point for us. We wanted Little Red's antagonist to be portrayed as a real wolf character, not as a human villain or symbol.

As you can see, the story was as much a thought experiment as it was a new take on a familiar tale.

**More Changes and More Research**

Somewhere about this time in the writing, we realized that we were twisting two story elements at once: character and setting. It was as if we had two pointers on one storytwisting dial, not unlike the minute and second hands on a clock. The primary fracture point, character, was our main focus, but there was a secondary focus on setting. In this case, re-setting the tale in a contemporary time period. This made the process more complicated, and wickedly fun.

Since our twisted tale now had a new setting—a modern world with a forest backdrop—we had to make sure that our descriptions of contemporary skateboard culture were correct. For that we needed authentic details. (See Chapter Three, "Fracture Point: Setting") We fell into a research wormhole, and learned language, slang, and tidbits about culture and celebrities. Our representation of skateboarding had to be on point. Otherwise, skateboarding audience members would notice mistakes and at best, stop listening. At worst, they might be offended by our innocent misrepresentations.

Like other sports and subcultures, skateboarding culture is steeped in jargon. Use of that language would delight any boarders in our audience, but the bulk of our audiences won't know these words or ideas. We had to strike a delicate balance, using a limited number of interpretable words and phrases to keep non-skateboarders connected to the story, but enough to add legitimacy for skateboarders.

### Twisting Tip

*Determine whether your linguistic turns of phrase fit new cultural contexts.* If your story explores a cultural context like skateboarding culture, consult with people who are active in those contexts. Information you find in online dictionaries, websites, and blogs is helpful, but it may not reflect actual spoken language. There also might be regional variations among words and phrases, as we discovered when we checked skateboarding terminology for our "Little Red Riding Dude."

In addition to changes in plot and setting that came as a result of the character fracture point, there were others. Once we changed the gender of the protagonist—Little Red—we explored the possibility of gender switching other characters. If this became another theme, our tale could parody the issue of gender in the fairy tale canon.[14] In most well-known versions of this story, the characters are Little Red, her mother, and Granny. We gender-bent the traditional parental roles. Little Red's stay-at-home father is the caregiver, and his mother works outside the home.

Next we looked at the Wolf. This antagonist, the classic troublemaker, was now cast as a female. The gender swap brought additional depth to the Wolf character, which deepened the story. In fact, our she-wolf supplies near-poignant content in "Little Red Riding Dude Rap."

## On Explanations and Making Sense While Telling Stories

Traditional stories don't have to flow with the logical precision of a legal argument. Every last detail in folk and fairy tales is not explained and justified. Leaps of faith are part of the story journey because they evoke the fantastic. Furthermore, in-depth explanations of story details can increase a folktale-length piece beyond the scope of its genre.

### Twisting Tip

*Check back to make sure that all of your changes harmonize* with your twisted story's moral, message, or theme. Alterations to your narrative arc, shifts in setting or character, updated symbols all need to interlink and be consistent with meaning for a story to work well. In this case, it really helps to sweat the small stuff. Even tiny changes, like what a character wears, supports meaning and the integrity of a new tale.

Mysterious details and legal arguments notwithstanding, stories must make sense. This is especially true in a reinvention of a well-known story. Twisted tales can't be total pastiches of seemingly random details or they lose their story-ness. Narrative integrity must be in place so that the tale hangs together. But the numinous quality of *story*, that ineffable fluffy borderland where imagination and truth meet, inspires suspension of disbelief. That is why certain plot leaps or well-placed wrinkles in a twisted narrative work. Listeners accept the simple maxim that things just happen that way in story worlds. Time moves how it moves. We accept these conventions because we are familiar with how it goes in such worlds. Scholars call this idea *chronotope,* the time and space where story happens[15]. Exposure to literature teaches us how things go in story worlds. When familiar chronotopes, like fairy tale kingdoms, show up in other stories, we understand and accept their conventions and willingly suspend our disbelief.

Familiarity with the numinousness of story grants some inexplicable details a free pass. In the famous "Little Red Riding Hood" story, nobody stops mid-story to wonder why a granny lives all alone in a house in the woods. As strange as it might seem in real life, we fully accept it in the story. That a mom sends a little girl into the woods all by herself is another strange idea from reality that works in folklore and fairy tales. This same free pass privilege extends to adaptations as well. We don't have to explain every last detail in fractured fantasies.

Though tempting, we can't leave everything to the numinous. We have to explain some of what is unexpected. It is necessary to clarify outlandish ideas, especially when there is other content that tinkers with the chronotope. This is where instinct rules the day. If it bothers you, it is likely to bother others.

Like other twisted stories, "Little Red Riding Dude" diverges from the popular tale in many ways. One way is that he was a skateboard riding dude. We firmly believed that leaving the riding question unanswered would prickle the mind like a chocolate craving. It surely bothered us.

*Teaching Twist*

*When given a chance to rewrite a classic story with new characters, students often gravitate to popular culture, such as favorite movies, celebrities, and television shows. Set careful parameters for character-changing exercises if you prefer that they create characters from classroom materials.*

Discerning between details that require explanation and those that can slip by unnoticed is especially important in stories that are performed for live audiences. Listeners have but one chance to hear the tale and grasp its meaning. If they get lost in thought, trying to figure out the whats and whys, they lose the story thread and, ultimately, the meaning of the tale.

Even when you think a tale is ready to tell, test it out. Spoken and written stories benefit from test performances of early drafts, and/or consultation with others, to find and repair bumps in the story road. We can only smooth out bumps when we know they are there.

## *Little Red Riding Dude Rap*

By Jeri Burns and Barry Marshall,
Copyright 2004, 2018 The Storycrafters

Once upon a time at the edge of the wood,
A boy lived with his family and life was good.

His Dad worked at home, His mom worked outside it—
The boy had a skateboard and he liked to ride it.

He practiced tricks every day until dark—
On the streets and sidewalks, and at the skate park.

He wore a red hoodie so he streaked like a flame—
And that's how he got his famous nickname—
A great skate boarder—always apple-hued—
Had to be called Little Red Riding Dude.

One day his Daddy said, "You're Granny is sick
She needs some food and she needs it quick!"
Dad packed a picnic basket with gluten-free foccacia,
Kombucha, crispy kale, and buckwheat kasha.

"Take this to your Granny, it will do her some good—
But you'll have to be careful as you cruise through the wood!
Wear your pads and helmet! Never talk to strangers!
Avoid fallen trees, Lyme disease and other dangers."

Little Red said, "It's all good!"
Hugged his dad and skateboarded into the wood.
The basket was his backpack; the board his steed—
And he pushed through the forest at a comfy speed.

But the weather that day was hot as high summer—
The basket made him sweaty, the helmet was a bummer.
He shed that stuff, chillaxed 'neath a tree—
Splashed his pits with bottled water and sipped a green tea.

Then the snap of a twig disturbed his solitude
He said, "Don't mess with Little Red Riding Dude!"

Now you know who was lurking, looking to engulf
Little Red Riding Dude—it was the big, bad wolf!
Red had the willies while Wolfie peek-a-booed
"I said, don't mess with Little Red Riding Dude!"

Now that wolf was a Mama hunting wolf pup food
"I'll need a main course to go with this scrawny dude."
She sniffed at the basket to see what she could glean—
"My kids eat meat, not hipster cuisine!"
Then the wolf spied a note, a "Dear Granny letter"
"Aged like wine and cheddar, Granny's taste much better."
So that clever she-wolf hatched a plot
To take down a pumped up sports hotshot.
The wolf jumped out

Red said, "That's rude"
"Don't mess with Little Red Ridin' Dude!"
The wolf said, "Yo, think you're so great?
I can show you real tricks—let's play skate!"

That Wolf was sketchy, the words his Daddy said—
"Don't talk to strangers," ran in his head.
But Red loved a challenge, like wolves love hunts—
"I can talk to a stranger, just this once!"

Then he said with a bit of an attitude
"Don't mess with Little Red Riding Dude!"
Red ditched his helmet and all his pads—
"Can't hurt, just once and I'll look rad!"

Wolfie grabbed Red's board and ollied over rocks—
Red did the same and rolled away stocked.
The game went back and forth, Red landed every trick
Then the Wolf said, "You'll never do this, it's sick."

She bombed down a hill, her tricks were tweaked,
Little Red was worried—he was really freaked—
"I gotta take my time, there are roots on that hill."
"No problem," said the Wolf, "I'll hang and chill."

Red studied and saw what to do
He spat on his hands and tied his shoe
"I see my line, going for it, I am!"
But his board hit a root and he went SLAM!
He had a case of road rash, he was truly bruised—
Who messed up? Little Red Riding Dude!

He looked for the wolf, but she was long gone
"I'd better get to Granny's—time to move on."

In the meantime, the Wolf ran to Granny's place
Scooped her up and the Wolf stuffed her face—
Put on a cap and gown, her Granny token
And looked at the mirror, "Oooh, baby you're smokin'!"
She jumped into bed and waited for the knock—
"That boy is in for a terrible shock!"

Red dragged himself to Granny's, he was really bummin'
Knocked on the door and the Wolf said "come in!"

He went inside, the wolf was in the bed—
"Granny needs a shave or I really bumped my head!"
"Yo, Granny, why are your eyes bugging out?"
Wolf said, "I must have caught a touch of the gout."

"Granny, your ears are hanging like socks."
Wolf said, "I must have caught a touch of small pox."
"Granny, your breath smells like a rotten egg."
"I must have caught a touch of bubonic plague."
"Granny, your teeth are sharp and well carved."
"You hit the nail on the head, Little Red, I'm starved!"
The wolf leaped out of bed, teeth bared—it was crude
"I'm gonna mess you up Red Ridin' Dude!"

"You are nothing but a poser, where's Granny, gimme a hint?"
"She was quite delicious, you're the after-dinner mint."
She chased him round the room, while Red gave a shout—
Then he jumped on his board and popped a nose grind on her snout!

Red's Mama was working with loggers in the wood
She heard that shout, "Someone's up to no good!"
Every Mama knows the sound of her child's cry
So she came to the rescue, her axe held high!

The wolf saw angry Mama with a swinging axe—
"It's time for me to make some tracks!
You work with all those loggers, yo what's up with that?
Don't you know that you are trashing our habitat?"

Wolf coughed up Granny, ran to the fridge
And scarfed some ham and pot roast to feed the kids.
She heard them call as she ran with the food
"Don't mess with Little Red Riding Dude!"

Granny was a slippery, slimy, slobbery mess
She took a hot shower, put on a clean dress.
She said, "What jivin' medicine, I feel so alive, I
Think I'll start selling homeopathic wolf saliva."

Then they all ate the gluten-free focaccia,
Kombucha, crispy kale, and buckwheat kasha.
Then Red and his Mama said goodbye and headed out—
Mama read Little Red the riot act, no doubt.

From that day forth, Red's ego was deflated
He stopped showing off whenever he skated.

Nowadays, Little Red does YouTube ads
Telling kids to listen to their Moms and their Dads—

"When you cruise through the world be sharp and shrewd
So you don't mess up like Little Red Ridin' Dude!"
Don't mess up like Little Red Ridin' Dude,
Yeah, don't mess up like Little Red Ridin' Dude."

## TWISTING TIPS: CHARACTER

*Make gender changes with purposeful intention.* It may be tempting to "have at" a story and change the genders willy-nilly. Be mindful. Are your choices guided by purpose? Do you make social commentary or values statements with each change? Do you swap gender to be clever without other purpose? Is it random? Ask these questions at each creative crossroads. The integrity of your twisted story and its resonance for audiences depends on this. Although it is fun to change a character to be clever once in a while, meaning must be the ultimate referee.

*Be aware of gender assumptions that bubble up* when you flip characters based on their gender. It is easy to stumble into stereotypical characterizations when working with gender. Do your changes reflect any of your own gender biases?[16] Is this acceptable to you or your potential audiences? Be aware of the assumptions that underlie every change. Choose your words and ideas consciously. For example, Little Red Riding Dude's competitive nature could be construed as a male stereotype. But because his behavior is consistent with expectations in skateboarding culture (according to members of boarding culture with whom we consulted) it is a cultural characteristic, not a gender stereotype.

*Make sure your changed character acts in ways that are consistent* to their natures. If you change from human to animal characters, for example, determine whether the behaviors enacted in the story match the nature of the animal who now must engage in them. If not, you may need to explain why your (herbivorous) sheep, for example, eats meat. The reverse is true as well. If you decide to twist "The Three Little Pigs" into a human-based variant, unless it is a vampire story or a dark, cannibalistic tale of serial murder, consider an alternative to the nasty, literal consumption of one human by another. You can translate the idea of "devouring" to make it representative of human nature by substituting metaphors, such as buying up local businesses to make a monopoly.

*Explore your characters, their backgrounds, and their motivations.* This information provides juicy tidbits that enliven any story and is vital in twisted versions of familiar stories and story genres. First, these tidbits provide the raw materials for original characterization. Second, a review of your insights will help you note patterns that can be used to state (or imply) subtle or biting social commentary.

### Twist for Thought: Lost in Translation—Collector Bias

The folk and fairy tales that everyone knows carry imagery and meaning that sears into the hearts and minds of people in many different cultures. People adore some of images and messages, tolerate others, and some are rejected outright. Some tales fall out of favor, but time's sifting process has kept many beloved stories in literary and oral vogue.

These and other tales are cultural mirrors for the people who told them.[17] Even the seemingly innocent stories that have formed the fabric of the nursery and classroom story hours have roots in social and historical contexts that reflect the past. To understand the stories, we must understand the socio-historical contexts that gave rise to them. Scholars such as Jack Zipes have studied this in great depth.[18]

Societal values and biases are reflected in the stories. Sexism, ableism, and classism, for example, strong and robust cultural forces in times gone by—and which unfortunately persist today—are showcased in story themes and characters. Even when subtle, these forces are recognizable. In contrast, there are other biases that are not so apparent.

In addition to affecting the behavior of characters and the messages in stories, socio-historical context affects the collection and distribution of the stories themselves. As nationalism rose during the Nineteenth Century, nations championed their own folklore to claim cultural identity. The brothers Jacob and Wilhelm Grimm were trailblazers in gathering and disseminating the folklore of their own nation—many others followed in their wake.

This impulse extended outward into the world. Europeans collected stories from Non-Western populations. In the Nineteenth and early Twentieth centuries, when folklore was first actively collected and written down, the task was primarily accomplished by white Westerners, predominantly men. Western collectors viewed the storytellers who shared their culture's tales, the stories, translations and edited texts, through the lens of white-male hegemony. Furthermore, literary and editorial choices were influenced by these values and viewpoints. A great deal of scholarly effort is devoted to unraveling the cultural bias of collectors and publishers and evaluating story collections with that in mind.[19]

Colonizers and other Western collectors stated a desire to preserve the folklore of dying cultures. Ironically, the cultures of interest were dying in part because of the colonizing regimes. Usually designed for a Western audience, these collections were not accurate representations of folklore because key cultural and linguistic details were lost in translation.[20] In short, many folk and fairy tale collections suffer from collector bias.

Andrew Lang, a famous Scottish folk and fairy tale editor[21] from the late Nineteenth Century and early Twentieth Century, presents translations of traditional tales from many cultures.[22] In the preface to the *Violet Fairy Book* book, he states: "They are narrated by naked savage women to naked savage children."[23] Although "savage" was a commonly used word in Lang's day to describe indigenous peoples, it is offensive to modern ears. Not only does it reflect a broadly held cultural attitude of his time, but it also probably influenced what stories were chosen for the collection and how they were presented.

Similarly, in her 1914 collection of South African folktales, Sanni

Metelerkamp emblazons this same attitude on the first page of her book when she refers to the stories as "tales of a childlike race" and to the people who tell them as "primitive."[24] The negative connotations of her words fling patronizing disrespect onto those who told the stories.

K. Langloh Parker was a white woman who lived on a sheep station in Australia. Her neighbors wondered why she would publish a collection of stories from Aboriginal Australians, asking, "But do the blacks have legends?"[25] The attitude among her fellow colonists suggests an attitude of cultural superiority.

Even if readers don't review the prefaces of folkloric collections and are not consciously aware of the biases of the collectors, they are still affected by them. Collector bias about the "primitive" people who tell the tales likely influenced the selection of stories for the collection. A condescending colonialist attitude can permeate the work done by transcribers and collectors. The stories may not be representative of the kinds of tales told in the time and place in which they were collected. They also may have been chosen for the collection because they fit—and reinforced—preconceived notions about the people who tell them. Words and meaning in the tales themselves may not reflect the culture but the opinions of the writer. The colonialist, racial, and ethnocentric bias of the authors makes the authenticity and representativeness of the stories selected for some collections suspect.

Lang, Parker, and Metelerkamp wanted to preserve and spread the stories of little-known cultures of the world. But each author was a product of a time and place in which Westerners believed they were more civilized than other peoples. This attitude of superiority implied that the work and thought of Westerners was of primary importance and the world of non-Western peoples was of diminished value.

In the preface to her translation of the newly discovered German fairy tale collection of Franz Xavier von Schönewirth, Maria Tatar states that Schönewirth's tales are raw, that they reflect the words of informants rather than the literary style of the collector. She contrasts his collection to the stories of the Brothers Grimm and Charles Perrault, the most famous sources of collected folk and fairy tales. Their tales were not raw, but adapted with literary flare. Where the Schönewirth collection has stories of struggling lads and lasses,[26] male Cinderella types, and women saviors, the others feature dependent women and strong and capable men.[27] The Schönewirth collection suggests that a broader range of tales were in existence but not always collected and/or published.

And so we come to an important question. If story collections are suspect, and not only older ones, why share the tales at all?

There is no easy answer. Some of the stories are iconic in the minds and hearts of generations of people across cultures, and sharing them connects us to our past. Tales in older, not so well-known collections, contain versions of stories that may be cultural legacies that exist nowhere else. All of these tales are also free of copyright restrictions. Although they aren't perfect historical documents, they provide social and cultural information about other times and places.

We can use these tales as research tools, springboards for finding other versions of the same and similar stories. And whenever we approach this material—for research or for telling—we should view it with an educated eye. Read the prefaces, evaluate source material, and be aware that the folktales might be marbled with bias.

### Teaching Twist

*Students enjoy writing stories with familiar characters. In classroom exercises, encourage them to transplant characters from history or literature and insert them into fairy tales. The story will change somewhat as will character actions when the personalities of literary or historical characters are taken into account. Making it all come together sensibly is their twisting challenge.*

If we choose to tell these stories, let's do our homework. Learn about social and historical conditions at the time when tales were told and discover the manner in which they were collected. This knowledge can influence the way we craft a retelling, adapted retelling, or fractured version of such a tale. Or it can be shared in an introduction to the story itself.

We believe that it is important for anyone engaged in the art of storytelling to ask themselves why they are working with any story. Scrutiny of the self, the story, and the way stories are collected or written is a process that raises hard questions with no easy answers. But such scrutiny also raises the ethical bar for the profession, which elevates this art form and our place within it.

## A Few Words About Representation

Story characters are models for how we see ourselves and for how others see us. That is why the portrayal of women characters in traditional stories has been a longstanding issue of concern to academics and storytellers.[28] In response, writers *re-present* them in ways that better fit our times. Turning a passive folktale wife into an active one or changing the gender of a heroic rescuer from male to female are transformative processes that paint different expectations about who women are and who they can become. In that spirit, this chapter looks at gender representation in stories. But representation in traditional stories doesn't stop there.

When our son was little, there were few illustrated fairy tales that represented people of color. So, when we started watching movies with him, we purposely chose the 1997 musical version of Cinderella. It features a multicultural cast. In this way, Zack's heart and mind were imprinted with positive diversity in the world of Cinderella, which we hoped would somehow contribute to his conception of the real world. Today, thankfully, there are many culturally diverse children's books featuring characters of color.

The issue of representation is important. It is broad. To cover it fully, given this chapter's scope, is impossible. Representation in stories deserves a book of its own. But there are a few items that should be mentioned here.

In any conversation about gender, it is important to discuss *heteronormativity*, which is, in part, the socio-cultural expectation that people conform to being either male or female.[29] Heteronormativity impacts our world in many ways. The use of the pronouns "he" and "she" is an example. Implicit in those words are assumptions about gender, which are unfair for people who don't identify with the gender binary. Instead, the pronoun "they" presents a beautiful alternative, one that is free of classic gender expectations. While stories can have nonbinary or "they" characters, not every story is about gender. It is liberating when characters are free to act without gender expectations.

A parallel issue involves people's abilities. Society is designed for people who are able-bodied, and literature reflects this ableist bias. Classic story characters ride on horses, not in wheelchairs. Perfect physical bodies are idolized. Intellectual and emotional struggles are obstacles to be overcome. Traits that don't fit cookie-cutter standards are often wished away in stories after characters complete their quests. In contrast, real people with disabilities are capable and contributing members of society, and they can and should be reflected and honored in stories.

It is heartening to know that there are traditional stories with positive representations of typically underrepresented characters, like caring step parents. Diversity exists, if you scour the literature. Thankfully, someone has started that process for us. Storyteller Csenge Zalka has a series on her blog in which she shares many traditional tales that are inclusive, diverse, and representative.[30] Her work is a wonderful resource.

We can also approach this problem in another way. As new stories are crafted—original creations, retellings, or twisted ones—we can be aware of these considerations. Heroes can have disabilities. They can be gender fluid. By keeping these issues in mind, we can battle our own biases. We can also open other eyes and hearts to those who do not identify with "he" and "she" or whose bodies are unique. With awareness and respect, more people can see themselves in stories and others can bear witness to the diverse palette of human potential. Then we can move toward fuller and fairer representation in stories, and most importantly, in life.

# NOTES

1. Lewis Carroll, *Alice's Adventures in Wonderland*, full text of *Alice's Adventures in Wonderland*, August 12, 2006, accessed July 10, 2016, https://archive.org/stream/alicesadventures19033gut/19033.txt.

2. Characters are often described as "persons," implying that they are often defined as human beings. Chris Baldick, *The Concise Oxford Dictionary of Literary Terms*, (Oxford University Press: Oxford, New York, 1990), 33; J.A. Cudden et al., *Dictionary of Literary Terms and Literary Theory*,.rev. by M.A.R. Habib, (Penguin Group: London, 2013), 116.

3. Chris Baldick, *The Concise Oxford Dictionary of Literary Terms*, p. 34.

4. In the beloved Broadway musical, *Into the Woods*, with words and music by Stephen Sondheim and book by James Lapine, several traditional fairy tales are intertwined with an original one. In this theatrical narrative, Prince Charming is the wolf who leads girls and women astray in the forest.

5. David Adams Leeming, ed. *Storytelling Encyclopedia: Historical, Cultural, and Multiethnic Approaches to Oral Traditions Around the World*. (Pheonix: Oryx Press, 1997), 58.

6. "Archetype," Literary Devices, accessed February 6, 2016. http://literarydevices.net/archetype/.

7. R. Seth C. Knox, "Archetype," in *The Greenwood Encyclopedia of Folktales and Fairy Tales*, ed. Donald Haase, (Westport: Greenwood Press, 2008), 64-66. Some examples of archetypes that relate to storytelling include the Mother and the Trickster.

8. See generally, Joseph Campbell, *The Hero with a Thousand Faces, Third Edition*. (Novato: New World Library, 2008). Campbell is famously recognized for his comparative work on the hero's journey, an archetypal adventure story structure that is found in mythology around the world.

9. See, generally, Marie-Louise von Franz, *Archetypal Patterns in Fairy Tales*, Toronto: Inner City Books, 1997 and Rudolf Meyer, *The Wisdom of Fairy Tales*,( Edinburgh: Floris Books, 1997), first published in German under the title *Die Weisheit der deutschen Volksmärchen*. Stuttgart: Verlag Urachhaus, 1935.

   Each of these are examples of books that analyze fairy tales for archetypal imagery and patterns. Von Franz was renowned for her psychological interpretation of fairy tales. Meyer, who was also influenced by the work of Rudolf Steiner, argues that such stories are important for the spiritual development of children.

10. E.M. Forster, *Aspects of the Novel*, (New York: Harcourt, Brace & Company, 1927), 77-78.

11. Chris Baldick, *The Concise Oxford*, 34 and J.A. Cuddon et al, *Dictionary of Literary Terms*, 280.

Sometimes these distinctions are broken down further, differentiating flat from static and round from dynamic characters. See for example, Lyman Baker, "Flat vs Round Characterization," 2001, last updated September 6, 2001, http://www.k-state.edu/english/baker/english320/cc-flat_vs_round_characterization.htm, and Lyman Baker, "Static vs. Dynamic Characterization," last updated March 7, 2001, http://www.k -state.edu/english/baker/english320/cc-static_vs_dynamic_characterization.htm.

12. Thanks to the work of the French folklorist Robert Delarue, the world is fairly confident that the story we know as "Little Red Riding Hood" emerged out of folklore. Her famous "riding hood" is an irrelevant (though iconic) detail invented by Charles Perrault in his 1697 collection of fairy tales that also included "Cinderella" and "Sleeping Beauty." The tale that Delarue studied is dubbed "The Grandmother's Tale," a bawdy version from the oral tradition. In that narrative, the girl enters her grandmother's house to discover the wolf in bed. After performing a strip tease, she climbs into the bed with him. This is not the children's tale we know. Unlike the version of the story popularized in the pre and post-industrial years by Perrault and later by the Brothers Grimm, this young girl escapes her plight due to her own wits. See, generally, Alan Dundes, *Little Red Riding Hood: A Casebook*. (Madison: University of Wisconsin Press, 1989), Jack Zipes, ed. *The Trials and Tribulations of Little Red Riding Hood*, 2nd Edition, (New York: Routledge, 1993), and Catherine Orenstein, *Little Red Riding Hood Uncloaked: Sex, Morality, and the Evolution of a Fairy Tale*, (New York: Basic Books 2002) for more insight.

Not only was the story part of the oral tradition in Europe before Perrault's literary version, but variants also existed in China, Korea, and Japan prior to 1697, (Alan Dundes, *A Casebook*, 13 and 21-63.)

13. "Riding Hood." Merriam Webster, accessed 12/1/15, http://www.merriam-webster.com/dictionary/riding%20hood.

14. A thumbnail history of feminist fairy tale literature could fill a chapter; a full history could fill an old-school encyclopedia set. Here are some highlights and suggestions for further reading. The poet Anne Sexton (1971) and the writer Angela Carter (1978) authored literary works that turned fairy tales on their heads. Their reinterpretations of the old stories and the roles women played in them sizzle with critical insight and bold social commentary. Their works, along with numerous others, such as the novels of Robert Coover (1996) and Gregory Maguire (1995), constitute an ever-growing body of fairy-tale reimaginings. These and other works have been studied deeply by scholars such as Sandra Gilbert and Susan Gubar (Gilbert and Gubar 1979), Cristina Bacchilega (1997), and Catherine Orenstein (2002). More recent edited compilations include *Fairy Tales and Feminisim* (Haase 2004), which addresses a number of issues related to the topic, and *Transgressive Fairy Tales* (Turner and Greenhill 2012), a collection that looks unflinchingly at gender and sexuality (it also has a glorious appendix with an index of trans and drag folktales), Susan Redington Bobby's (Bobby 2009) excellent collection of essays covers a variety of issues, including gender.

In the storytelling world, awareness of the biased representation of women in folkloric collections has resulted in conscious compilations with a feminist cast, including (and possibly started by) Ethel Johnston Phelps (1978 and 1982) and

Angela Carter (1990 and 1993). More recent compilations include collections by Kathleen Ragan (2000) and Jane Yolen (2000). Professional storytellers are also in on the act, curating shows that challenge the folktale status quo. For example, Milbre Burch's "Changing Skins: Folktales about Gender, Identity and Humanity" is a shining example of a storyteller's effort to awaken audiences to these important issues. Accessed 5/22.16.
http://www.kindcrone.com/

15. Maria Nikolajeva, *Children's Literature Comes of Age: Toward a New Aesthetic.* (New York and London: Garland Publishing, 1996).

16. Despite the politically-correct staff of life that burns in so many of us, we all have biases. We may not think we do, but as members of the human race, we are affected by them. The best way to combat bias is to honestly acknowledge the ones we have so that we can mitigate against them. See, for example, Clark, Pat, "I Don't Think I'm Biased," *Teaching Tolerance Magazine*, No. 37, Spring 2010, accessed 5/22/16. http://www.tolerance.org/magazine/number-37-spring-2010/feature/i-don-t-think-i-m-biased.

17. See, for example, Alan Dundes, author and Simon J. Bronner, ed."Folklore as a Mirror of Culture." *The Meaning of Folklore: The Analytics of Alan Dundes,* (Logan: Utah University Press, 2007), 55-60; Anne Goding,. *Storytelling: Reflecting on Oral Narratives and Cultures*, 2nd ed. (San Diego: Cognella Publishing, 2016).

So many scholars maintain that this is the case that one might argue that this information has reached the status of common knowledge.

18. Jack Zipes is a prolific scholar who has published volume after volume about the socio-historical study of fairy tales. See in particular Jack Zipes, *Fairy Tales and the Art of Subversion: The Classical Genre for Children and the Process of Civilization.* (New York: Wildman Press, 1983); Jack Zipes, *Fairy Tale as Myth/Myth as Fairy Tale: (*Lexington: University Press of Kentucky, 1994); Jack Zipes, *The Irresistible Fairy Tale: The Cultural and Social History of a Genre,* (Princeton University Press: Princeton and Oxford, 2012). Jack Zipes, ed. *The Trials and Tribulations of Little Red Riding Hood,* 2nd Edition. (New York: Routledge. 1993); Jack Zipes, *Why Fairy Tales Stick: The Evolution and Relevance of a Genre.* (New York: Routledge, 2006).

19. For example, Donald Haase argues for the decolonization of folk and fairy tale studies since so many were gathered under colonial conditions. In her celebrated cultural tome, *From the Beast to the Blonde,* Marina Warner interprets fairy tales told by and about women. Haase, Donald. "Decolonizing Fairy-Tale Studies," (*Marvels & Tales* 24, no.1, 2010): 17-38, accessed 5/16/16,. http://digitalcommons.wayne.edu/marvels/vol24/iss1/1 and Warner, Marina, *From the Beast to the Blonde,* (New York: Farrar, Strauss, and Giroux, 1994).

20. Haase, "Decolonizing Fairy-Tale Studies," 2010.

21. Andrew Lang is famous for his multicultural collection of stories from around the world, which Heidi Anne Heiner refers to as "Andrew Lang's Colored Fairy Books" (http://www.surlalunefairytales.com/bookstore/langbooks.html). *The Yellow Fairy Book, The Red Fairy Book, The Lilac Fairy Book* are examples of some additional titles.

22. Most of the tales were translated by women, including Mr. Lang's wife. For an in depth consideration of women storytellers, see Warner *Beast*, 1994, 3-197.

23. Andrew Lang, ed. "Preface," *The Violet Fairy Book*. New York: Dover Publications, Inc., 1966. Originally published in Andrew Lang, *The Violet Fairy Book*, (London: Longmans, Green and Co.,1901, vii.

24. Sanni Metelerkamp, Preface to *Outa Karel's Stories: South African Folk-lore Tales*. (London: Macmillan and Co., Limited St. Martin's Street, 1914), accessed 5/16/16, http://www.worldoftales.com/African_folktales/South_African_tales_preface.html.

25. K. Langloh Parker, Preface to *Australian Legendary Tales*. Notes: Folk-lore of the Noongahburrahs as told to the Piccaninnies. Features 31 Australian folktales, 1896. London: David Nutt; Melbourne: Melville, Mulle & Slade, 1896. Accessed 5/16/16. http://www.sacred-texts.com/aus/alt/alt02.htm.

26. We have not discovered a satisfying male equivalent for the phrase "damsel in distress." Would "man in a mess" or "gent in jeopardy" do?

27. Maria Tatar, Introduction to *The Turnip Princess and Other Newly Discovered Fairy Tales* by Franz Xavier von Schönewirth, (London: Penguin Classics, 2015), vi-xviii.

28. See for example, Donald Haase, *Fairy Tales and Feminism: New Approaches* (Detroit, MI: Wayne State University Press, 2004).

29. In addition to the socio-cultural expectation that people conform to biological gender assignments, many definitions of heteronormativity include societal expectations about gender roles and heterosexuality. For purposes of the chapter inset, "A Few Words About Representation," we narrowed the focus for two reasons: (1) discussions about gender role expectations arise throughout the chapter, and (2) society's heterosexual bias is also defined by a separate term, "heterosexism." Furthermore, the heterosexist bias of classic fairy tales is upended in a story in Chapter Eight. While we cannot fully address the huge topic of representation in this book, it cannot be overlooked either. It is our hope that issues raised throughout the book about gender, ability, race, and class stimulate important discussions about representation among storytellers and writers.

30. Csenge Virag Zalka, "Representation," *Multicolored Diary*, April 2016, accessed September 29, 2017, http://multicoloreddiary.blogspot.com/search/label/representation.

*Curiouser and curiouser.*

LEWIS CARROLL[1]

CHAPTER EIGHT

# Fracture Point & Plot to Mash-up

PEOPLE LEARN BEST ABOUT MASH-UP STORIES BY DOING. It is also how we write them. Intuitive sense makes a better teacher than formulaic rigidity. There is no "click and share" mash-up recipe. Mash-ups arise organically. All the pieces tumble into place. Eventually.

What exactly is a mash-up? A mash-up is a new work that is "created by combining two or more elements from different sources."[2] The mash-up idea is often associated with music. Song mash-ups include samples, which are words or snatches of melody from one piece that are overlaid onto a musical track from another. In similar fashion, literary mash-ups also sample pre-existing material.

Mash-ups are not cutesy or superficial amalgamations of random images and motifs. They are carefully crafted works that create something new. Done well, mash-ups are playful, perceptive, and purposeful.[3] They can also be powerful.

For our purposes, a story mash-up is created when elements from different stories, such as character, plot line, or setting, are layered one on top of each other. For example, the spines of two or more plots might intertwine to create a mash-up. Alternatively, the characters from one story might leap into another. Setting can also form a point of commonality as it does with Stephen

Sondheim and James Lapine's beloved musical, *Into the Woods*. The alchemical possibilities are boundless with mash-ups. Each gentle twist of the tale gives rise to a multiplicity of new meanings. Students in our workshops have crafted so many hilarious mash-ups of familiar stories that we remain dazzled by the depth and vastness of the mash-up's literary potential. A limitless well of stories awaits the next brave soul.

## A Little Bit About "The Frog Prince Mash"

The first mash-up in this chapter, "The Frog Prince Mash," blends two tale types from the fairy tale canon, "The Frog Prince"[4] and the lesser-known "Diamonds and Toads,"[5] both of which are summarized below. Blending fairy tale motifs from different stories is not new to storytelling—it reflects a long-standing tradition in the composition of literary fairy tales.

In our merger of relatively straight retellings, most patterns of action, setting details, and key characterizations remain the same. In addition to keeping the mash-up themes faithful to the meaning of the folktales, we also strive to preserve the fairy tale feel. Yet weaving fairy tales together is a process that demands change. In "The Frog Prince Mash," we depart from folkloric fidelity in two ways. First, not every element from the source stories is included in the blended one. Such is the way with any adaptation process. Numerous decisions and choices are made along the way, including changes or exclusions. Our second departure is the inference we make at the end of the new tale. Adaptations are satisfying when they bring familiar stories to a new place.

## A Little Bit About "Redi-Locks and Goldi-Hood"

The second story we offer in this chapter is "Redi-Locks and Goldi-Hood," a wacky mash-up of three famous nursery tales: "The Three Pigs," "Little Red Riding Hood," and "Goldilocks and the Three Bears." This tale is a parody. Replete with cameo appearances by famous characters from numerous familiar stories, "Redi-Locks" confronts, makes fun, and wreaks havoc on specific fairy tales and the genre itself.[6] It also aligns with postmodern sensibility.

We include both mash-up styles to illustrate two different writing approaches, but there is another more important reason. The pieces are starkly different in tone. Presenting both pieces shows that mash-ups can work whether they are serious and lyrical or spunky and comic.

**Twist the Dial: From Single Plot to Mash-up**

*Plot.* While it is possible to write a mash-up that is character-driven, theme-based, or object oriented, we find that focusing on plot has a two-pronged advantage. It channels creativity by keeping narrative integrity at the forefront of the writing process. It fosters a conversation among tales, or intertextuality. Plot also provides glorious grounding in the Wild West of mash-up creativity.

In its most simple terms, plot is a story's sequence of events: the set-up, the trouble, the fallout.[7] It includes setting, characters, actions, and events. Successful plots seize attention and unfurl coherently.

In educational contexts, plot is often broken down into five components:
- exposition
- rising action
- climax
- falling action
- resolution.[8]

*Exposition.* Sometimes called the Introduction, the Exposition is when the setting is described and characters first appear. Everyday normality in a story's world is presented so that outsiders understand how things are before trouble comes.

*Rising Action.* Often the longest part of the story, rising action refers to when the conflict, problem, or inciting incident is revealed. Tension increases. Things get complicated. Tension climbs higher and higher until it reaches the climax.

*Climax.* When tension is at its peak and we are in the most gripping part of the story, it is the climax. Conflict increases, trouble erupts, and everyone wonders what will happen next.

*Falling Action.* The moment we learn what happens, there is a release. Tensions dials down, struggles unwind. This part of the plot is called falling action.

*Resolution.* When things settle to a new normal, the problem is solved. The resolution is when we learn who leaves town, who lives or dies, who gets married or punished, and so forth. Resolution is the happily ever after, or not.

## Bones: A Metaphor for Plot

Storytellers often refer to the plot of a story as the bones. When bones are pieced together in a certain way, a skeleton emerges. In the scientific world, some skeletons are immediately recognizable, like those of fish or dogs. But, with a little imagination, a dog's bones could be rearranged so that they appear to be the skeleton of a groundhog.

The salience of this metaphor for oral storytellers is that it depicts what we do to retell existing stories. Bones are recognizable symbols that create recognizable patterns. In terms of a story, when a certain story's bones are arranged just so, the tale is recognized as "Beauty and the Beast" in much the same way that museum goers can identify a dinosaur skeleton on sight. There might be variations, but the basic structure remains intact and recognizable.

Storytellers construct the bones of every story anew. We lift them from an existing story and reposition them for our own unique, oral rendition. Whether the story is our own original writing, personal memoir, myth, folktale or historical piece, that story already exists in some form. The plot is already in place. Plot elements, such as rising action, are already set forth. The challenge for storytellers is to translate those pre-existing story elements into their own words and sequences.

Although changes are a natural part of this adaptation process, the spoken story remains recognizable as a retelling of a pre-existing one. The term "bones" refers to the recognizable components that a storyteller reanimates in a retelling of a story.

Renowned screenwriter and story design expert Robert McKee describes plot as "... an accurate term that names the internally consistent, interrelated pattern of events that move through time to shape and design a story."[9] If

*Teaching Twist*

*Blend two favorite tales.*

1. Select a pair of stories with at least one obvious bonding point. Character or setting are excellent bonding points, as are patterns of actions, such as chases, climbs or quests.

2. Select a primary bonding point.

3. Write out the bones of each source tale.

4. Overlay the story spines and highlight every other bonding point that you see.

5. Select one story spine to act as the baseline for the fractured tale—if your stories are not sequential—and write out the story bones of the blended new story.

6. Now comes the real fun—cut, paste, and puzzle out a story that makes sense.

the bones of a storytwisted tale are not internally consistent and interrelated, then the story won't make sense. Furthermore, a fractured tale won't echo the pre-existing tale if the plots of each aren't consistent.

Mash-ups work with multiple stories all at once. A myriad of symbols and patterns from existing stories are available to feed the new one. The author's challenge lies in multi-tasking: (1) understanding the bones and symbols of the old stories; (2) considering how they will be built in or excluded from a new story; (3) preserving chunks of the familiar story to make the mash-up recognizable and; (4) saying something new and relevant to today's audiences.

## A Blend of Two Faithfully-Told Tales: "The Frog Prince Mash"

### Do the Twist: Building Bonding Points

The approach to writing mash-ups differs slightly from general storytwisting. Instead of breaking or fracturing existing bonds, mash-ups form new ones. Like children are born from the unity of their parents, bonding points are the common elements in different stories. They can be characters, settings, actions, objects, symbols, gestures, and more.

### How We Did It

**Phase One: Identify source tales.** We started by identifying the tales for the foundation of the mash-up.

"The Frog Prince Mash," which sounds more like a recipe for a potion than an engaging story, blends a Scottish variant of "The Frog Prince" and an English version of the fairy tale type nicknamed "Diamonds and Toads." The Scottish tale tells about a young woman who keeps her promise to spend the night with a frog only to discover that he is an enchanted prince.[10] The English story is about a generous sister whose kindness to others is rewarded with the magical ability to produce jewels whenever she speaks. In contrast, her unkind sister is punished. Whenever she speaks, toads and snakes burst from her mouth.[12] Scottish and English folktale versions of these tale types appealed to us because they reflect Barry's heritage.

**Phase Two: Review source tales and related variants.** In addition to reviewing both source tales, we also reviewed the better-known story counterparts from the classical fairy tale canon, "The Frog Prince" and "Diamonds and

Toads."[13] This process served two purposes: to unveil commonalities among the stories and to find widely recognized images and ideas.

**Phase Three: Identify and refine bonding points.** Here are four examples of bonding points between the source tales.

*Young woman on a quest.* Both tales feature this motif, but in different ways. In the Scottish "Frog Prince," a young woman seeks healing water from a well after her siblings fail to achieve the task. In the English "Diamonds and Toads" the youngest daughter goes on the quest before her sisters get to go. We had a choice to make. Because it is consistent with the structure of better-known classic,[14] the successful sister tackles the task first in our mash-up.

*Magical helper.* Each source story has magical helpers. In one story, the helper is a frog. The other tale has a trio of helpers—three golden heads who live in the well. Instead of flipping a coin and choosing heads or frogs, we included both sets of helpers for three reasons. First, our story goal was to adhere to the widespread and well-known image that a prince is an enchanted frog. We needed him in our story to fulfill that purpose. Second, the three golden heads, or in the case of our tale, filthy—or dirty—old men, offers an opportunity for humor and/or darkness, depending on the audience. The third and most important reason to include the men is that they are the source of both sisters' rewards and punishments.[15]

*Amphibians.* In one tale, the frog was a bewitched, princely reward for promises kept. In the other, toads and snakes were the older sister's (literal) tongue-in-cheek punishment. We left the punishment intact except that we replaced the snakes with frogs. This bonding point, along with the well, was the inspiration for choosing these two fairy tale types.

*Rewards.* While thinking about bonding points, we continually thought about the overarching message of our tale. A young woman who finds her life partner wrapped up in amphibious garb is all well and good, but it is not the primary message of our tale. Our interpretation highlights the unexpected gifts that simple, caring gestures bring. By correlation, it is also about a self-involved, lazy sister's comeuppance. To match the message of the story, we needed a reward-punishment system to recognize the caring/uncaring gestures. That meant we needed our protagonist to win something other than the hand of an enchanted prince. We needed other rewards, like diamonds and rubies.

**Phase Four: Intertwine the plots.** This phase is as involved as a presidential election, so it is divided it into five separate steps (but there is no electoral college).

🐸 *Step One: Name the bones and line them up.* For each source tale, we identified every character, plot event, setting detail, object—the story's bones—and wrote them on separate pieces of paper. Next we lined up each piece of paper in sequential order, spreading them all over the living room floor, nearby furniture, and sleeping cat.

🐸 *Step Two: Compare and contrast stories.* We noted similarities and differences among the tales. Both featured a well, but the water in one well was healing water and in the other it was not labeled as such. The well is a powerful symbol in folklore: many traditions believed that guardian spirits resided in wells, others believed in the healing properties of wells.[16] Since there was precedent in one source folktale for a well to have healing waters and an enchanted frog, we included a well with healing waters and guardian spirits in the mash-up.

---

### Teaching Twist

*Review "The Little Red Hen" and "The Gingerbread Man." Identify the bones and characters from each story and line them up on the board or on newsprint. One possible bonding point is the farm; another is the kitchen. One pattern in both tales is the act of baking. What other shared patterns or characters do you or your students observe? (Animal companions who chase the cookie or refuse to help the Little Red Hen). Can you or your students identify a story theme in common? (A greedy desire to eat appears in both tales). Will your mash-up create a brand new message?*

*A human doesn't have to bake the Gingerbread Man—the Little Red Hen can do it instead. All of her lazy barnyard companions can chase him down. Will a fox be the one to devour him? Will the Little Red Hen eat him up all by herself? Is there a different ending altogether? Enjoy the discovery!*

---

🐸 *Step Three: Select the spine of the mash-up.* To streamline the story writing process and link the mash-up to a familiar source story, we foregrounded one plot. It became the spine of the mash-up. Since "The Frog Prince" storyline is more familiar to general audiences than "Diamonds and Toads," the Scottish Frog Prince tale was chosen.

    *Step Four: Arrange and rearrange the bones.* We copied the Scottish story's bones and arranged them sequentially below the other two sets. Now we had three, visual, parallel plots lined up one on top of the other, like lines on a musical staff. After adjusting the papers so that the bonding points lined up as much as possible, we started to play.

    The duplicate "Frog Prince" plot line was the canvas upon which we painted our mash-up. In an old-school version of word processing, the paper pieces all over our living room were moved around, crumpled up, changed, overlaid and/or pasted onto the mash-up's spine to create a fully blended plot.

    *Step Five: Review all sources for additional material.* After we settled on the basic blended plot, we reviewed the sources again to find additional elements that would improve the blended story and/or preserve the essence of the source tales. Ideas popped into our heads like frogs popped out of the unkind sister's mouth. A favorite was when Barry decided to turn the mash-up into a *pourquoi* story.[17] In the traditional tale, the frog disappears from the story when the prince is released from the enchantment. We tweaked this. Our tale implies that an enchanted frog is produced from the punished sister's mouth. Like a ribbon on a package, it ties the two frog "legs" of the story together. It also adds a slightly mind-bending, allegorical ending.

    *Phase Five: Mash it up.* Step by step and bone by bone, we built a new narrative, swapping characters and plot devices until the bones fit together in a new plotline that was internally consistent and meaningful. To referee hard-to-make decisions and fill narrative holes, we consulted other well-known fairy tale versions of each tale[18] and our imaginations to add meaningful details.

    Scottish folklore forms the backbone of our mash-up, so we accompany the tale with a traditional Scottish air called "Fingall's Lamentation." Since we add text to the song and its meaning morphs from lament to strange humor over the course of the story, we begin every telling of the tale with a Scottish harp solo to salute the tune and the instrumental tradition.

## Storytwist

### *Frog Prince Mash*

By Jeri Burns and Barry Marshall
Copyright The Storycrafters 2010, 2018

Once upon a time, a mother lived with her two daughters who were as different from each other as night and day. The mother was very sick. She had not spoken, moved out of bed, or done anything for herself for as long as they remembered. The younger daughter did everything for her mother, and took care of her from dawn until dusk. The older sister did nothing for her mother and cared only for herself.

One evening, the two girls were sitting at the kitchen table when they heard a sound that they had not heard for a long time. They heard their mother's voice, coming from the bedroom, singing:

> *Oh bonnie maids, won't you hear my plea*
> *Bring healing water and make me well*

They rushed into the bedroom and found their mother prone on the pillow, as she had been for a long time past. Her eyes were dim and her cheeks pale as the waning moon. But her mouth was open just enough to whisper, "My darling daughters I will not survive to see the heather blooming on the hill unless one of you go to the healing well and bring me the healing waters to drink."

The moment it was said, the younger daughter set out to find the well. She walked for many a day until she came to the place where the sun kissed the earth. There was the well. She stretched her arms to reach the water with her dipper, but it was too far down.

She gazed at the distant water, waiting for an idea to come. It wasn't an idea that came, but one, two, three dirty, old, men who climbed out of the depths of the well and sat on its stone wall. Their heads were slimy and festering, their mouths were foul and filthy, and their backs were covered with mold and ooze. They sang:

> *Oh bonnie maid, will you hear our plea*
> *Wash us now and make us clean*

Revulsion coursed through her, but compassion washed it instantly away. How horrid for them! Using the hem of her dress, she rubbed their heads until they gleamed, scrubbed their backs until they shone, and polished their teeth until they sparkled. Then the three men smiled at the girl and said, "In reward for your kindness, whenever you speak, diamonds and rubies will fall from your tongue." Then they took the dipper and splashed into the well.

She waited for them to come back with the dipper. And soon, a full dipper rose from the depths. And holding the dipper was a frog. He climbed out of the well, and said, "You can't have this dipper unless you promise to do everything I ask of you for one night."

She thought about it. After caring for her mother's every need for many years and cleaning the filthy men, there was little that the frog could require of her that she couldn't manage. The girl agreed, and the frog gave her the dipper.

She walked again for many a day until she reached her mother's house. When she poured the water into her mother's mouth, the color returned to her cheek and the light came back into her eyes. She sat up, and for the first time in many years, she hugged her children. Then she asked the younger daughter to tell her how she'd gotten the water.

But when the younger daughter opened her mouth, diamonds and rubies fell from her lips upon the floor. Everyone lost interest in the story, and cried "Just say anything!" Excitedly they gathered the fallen jewels and stored them in a closet. Then the three women went into the front room to eat supper. They sat at the table as a family for the first time in many years and were just about to eat when there was a knock at the door.

The older daughter went to answer the door. But when saw who was there, she shrieked. "I am NOT answering the door for a frog!"

Just then, the frog, outside the door, sang:

*Oh bonnie maid, will you hear my plea*
*Bring me in out of the cold*

The younger daughter knew who it was. She had promised to do his bidding for a night. And a promise is, after all, a promise. After she opened the door, the frog hopped inside. She sat at the table and was about to eat when the frog sang:

> *Oh bonnie maid, will you hear my plea*
> *Sit me down upon your knee*

A promise is a promise. The girl lifted the frog and put him on her knee. She was about to, once again, eat her dinner, when the frog sang:

> *Oh bonnie maid, will you hear my plea*
> *Feed me well from your dinner plate*

A promise is a promise. The younger daughter got another dinner plate for the frog. She served him food from the table, and put the plate on her other knee. She and her family ate dinner while the frog ate his meal from the plate on her knee.

Afterward, they cleaned up the kitchen, put the dishes away, and said "good night." The younger daughter went off to her bedroom. She brushed her hair and climbed into bed. She was just about to fall asleep, when the frog, at the foot of her bed, sang:

> *Oh bonnie maid, will you hear my plea*
> *Let me sleep on your lovely bed*

A promise is a promise. The girl reached down and put the frog on the bed. She took an extra blanket and climbed into an armchair in the corner of her bedroom. She pulled the blanket up and leaned back in the chair. She was about to go to sleep when the frog sang:

> *Oh bonnie maid, will you hear my plea*
> *Sleep with me on your lovely bed*

A promise is a promise. She climbed back into bed. She picked up the frog and put him in the arms of the stuffed teddy bear on the headboard of the bed. She was about to go to sleep when the frog sang again:

> *Oh bonnie maid, will you hear my plea*
> *And swiftly chop off my tiny head*

A promise is a promise. But this was going a bit too far. She was a non-violent person. And besides, she didn't own a sword. Or so she thought.

The frog said, "Look behind the bed." There, tucked between the bed and wall was a sharp sword. She lifted it. The frog nodded vigorously, pointed to his neck, and mimed slicing motions. She held the sword up, closed her eyes, and let it fall onto the frog's neck.

Then something happened that made the girl's life seem as different as night and day. When she opened her eyes, instead of a frog on her bed, she saw a man. With a head. He was wearing a crown.

So she married the prince, moved into the castle, and invited her mother and her older sister to live there as well.

Life was lovely in the castle. They had servants and fine linens. They had jewels and riches. The younger daughter had many children, and none of the children were tadpoles. Everyone lived happily ever after. Everyone except the older sister.

She was bitterly jealous of her younger sister's fortunes. So she, too, decided to look for the healing well. She walked for many a day until she came to the place where the sun kissed the earth. She raced to the well and cried, "Come to me, froggie." But no frog came.

Instead, one, two, three, dirty, old men climbed out of the well, singing,

*Oh bonnie maid, will you hear our plea*
*And wash us now to make us clean*

She took one look and said, "You are filthy, foul, and disgusting. Clean yourselves, I don't do manual labor!" Then the three dirty, old men smiled at the girl. "In punishment for your unkindness, whenever you speak, frogs and toads will fall from your tongue."

The girl opened her mouth to laugh. But when she did, a frog hopped from her mouth and landed on the wall of the well. With one more hop, the frog jumped into the well. The older daughter ran away from the well. She ran for many a day, and was never seen again.

And so, somewhere, out there, where the sun kisses the earth, there is a well with a frog in it. If you happen to find that well and a frog offers you a dipper filled with water, remember this story. Something might just happen to make your life seem as different as night and day.

ॐ

## Twisting Tips: Blended Story Mash-up

*Scour stories to find commonalities that can serve as bonding points.* Sometimes bonding points are exact and literal, like a big, bad wolf in "Little Red Riding Hood" and "The Three Little Pigs." Sometimes they are not exact, but fall into a common category. While a big, bad wolf and an evil stepmother are not exactly the same, they are fine examples of the villain archetype. As you will recall from "Chapter Seven: Characterization" archetypes are symbols, characters, and patterns that endure throughout time and across cultures. They can also be patterns of story action, like fighting evil, tricking the powerful, or hunting magical objects. Archetypes make excellent bonding points when exact commonalities between tales are not to be found.

---

### Less is More–More or Less

"Less is more" is one of our prime directives as artists. It is ironic, considering that we complicate the art of storytelling by speaking in two voices and by accompanying ourselves on a variety of instruments, sometimes more than one at a time. The multi-vocality of our performance work belongs firmly in the *more* category. That is why we are particularly careful with twisted stories. We perform many fractured stories without musical instruments, although the raps are always accompanied by a single hand drum. The simplicity of the performance highlights the story, its commentary, and humor.

Overtwisting can sludge up the works and obfuscate meaningful content. With a host of ideas scrambling to appear on the story stage, it is tempting to appease their selfish wishes and include every last one in a new story. But the addition of multiple ideas takes away from the product's overall integrity. It is about *more* than inventive ideas. A volley of jokes tilts the audience's attention away from the story and onto the jokes. Too much description, no matter how poetic or clever, sucks momentum out of the narrative.

Unfortunately, there are no objective guidelines to measure exactly when less becomes more. The least we can do is share is our rudimentary approach. If we are unsure if an idea works, we scrap it. If an idea continues to press itself into our heads or onto our documents like a whining, spoiled child, we reconsider the decision and try it with a safe, forgiving audience–in case our initial instincts to cut it were right. Any content that distracts us from the storyline is also scrapped.

---

*Organize your plots in a visual manner.* In a blended story, like "The Frog Prince Mash," we had two distinct storylines to entwine. We also had stories from the classical fairy tale canon to consider as well. As we described earlier, we lined up our story bones all over the living room. This same process can be achieved in a computer spreadsheet, if that is your preference, or on a traditional story board. Because two of us worked on this at the same time, it was helpful to have a room-sized process as it allowed both of us to move papers around.

*Carefully review stories from the classical canon of folk and fairy tales before starting your mash-up.* They are sound signposts for your literary adventure in mash-up land. We consult various sources, like Grimm and Perrault. However, we also look at annotated compilations like Maria Tatar's *The Annotated Classics*[19] and Heidi Anne Heiner's excellent online website "Surlalune Fairy Tales."[20] In this manner, we identify a preferred version (or versions) for our mash-up. This process reminds us of forgotten details, and is also a glorified writing prompt. Last but not least, it helps to distinguish traditional stories from versions that are not in the public domain. See Chapter One, "Ethics and Culture" for more on this.

*Look for loose ends, even when you think you are finished with your mash-up.* Mash-ups quilt together many story elements, so even when we think we have made the whole thing smooth, often it just isn't. Sometimes seams show or characters dangle like threads. Expect loose ends. Embrace them. Look for them. Only when you find then can you smooth them out. Yes, it may involve some revision—we revise our mash-ups again and again. It is part of the process, part of the creative challenge. We find loose ends in several stages. Even after we both review it multiple times, we read the story to other people. Those who aren't part of the creative process are the best loose-end spotters.

*Monitor the changes made to familiar storylines diligently.* As your alterations accumulate, they can mask imagery from familiar stories. The interweaving story lines and disconnected characters make a very complex narrative. Complexity works, but it can accelerate to confusion in a keystroke. That is why we keep a close eye on the changes to be sure that plot and meaning shines through.

*Be aware that less is sometimes less.* Less is more, is desirable in most situations, as we describe in the inset, ""Less is More-More or Less"" Lean stories carry punch. Artifice or cleverness is clunky when overdone. But sometimes, less really is less. As we wrote "The Frog Prince Mash," we toyed with cutting the diamonds/toads aspect to tighten the plot. We thought we could concentrate on the Frog Prince storyline with the healing well and good sister plot devices and boom, fairy tale done. But deeper consideration revealed serious flaws. In such a mash-up, marriage would be the younger sister's only reward. The older sister's unmarried state would be her only punishment. This implies that getting a partner is highly valued where single life is devalued. We rejected that message as out-of-step with contemporary America. It also didn't meet our vision for the story. Ultimately we found a way to smoothly include the other reward/punishment scenario. It makes the tale stand on its own, encourages dialogue between two classic stories and the mash-up, and it de-emphasizes marriage as a prize for good deeds done.

## AN INTUITIVELY-COMPOSED MULTI-PLOT MASH-UP: "REDI-LOCKS AND GOLDI-HOOD"

### Do the Twist

The process for writing this story was different than for "The Frog Prince Mash." While both stories were inspired by a bonding point, "The Frog Prince Mash" creative process focused on a small pool of stories to meld and mold. "Redi-Locks and Goldi-Hood" didn't begin with even one tale to twist. We started with a single, solitary bonding point. From there we let images and stories collide. Intuition was our only guide.

The finished "Redi-Locks" contains allusions to eight popular stories. The intertwined bones of three famous tales form the plot of our mash-up: "Little Red Riding Hood," "Goldilocks," and "The Three Little Pigs." But to go from a single bonding point to a textured mash-up, we allowed the story to arise organically from the writing process.

### Let Your Fingers Tell the Tale

It all started with one single bonding point, a forest path. From there, we brainstormed famous characters who head down such fabled paths: The Big, Bad Wolf, Goldilocks, Three Bears, Hansel and Gretel, one or more of the Three Little Pigs, Chicken Little and his companions, Little Red Riding Hood, Rapunzel's witch or prince, and Seven Dwarfs. Next we identified settings on a forest path: a palace at the edge of a clearing with a thorny hedge all around it, houses of sticks or bricks, a gingerbread house, Rapunzel's tower, Granny's house or the house of the Three Bears. The list stopped there because an idea began to form.

Little Red Riding Hood swirled out of this tornado of images. We stopped thinking, started writing, and let our fingers tell the tale. She walked down the forest path. The wolf trailed after her. He was the link to bond her story to another one: "The Three Little Pigs."

Like a set of dominoes, one image crashed into the next. The wolf huffed and puffed at the home of Little Red Riding Hood's Granny. Granny was in the house. None of this was planned.

---

### Twisting Tip

*Carry old and new school recording devices wherever you go.* We keep pen and paper in every room of our house. We record ideas into the voice recorder of our mobile phones or text phrases to our emails—we do whatever it takes to capture the whimsy of creative moments. Ideas are fleeting and easily forgotten, even when we think we won't forget them.

---

At this stage, we stopped to consider our reason for doing this mash-up. Our work needed purpose beyond kitsch and cleverness. We asked ourselves if there was something new we wanted to say about the Little Red Riding Hood tale or any of the characters. Jeri felt strongly about this.

> So many of the most famous stories in the classical canon showcase female dependency. Wouldn't it be wonderful if our story turned that notion on its head? What if we go back in time, to older versions of this tale, where Red is more autonomous? Could we do a revisionist piece in the feminist tradition and showcase female independence?

Themes of dependency and "parents and wolves know best" stem from the famous Perrault story and one of the Grimms' versions of the tale.[21] Widely-known retellings often preserve these iconic themes that were penned in the books by Perrault and Grimm.[22] An older version of "Little Red Riding Hood," pre-dating Perrault's, is quite different. It features an independent girl who finds her way into a lecherous wolf's bed. Through her own cleverness, she escapes from her tormentor.[23] The story's message, that a girl can be the agent of her own rescue, was the one we wanted to rekindle in our version. Not only is that message consistent with the folkloric roots of the story, it is also relevant to modern society's expectations for girls and women.

So we agreed that our Little Red Riding Hood would not be a helpless child at the mercy of parental prohibition, wolfish pressure, and childhood lessons. Once Little Red Riding Hood was swallowed by the wolf, she had to escape from the wolf's belly. To be consistent with the message in our mash-up, Little Red Riding Hood couldn't rely on a princely savior. She had to be the agent of her own rescue. In an early draft, she used a pocket knife to cut herself out, but a question hovered over us like a low-hanging cloud. Wouldn't the underlying message of the story be deepened if there were multiple female character models? Could another girl or woman be involved?

### *Femme Fougueuse:* A New Term for New Times

An *independent women* motif excited us. But that moniker was wrong. Despite the older versions of the story, Little Red Riding Hood is typically not a grown woman in post-Perrault versions of the children's story. The use of the word "girl" didn't work, since other independent female characters in our mash-up were adult women. After some consideration, we tinkered with the well-known phrase *femme fatale* and came up with femme fougueuse. The word fougueuse (pronounced foo-joose) means fiery, passionate, and spirited. Femme fouguese is a term that describes the modern female spirit, in life and stories.

Energized, we listed traditionally passive princesses who could be wedged into the mash-up. Rapunzel could let her hair down the wolf's throat as a life-line and pull Little Red to safety. Snow White could break out of her glass coffin, brandish a shard of coffin glass, and save the day. The ideas were thrumming. Each idea was attractive, but none were logically connected to our story.

So we looked directly at the story and our brainstorming list. There was one character who could logically rescue Little Red Riding Hood if we incorporated a third main story to the mash-up, aligned at the forest path bonding point. Goldilocks could visit Granny's house a la "The Three Bears." Instead of being sick in bed, Granny would make porridge. Goldilocks as freedom fighter matched our message just right.

The femme fougueuse theme spread to other characters who do not usually have agency in their fairy tale lives. This story motif would unseat an audience's expectations about fairy tale characters who "can't think for themselves." Our twisted variant became a snapshot of autonomous young girls with wherewithal and spunk, and a parody of the fairy tale genre.

## Ironing the Wrinkles

There were many details crumpled up in the newly tailored tale. We had ironing to do.

---

### The Success of Failure: Outtakes

Every mash-up is an experiment with brand new ideas. You can expect flagrant failures, middling maybes, and a few succulent successes. There is no sugar-coating this: some things work and many things don't. Your challenge is to approach the creative process with a playful, open mindset.

It is delightful when carefully crafted jokes land or subtle ironies are applauded by others. But every new idea doesn't work. Reframe your brain to view this type of "failure" as a glorious opportunity to sculpt an elegant, workable tale. Turn failures into triumphs.

In the Little Red mash-up, we highlight moments of feminine agency. Little Red Riding Hood chooses, on her own, to pick flowers for Granny. She initiates her own rescue from the wolf's belly. To orient an audience to the importance of this theme, we wanted a repetitive phrase or idea that would link those moments thematically to emphasize that feminine characters don't need to be told what to do, but could think for themselves and "write their own story." Our first attempt was a simple phrase for each event: "The wolf didn't tell her, at all," or "She didn't pine for rescue, at all."

It didn't work, at all. Next, we tried couplets based on the "Jack be nimble" nursery rhyme. "Goldi be nimble, Goldi be quick, cooked up a plan and locked it, click!" and "Pig be nimble, Pig be quick, built a strong house out of brick!" We crafted one poem for every story event with femme fouguese motifs. The couplet balloon burst in the first test run. Audience feedback indicated that the rhymes muddied the story and didn't highlight any motif or theme. So we went back to the drawing board and ultimately devised a repetitive phrase that was just right for the tale. These "failures" honed our understanding of the salient message of the story and helped us focus.

Try out your ideas one by one. Does the story work better with that idea or without? Which way flows better? Do both ways make sense? Find a local story group or initiate a gathering where you can test out your material and get more feedback. Failure is a process that yields golden success if you let it.

---

With a heroic Goldilocks, Little Red Riding Hood seemed passive by association. She had to be involved in her own rescue. Looking at how people save themselves from trouble in modern times brought the obvious answer, cell phones—that was the easy wrinkle.

The character of Granny, ironically, had the most wrinkles of all. Was she Red's traditional, sick Granny? Was she a cook like Mama Bear? Would she fit best as one of the Three Little Pigs? Could she be a blended character? To balance out the story, we wanted her to be a bonding point—a spunky, porridge-cooking Granny who happened to be the clever third Little Pig. But giving Red a pig for a granny required some serious thought.

Story purists might argue with our decision to make a pig the grandparent of human children. But twisted stories are fantasies based on fantasies. The genre is dominated by suspension of disbelief. And although a porcine granny departs from the traditional stories markedly, we embraced the idea for other reasons as well.

First, the character isn't a literal pig or a granny. Like other fairy tale characters, she is symbolic. So, what does the Granny represent in our story? Granny's role in the mash-up is consistent with her role as a porridge-making parent in "Goldilocks." She represents a caring, maternal figure. Even though Granny is ill in the popular "Little Red Riding Hood" tale, we have no reason to believe that she isn't a caring granny when healthy. Why else would the family be committed to caring for her in times of need?

Second, although Hansel and Gretel are human children, their behavior in their traditional story is arguably pig-like. They snuffle around a gingerbread house and greedily devour window-panes and chunks of walls. Though subtle, it is thematic to imply that they could be pigs.

Third, Granny as the third little pig is consistent with the theme of the mash-up—that female characters in stories can be independent and inventive. The third little pig thwarted the wolf in "The Three Little Pigs." This earlier escapade foreshadows her escape in the new tale. In this way, our twisted version with Goldilocks, Little Red, and Granny conjures up a sisterhood of women who win the day for themselves.

Finally, the addition of Hansel and Gretel opened up new narrative avenues. For instance, the gingerbread house from the traditional Hansel and Gretel provided the raw materials for the Gingerbread Man.

One of the most gripping aspects of mash-ups is the element of surprise when expectations are shaken. Casting Granny as a pig does just this. Furthermore, her relationship to Hansel and Gretel makes Red their cousin, another surprise. Careful narrative ironing makes it all work.

## *Redi-Locks and Goldi-Hood*

By Jeri Burns and Barry Marshall
Copyright The Storycrafters 2016, 2018

One fine sunny, day, a girl in a red cape set off down the forest path to visit her grandmother *because that's what they do.* She came upon a wolf.

"Where are you going, little girl?" asked the wolf.

"I'm off to visit my Granny and have brunch with my cousins."

"Oh the lovely brick house at the end of the path? I pass that house every morning. It looks lonely because all the window boxes are empty."

Little Red was sad to hear that. Granny loved having cheerful flowers in her window boxes. Just then, she noticed a big patch of flowers growing in the woods just off the forest path. Little Red decided to gather a big bunch to surprise her Granny.

The wolf didn't tell her to pick flowers, she decided to that on her own.

Little girls can think for themselves.

Now that wolf may not have been clever as a fox, but he was an opportunist. When he saw Little Red Riding Hood stepping off the forest path, he ran through the woods to Grandmother's house. Then, for the first time, he crept close and looked in through the window. He was awfully surprised to discover that the little girl's grandmother was a pig. You see, the Wolf was of that persuasion that is still taken aback when faced with mixed marriages.

Granny was busy making breakfast for Little Red Riding Hood and her other two grandchildren who lived on another forest path. Their names were Hansel and Gretel. That may be surprising, but if you stop to think about it, if there is any story character who has a pig for a parent, it is Hansel and Gretel. And if there ever were two little children who behaved like pigs, well they would be Hansel and Gretel.

Granny made a big pot of porridge. She set out a big bowl for Hansel because she thought he needed some fattening up, the medium bowl for Gretel, because she was also known for her appetite, and the smallest bowl for Little Red Riding Hood since she was, after all, little.

Granny filled their bowls with porridge so they could cool when she heard a knock on the door.

"Little pig, little pig let me in."

She thought, oh no, not again and then said, "Not by the hair on my chinny-chin-chin."

The wolf thought that Grandmother was due for a waxing.

"Then I'll huff and I'll puff and I'll blow your house in."

Granny used to have two brothers, but she was the only surviving family member because she was smart and industrious enough to avoid building her house out of straw or sticks. She was also smart enough not to wait around for a wolf to break in. Granny broke out the back door and hightailed it, wee-wee-wee-wee to Hansel and Gretel's house.

In the meantime, the Wolf didn't try to enter through the front door or window. He climbed up to Granny's roof and slid down the chimney *because that's what they do.* He went straight to Granny's room, put on one of her dress-up wigs, and tucked himself into her bed *because that's what they do.*

When Little Red arrived, being in desperate need of an eye exam, she mistook the wolf for Granny and was swallowed whole. But Little Red didn't wait around hoping that someone would magically find her. She wasn't longing for a handsome prince. There wasn't a genie lamp in the wolf's belly. She couldn't consult a magic mirror. There was something else she could do.

Little Red pulled out her cell phone and Tweeted: "Stuck inside #wolf. Need #911. #Grannyshomeontheforestpath." Little girls can think for themselves *because that's what they do.*

It wasn't long before someone saw the tweet, came to the house, checked out the porridge on the table, and then saw the chairs. The hardest chair was just right. She went up to the bedroom, and saw fifteen mattresses stacked one upon the other. And on top of that stack, like a cherry on a cake, was the Wolf. Faster than you can say, "Granny what big eyes you have," she climbed the mattress stack and sat on top. It was lumpy, bumpy, and rather painful. She raised up the chair and forced open the Wolf's throat. The Wolf coughed up Little Red and ran far, far away … *because that's what they do.*

Little Red and Goldilocks jumped off the bed. Goldilocks thrust her hand under the mattress and found what was troubling her. It was a bean. She tossed it out the window. Then, they went downstairs, ate the porridge, and skipped down the forest path *because that's what they do.*

In the meantime, when Granny got to Hansel and Gretel's house she told them about the Wolf. Gretel had an idea because little girls can think for themselves. She took them by hand and trotter and skipped down the forest path because that's they do. They arrived at a house in the woods made of gingerbread. They worked and worked and fashioned the very thing that would rid Granny of the wolf. It wasn't a Golem or tar baby. It was a Papa Bear-sized Gingerbread Man. They put him on a leash and went back to Granny's house.

Their plan was simple. They would unleash the cookie the moment the Wolf saw him. The Gingerbread Man would run and the Wolf would chase him far, far away. Granny would be safe.

But when they got inside Granny's house, they combed it from top to bottom. There was no sign of the Wolf anywhere.

So they went back to the kitchen and looked hungrily at the Gingerbread Man. He gazed at them with terror in his raisin eyes. One was a pig and the other two were infamous gluttons, his goose was cooked. He was about to run away *because that's what they do* when Granny said, "Not to worry my dear, we are on low carb diets—bread is for the birds and we stopped eating sweets long ago, they are nothing but trouble." Hansel and Gretel nodded knowingly. So they all enjoyed a Paleo supper and went upstairs to play video games. They invited the Seven Dwarfs to join them. They gave the guests the choice of games to play and the Dwarfs chose Minecraft *because that's what they do.*

It turned out that Little Red Riding Hood and Goldilocks became close friends. They were both independent, bold girls who could think for themselves. They stayed in touch throughout their youth and when they grew up it should come as no surprise that they had a fairy tale wedding, *because that's what they do.* By then, the beanstalk outside Granny's house grew very tall and there were more adventures. But that is a giant of a story best saved for another time. As for this one, they all lived happily ever after, *because that's what they do.*

ॐ

## TWISTING TIPS: MASH-UP STORYTWISTING TIPS

*Expect to make one decision after another while composing a mash-up.* When you overlay the spines of two or more stories, you have double or more events, settings, objects or characters—many more than you can include in a fractured tale. You have to choose what to include, what to exclude, and how to navigate tricky spots.

In "Redi-Locks and Goldi-Hood," we had choices about how to handle the wolf's arrival at Granny's house. He could have swallowed her—à la "Little Red Riding Hood," she could have been out walking in the woods when he arrived—as in "The Three Bears," or she could have cooked the wolf in a stew —in the manner of "The Three Little Pigs". We chose none of those. Instead Granny escaped—it was consistent with the *women are independent* message of the story and it gave her a chance to realize her Gingerbread Man plan to rid the forest of that hungry, hateful wolf.

*Cue audiences when mash-up plots travel curlicue paths.* Multiple story lines and random allusions make mash-ups fun. But they can also be confusing unless listeners are given subtle guidance.

In "Redi-Locks and Goldi-Hood," Granny escapes when the wolf approaches her house. Without a cue, her escape can perplex those who expect him to devour Granny per the well-known "Little Red Riding Hood" tale. To minimize those expectations, our wolf doesn't knock and say he is Red Riding Hood. He threatens to blow down Granny's house instead. That tiny cue moves the "Three Little Pigs" story to the foreground and puts the "Little Red Riding Hood" story momentarily in the background. This makes Granny's escape expected according to the "Three Little Pigs" story formula.

*Keep the spine of your tale in mind at all times.* Make sure that all your story choices hang together according to the bones. Audiences are confused when the mash-up doesn't mesh up with the bones.

For example, in a draft of "Redi-Locks and Goldi-Hood," we deviated from the Little Red story spine and included the Straw and Sticks Pigs in the fractured piece. They had nothing to do with "Redi-Locks." Listeners got lost. So did we.

*Meta is better when it is goal-directed and brief.* Drawing attention purposely to writing and literary choices is what literary scholars call metafiction—when a story is overtly conscious about its own writing techniques or literary decisions.[24] A character who waxes poetic about being a story character or a storyteller who ponders the act of storytelling while telling a tale are examples of metafictional moments.

---

### Teaching Twist: Make a Mash-up

1. *Select two or more favorite story characters to meet up in a brand, new story.*

2. *Outline the plots of the source stories, overlay them, and identify where and how the characters meet. These will be the bonding points of the new tale.*

3. *Next, choose one character's storyline to serve as the spine of your fractured story.*

4. *The bonding point(s) will act as the outside character's entrance into the tale.*

*Suppose you choose Jack, of beanstalk fame, to meet Cinderella, with Jack's storyline as the spine and the ball at the castle as bonding point. When Jack climbs up the beanstalk, instead of finding a giant's castle, he finds a prince's palace instead. There are many possibilities here! Is the giant Cinderella's prince, or is Jack? Is Jack's beanstalk climb a metaphor for his climb out of the pit of poverty into the lap of luxury? Is there a way to integrate the fairy godmother as a bonding point? Perhaps the old man who gives him the beans for the cow is the fairy godmother in disguise. There are many ways that this story can travel. Permutations can be maximized when characters, objects, or patterns from other tales jump into this one. Maybe Jack has to guess Cinderella's name, as in Rumpelstiltskin. The possibilities are endless!*

---

Fractured stories, particularly mash-ups, are metafictional. Decisions that rearrange story motifs jolt an audience out of the story spell. Akin to breaking theater's fourth wall, these moments disrupt the flow of the narrative by stealing attention from the story and directing it to the moments themselves. We find that metafictional moments work best when they are crystalline and brief, like a perfectly gorgeous snowflake on woolen sleeve—it's there, it's beautiful, it's gone.

For example, when we perform "Redi-Locks" live, at the moment when Goldilocks removes a bean from under the bed—we allow listeners to guess "pea"—then we smile mischievously and state outright, "No it wasn't a pea, wrong story."

*Provide explanations when big changes are made* to a familiar story. You will alter traditional stories or their images to squeeze them into your mash-up. Offer tiny explanations for significant deviations from the source tale. The absence of an explanation can jar an audience out of the story and toss them into a cloud of confusion.

In "Redi-Locks and Goldi-Hood," there was only one pig from a tale about three pigs. Some people know versions of the story where the Straw and Sticks Pigs escape. Others know versions where they are devoured. To even the playing field, we offer this brief explanation for our solitary pig: "Granny used to have two brothers, but she was the only surviving family member because she was smart and industrious enough to avoid building her house out of straw or sticks."

## Twisting Tip

*Be judicious in the number of explanations you include in your twisted tale.* Revise your piece to require as few as possible or it will sound more like an annotated parody or an academic exercise than a story. People don't enjoy jokes that require extensive explanation. If you find you must explain yourself a bunch, it is time to dial back on those changes.

*Name mash-up motifs to coalesce creative thought.* In "Redi-Locks and Goldi-Hood," we observed that some of our characters skipped down roads. Initially, we named it "The Road Skipping Motif," but the name didn't feel right. We chewed on the thematic element therein and reviewed the entire story. Skipping down the road was a repeating motif in our tale, but there was more to it.

There were other fairy tale *tropes* (images or turns of phrase) in our story. When we realized that, we lumped them all into one category and named the motif Tropes. By looking at them together as a unit, we devised the repeating, foundational phrase of our tale "Because that's what they do." We might not have found it if we didn't play Name that Motif.

## Twist for Thought: Storytelling as a Springboard to Social Awareness

Postmodern storytelling is a literary phenomenon that spun into high fashion in the latter half of the Twentieth Century.[25] It's characterized by the fragmentation of previously existing works, intelligent borrowings and allusions, and both sub-textual and overt social or genre commentary—all of which fosters new cultural understanding and awakens us to important issues, but in unexpected, often amusing ways. Mash-ups fit right into this genre. Children's literature is full of role reversal stories and allusions to fairy and folktale tropes and motifs.[26] Adult literature also embraces postmodern expression. With mash-up novels that blend a classic story with a different genre, like horror, or books that roll multiple classics into one reformed narrative, reimagined stories are part of the literary scene.[27]

Mash-ups may be all the rage today, but the tendency to borrow from one genre to make a new story with social commentary is not a recent phenomenon. Many scholars point to the fairy tale tradition in France, where similar techniques were in use as far back as the Seventeenth Century.[28] In French salon gatherings, the verbal arts were on display in parlor games. There were gently competitive conversations peppered with literary references and allusions.

### Twisting Tip

*Keep a sharp eye out for what can be deleted.* A leaner story is a better story. Do better than Santa—check it more than twice. But ask yourself some questions when you delete content. Is the narrative still intact? Does the meaning of your new story reflect your intended meaning? Are the story seams hidden or does the deletion bring them out? If you wonder if a joke works, it probably doesn't. If you wonder if something strays from the path of the story, it probably does. If you can't fix the problem, then go ahead and delete it. But don't trash the deleted content! Save it for a future piece.

New fairy tales, crafted from motifs of pre-existing fairy tales or embellished, detailed variations of known stories, were sometimes formed and narrated on the spot.[29] Many of the tales reinvented the role of women, transforming them into more independent characters.[30] Furthermore, the stories made incisive, literary statements about the French aristocracy. Composed mostly by women

—and later published in books—salon fairy tales were political conversations veiled in literary motifs. Quilted together, they created wise new stories for their times.

---

### *Teaching Twist: Salon Story Game.*

*1. Brainstorm a list of story motifs, characters, patterns of action, objects, settings, magical helpers, and so forth from any and all fairy tales that you can think of.*

*2. Copy the list onto separate, small pieces of paper and put them into a hat.*

*3. Select at least eight papers from the hat.*

*4. With your class, incorporate all of those items into a mash-up story.*

*5 It can help to select a basic fairy tale plotline upon which to overlay those motifs.*

*6. While you are not limited to those eight items, it is fun to rise to the challenge of including them all in a tale of your reinvention.*

*For example, if you use a plot like Chicken Little, the tale might not start on a farm but in a village, say Hamelin of Pied Piper fame. The animals who run away with Chicken Little don't have to be farm animals, but a Gingerbread Man, Sleeping Beauty, a woodcutter, and a troll. In the mash-up, they do not fear the sky falling down, but rather the boy who cries wolf. Or the rats...*

---

The historical tendency to use narrative to make socio-political commentary is not confined to the salon era in aristocratic France. In ancient China, telling subversive folktales was a way to fan the flames of revolt. In their collection of Chinese folktales, Louise and Yuan His Kuo point out that "… discontent with the prevailing government or hatred of an alien king, were voiced in the stories, although the real thoughts were disguised by allegories and metaphors. The common people understood what was implied; officials usually did too, but were powerless to punish anyone."[31] Folklore carries other examples of stories told to impart a message about politics and society. African-American folktales, for example, warned children about unfairness and injustice in a white-dominated world.[32] Marina Warner, a writer of stories, history, and literary criticism, astutely notes that tales have been used to impart philosophy in times of censorship, to open minds to new ways of thinking through humor and satire.[33] Contemporary mash-ups continue this longstanding tradition. But interweaving humor, meaning, message, and satire isn't the province of mash-ups alone. All storytwisted tales stand on the same precipice of possibility. They can be entertaining and so much more. When composed carefully and consciously, twisted tales transform not only the canonical literature of childhood, but also the people who hear and tell them. Such is the power of story.

# NOTES

1. Lewis Carroll, *Alice's Adventures in Wonderland*, full text of *Alice's Adventures in Wonderland*, August 12, 2006, accessed July 10, 2016, https://archive.org/stream/alicesadventures19033gut/19033.txt.

2. "Mash-up," Merriam-Webster, accessed September 09, 2015, https://www.merriam-webster.com/dictionary/mash-up.

3. Jane Nardin, "The Literary Mash-up," Huffingtonpost.com (blog), November 27, 2012, accessed September 9, 2015, http://www.huffingtonpost.com/jane-nardin/the-literary-mash-up_b_2194133.html.

4. Jack Zipes, trans., "The Frog King, or Iron Heinrich," *The Complete Fairy Tales of the Brothers Grimm.* (Toronto: Bantam Books, 1987), 2-5.

5. Iona and Peter Opie, "The Fairy," *The Classic Fairy Tales.* (New York: Oxford University Press, 1980), 129-132. "The Fairy" is a translation of the Charles Perrault fairy tale, sometimes translated as "The Fairies." Over time, this tale type is more frequently called "Diamond and Toads." (Opie 1980, 128).

6. Linda Hutcheon, *A Theory of Adaptation*, (Abingdon, Oxon: Routledge, 2006), 3.

7. This is our shorthand for teaching the basics of plot. For more on our use of these terms, see Chapter Five: Fracture Point—Rhyme.

8. "Plot—Examples and Definition of Plot," Literary Devices. 2013, accessed June 29, 2016, http://literarydevices.net/plot/. For a discussion about plot in terms of mystery and causality, see E.M. Forster, *Aspects of the Novel,* (New York: Harcourt, Brace & Company, 1927), 83-103. These ideas allow for flexibility in sequential ordering of story elements, from the tightest of plots to episodic storylines.

9. Robert McKee, *Story: Substance, Structure, Style and the Principles of Screenwriting.* (New York: HarperCollins. 1997), 43.

10. John Francis Campbell, "The Tale of the Queen Who Sought a Drink from a Certain Well." *Popular Tales of the West Highlands Vol. II: XXXIII*, accessed December 03, 2015, http://www.sacred-texts.com/neu/celt/pt2/pt225.htm. *Popular Tales of the West Highlands* was originally published in 1890 and is in the public domain.

11. For a variant that does not have multiple daughters, see Robert Chambers, "The Paddo," *Popular Rhymes of Scotland: New Edition* (London and Edinburgh: W. and R. Chambers, 1870), 87-89, accessed January 14, 2016, http://www.pitt.edu/~dash/frog.html#chambers.

12. Joseph Jacobs, "The Three Heads of the Well," English Fairy Tales, accessed December 02, 2015. http://www.sacred-texts.com/neu/eng/eft/eft44.htm. Originally published with the same title, London: David Nutt, 1890.

13. Zipes, *The Complete Fairy Tales*, 1987, 2-5 and Opie, *The Classic Fairy Tales*, 1980, 129-132.

14. Ibid.

15. There are other stories of this type in which there is more than one task to perform before the kind daughter receives her reward. For example, in "The Three Little Gnomes in the Forest," the Grimm Brothers' variant, the daughter has to feed the men and then perform a household task. See Jack Zipes, trans. "The Three Little Gnomes in the Forest," in *The Complete Fairy Tales of the Brothers Grimm.* (Toronto: Bantam Books, 1987), 50-55.

16. David Pickering, *A Dictionary of Folklore*, (New York: Facts on File, 1999), 313-315.

17. A pourquoi story is a traditional folktale type that explains why things are the way they are, such as why rabbits have long ears. Pourquoi is the French word for "why."

18. We mostly referred to the Grimm and Perrault versions.

19. Maria Tatar, ed. and trans., *The Annotated Classic Fairy Tales*, (New York. W.W. Norton, 2002).

20. Heidi Anne Heiner, "SurLaLune Fairy Tales: Annotated Fairy Tales, Fairy Tale Books and Illustrations." SurLaLune Fairy Tales.com. Accessed June 01, 2016. http://surlalunefairytales.com/. Last updated 12/2/16.

21. Jack Zipes, ed., *The Trials and Tribulations of Little Red Riding Hood*, 2nd Edition, (New York: Routledge. 1993). Zipes presents about 35 versions of this tale from Charles Perrault's first literary adaption all the way into the later part of the 20th Century. In an analysis that precedes the stories (pages 17-81), Zipes describes the socializing process that the Perrault and Grimms' versions employed, and how those themes infiltrated many of the subsequent renderings of the tale. As the 20th Century proceeded, more versions parodied or contested his assumptions about women, male power, and following society's (and Mom and Dad's) rules.

22. Ibid, 137-138. Though in one edition of their collection, the Brothers Grimm offered a second story where Little Red Cap (as their story is translated) is bothered by the wolf. Thanks to Grandmother's plan, they lock themselves in the house. The wolf waits on the roof while they fill a trough with water that smells of sausage. The greedy wolf leans down to smell the water, falls in, and drowns.

23. Zipes, ed,, "The Story of Grandmother," in *The Trials and Tribulations of Little Red Riding Hood*, 2nd Edition, (New York: Routledge. 1993), 21-23.

24. Cudden. J. A. *Dictionary of Literary Terms and Literary Theory.* Revised by M.A.R. Habib. (Penguin Group: London, 2013), 431.

25. Stephen Benson, "Postmodernism," in *The Greenwood Encyclopedia of Folktales and Fairy Tales*, Vol. 2, edited by Donald Haase, (Westport, CT: Greenwood Press, 2008),

762-767; Cudden, *Dictionary,* 552-553.

26. Benson, "Postmodernism," 766.

27. A browser search of "mash-up novels" confirms this as a literary trend. For instance, Goodreads has a shelf devoted to the genre. Wikipedia, while not an authoritative resource from an academic perspective, but a reasonable indicator of popular culture, has a mash-up novel page as well.

28. Jack Zipes, *Fairy Tale as Myth/Myth as Fairy Tale,*.Lexington: University Press of Kentucky, 1994), 17-48.

29. Ibid. See also Marina Warner, *Once Upon a Time: A Short History of Fairy Tale,* (Oxford: Oxford University Press, 2014), 46-47.

30. This wholehearted reinvention of the role of women is subject to question. A deep look at the fairy tales of the time reveals that although the female protagonists defied societal conventions and acted independently, they typically found their "happily ever after" by sinking into societal expectations for marriage. See Lewis C. Seifert, "Feminist Approaches to Seventeenth Century *Contes de Fées,*" in *Fairy Tale sand Feminism: New Approaches,* edited by Donald Haase, (Detroit: Wayne State University Press, 2004), 65-68.

31. Louise Kuo, and Yuan-Hsi Kuo, *Chinese Folk Tales,* (Millbrae, CA: Celestial Arts, 1976), 10.

32. Roger D Abrahams, ed, *Afro-American Folktales: Stories from Black Traditions in the New World.* New York: Pantheon Books, 3-33.

33. Warner, *Once Upon a Time,* 156.

*Will you, won't you,*
*will you, won't you,*
*will you join the dance?*

Lewis Carroll[1]

# AFTERWORD

More often than not, the key to carrying an old story to a new place isn't immediately apparent when storytwisting begins. Every story has its own path. It is up to you to follow it.

The great writer Ray Bradbury captured the essence of this when he said, "Jump off the cliff and build your wings on the way down."[2]

We encourage you to take that leap. There will be times when rewriting is required to make your story flow or to clear up trouble spots. Sometimes the solution bubbles out of the research process. Though you may not know what the answer is when you start, one will pop up along the way.

So dive down the nearest rabbit hole, build those wings, and fly into the wonderland of storytwisting.

# APPENDIX A

### *Beeping Sleauty: Family Version*
By Jeri Burns and Barry Marshall
Copyright 1996, 2018, The Storycrafters

Once upon a time, a quing and keen lived together in a cancy fastle. They had everything they could ever want except for a bittle laby. How they longed for a bittle laby. How they wished for a bittle laby. And one fine day they were blessed with a bittle laby.

It was such a magnificent event that they decided to host a pig barty. They had a very long luest gist. It was so long that they forgot to invite the firteenth thairy. And the firteenth thairy was very angry at having been ooverloked. She grew so angry, that on the day of the pig barty she came anyway. But by then she turned herself into a wasty nitch.

And the wasty nitch cast a sperrible tell on the bittle laby. She said that when the bittle laby grew up to be a woung yoman, on her beighteenth irthday she would frick her pinger on a whinning speel and fall into a sleep dumber for hone yundred wears.

Well, the quing and keen took action. They ordered every whinning speel in the quingdom to be destroyed in a boring ronfire. And they were destroyed, all except for one.

In the teanmime, the bittle laby grew into a gittle lirl. Everyone loved her. Stories were spread war and fide about her. People said that she had a heautiful beart and heautiful bair. And as that gittle lirl grew up to be a woung yoman, her heautiful beart and bair grew even more heautiful.

But, on that woung yoman's beighteenth irthday she was overcome with a peculiar desire to explore the cancy fastle. She found a tidden hower that had steaky squairs. She climbed those steaky squairs all the way up to the toppy tip where she discovered a rusty doom. And there, in the middle of the rusty doom, was the last whinning speel in the quingdom. And sitting at the whinning speel was the wasty nitch.

The woung yoman stretched out her arm and fricked her pinger on the whinning speel and fell into a sleep dumber. And as she slept, the clocks on the wall tarted sticking. The mice in the corner narted stibbling. And the book in the cakery started booking. In no time at all, everyone in that cancy fastle, including the quing and keen, fell into a sleep dumber.

As they slept, a thedge of horns rose up around the cancy fastle. And legend of the sleeping woung yoman with the heautiful beart and bair was spread all throughout the quingdon. Soon everyone was saying that she was a regular Beeping Sleauty.

Prany a mince tried to cut through the thedge of horns, but the thedge was thick and the horns hurt. So no one succeeded.

Then a prucky lince came along. He cut through the thedge of horns, found the tidden hower, climbed the steaky squairs all the way up to the toppy tip where he discovered the rusty doom (which had grown even rustier over hone yundred wears). And there, in the middle of the room he saw that sleeping woung yoman with the heautiful beart and bair, that regular Beeping Sleauty. She really was a Sleauty.

The prucky lince walked near, bent over her, and fell leeply in dove. He had stutterflies in his bomach as he bent over and gave her a big, cat fiss. Then, right in the middle of his fiss, that woung yoman with the heautiful beart and bair, that regular Beeping Sleauty—well she might have been a sleauty but she wasn't beeping now—that regular Beeping Sleauty at sup.

When Beeping Sleauty at sup, the clocks on the wall tarted sticking. The mice in the corner narted stibbling. And the book in cakery starting booking. But was he ever in a masty nood because after hone yundred wears that cakery had gotten heally rot! Finally, everyone in the cancy fastle, including the quing and keen, all oke wup.

Beeping Sleauty shiled smyly, uttered her fleyes, got down on her knands and hees and asked the pruckly lince to marry her. The prucky lince was thrilled to have Beeping Sleauty become his wovely life. After hearing the couple's news, the quing and keen decided to throw another pig barty to celebrate, but that is another tairy fale entirely. As for this one, they all lived happily aver efter.

And the moral of the story? The next time you throw a pig party be sure to chouble deck the luest gist lest you too should forget to invite one very gowerful pest.

Ee Thend.

# APPENDIX B 🍀 TWIST YOUR OWN STORY

*Used with permission from Storytwisting: A Guide to Remixing and Reinventing*
*Stories. ©2017 by Jeri Burns and Barry Marshall, The Storycrafters*

| Story Element | Traditional | Twisted Sukkot | Twisted Fairy | Your Twisted Story |
|---|---|---|---|---|
| Upset character | Old woman/man | Andrew | Sleepy Fairy | |
| Advisor character | Rabbi | Cara | Father fairy | |
| Everyday house noise | Rocking chair, snoring, cat | Girls arguing, squirrels, whistling wind | Rain and breezes | |
| First addition to the house | Goat | Dogs | Ants | |
| Second addition to the house | Chicken | Popcorn maker | Caterpillar | |
| Third addition to the house | Cow | Lawnmower | Chipmunk | |

*I think I should understand that*
*better, if I had written it down: but I*
*can't quite follow it as you say it.*

LEWIS CARROLL[3]

# BIBLIOGRAPHY

Abrahams, Roger D., ed. *Afro-American Folktales: Stories from Black Traditions in the New World.* New York: Pantheon Books, 1985.

"Archetype." Literary Devices. Accessed February 6, 2016. http://literarydevices.net/archetype/.

Asbjørnsen, Peter Christen and Jørgen Moe. Trans. by George Webbe Dasent, *Popular Tales of the Norse.* Edinburgh: Edmonston and Douglas, 1859.

Aesop, Arthur Rackham, and Vernon Jones V. S., trans. *Aesop's Fables.* New York: Avenel Books, 1975. A Facsimile of the 1912 Edition.

Afanaśev, Aleksandr. *Russian Fairy Tales.* Translated by Norbert Guterman. New York: Pantheon Books, 1975.

Anshel, A., and D. A. Kipper. "The Influence of Group Singing on Trust and Cooperation." *Journal of Music Therapy* 25, no. 3 (1988): 145-55. doi:10.1093/jmt/25.3.145.

Ashliman, D. L. "Sleeping Beauty." Sleeping Beauty. Accessed May 30, 2016. http://www.pitt.edu/~dash/type0410.html. Last revised June 7, 2013.

Ausubel, Nathan ed. "It Could Always Be Worse." In *A Treasury of Jewish Folklore: The Stories, Traditions, Legends, Humor, Wisdom and Folk Songs of the Jewish People,* 69-70. New York: Crown Publishers, 1948.

Avins, Jenni. "The Do's and Don't's of Cultural Appropriation." *The Atlantic.* October 20, 2015. Accessed June 03, 2016. http://www.theatlantic.com/entertainment/archive/2015/10/the-dos-and-donts-of-cultural-appropriation/411292/.

Bacchilega, Cristina. *Fairy Tales Transformed? Twenty-First-Century Adaptations and the Politics of Wonder.* Detroit: Wayne State University Press, 2013.

Bacchilega, Crstina, *Postmodern Fairy Tales: Gender and Narrative Strategies.* Philadelphia: University of Pennsylvania Press, 1997.

Bailey, Lucanne Magill. "The Effects of Live Music versus Tape-Recorded Music on Hospitalized Cancer Patients." *Music Therapy* 3, no. 1 (1983): 17-28. https://academic.oup.com/musictherapy/article/3/1/17/2756890 /The-Effects-of-Live-Music-versus-Tape-Recorded.

Bailey, Betty A., and Jane W. Davidson. "Amateur Group Singing as a Therapeutic Instrument." *Nordic Journal of Music Therapy* 12, no. 1 (2003): 18-32. http://www.tandfonline.com/doi/abs/10.1080/08098130309478070.

Baker, Lyman. "Flat vs Round Characterization." Last updated September 6, 2001, http://www.k-state.edu/english/baker/english320/cc-flat_vs_round_ characterization.htm.

Baker, Lyman. "Static vs. Dynamic Characterization." Last updated March 7, 2001, http://www.k-state.edu/english/baker/english320/cc-static_vs_dynamic_ characterization.htm

Baker, Soren. *The History of Rap and Hip-Hop.* Detroit: Gale, Cengage Learning, 2012.

Baldick,Chris. *The Concise Oxford Dictionary of Literary Terms.* Oxford University Press: Oxford, New York, 1990.

Barnes-Murphy, Frances, Aesop, and Rowan Barnes-Murphy. *The Fables of Aesop.* New York: Lothrop, Lee & Shepard Books, 1994.

Bauman, Richard. *Verbal Art as Performance.* Prospect Heights: Waveland Press, Inc., 1997.

Benson, Stephen. "Postmodernism." In *The Greenwood Encyclopedia of Folktales and Fairy Tales*, Vol. 2, edited by Donald Haase, 762-767. Westport, CT: Greenwood Press, 2008.

"Bias." *Merriam-Webster.* Accessed May 31, 2016. http://www.merriam-webster.com /dictionary/bias.

Bobby, Susan Redington., ed. *Fairy Tales Reimagined: Essays on New Retellings.* Jefferson: McFarland, 2009.

Booss, Claire ed. "The Three Billy-Goats Who Went up into the Hills to Get Fat." In *Scandinavian Folk and Fairy Tales*, 29-30. Avenel: Gramercy Books, 1984.

Bottigheimer, Ruth. B. "Fractured Fairy Tales." In *The Oxford Companion to Fairy Tales: The Western Fairy Tale Tradition from Medieval to Modern*, edited by Jack Zipes, 172-173, Oxford, New York: Oxford University Press. 2010.

Bryant, P. E., L. Bradley, M. Maclean, and J. Crossland. "Nursery Rhymes, Phonological Skills and Reading." *Journal of Child Language* 16, no. 02 (1989): 407. https://www. cambridge.org/core/journals/journal-of-child-language/article/nursery-rhymes-phonological-skills-and-reading/53EE25F1E011C8090E659A8FABBB209E

Burns, Jeri and Barry Marshall. "Revitalizing Traditional Stories: A Cultural Imperative" Paper presented at Ananse SoundSplash Storytelling Conference and Festival, Kingston and Montego Bay, Jamaica, West Indies, November 19-25, 2014.

Campbell, John Francis. "Popular Tales of the West Highlands Vol. II: XXXIII. The Tale of the Queen Who Sought a Drink From a Certain Well." *Popular Tales of the West Highlands Vol. II: XXXIII.* "The Tale of the Queen Who Sought a Drink From a Certain Well." Accessed December 03, 2015. http://www.sacred-texts.com/neu /celt/pt2/pt225.htm.

Campbell, Joseph. *The Hero with a Thousand Faces, Third Edition.* Novato: New World Library, 2008.

Carpenter, Stephen, and Peter Christen Asbjørnsen. *The Three Billy Goats Gruff.* New York: HarperCollinsFestival, 1998.

Carroll, Lewis. *Alice's Adventures in Wonderland.* Full Text of *Alice's Adventures in Wonderland,* August 12, 2006, accessed July 10, 2016, https://archive.org/stream /alicesadventures19033gut/19033.txt.

Carter, Angela. *The Bloody Chamber and Other Stories.* New York: Harper and Row, 1978.

Carter, Angela, ed. *The Second Virago Book of Fairy Tales.* London: Virago Press, 1993.

Carter, Angela. *The Virago Book of Fairy Tales.* London: Virago Press, 1990.

Chalmers, Robert. "The Jataka, Volume I: Book I—Ekanipāta: No. 33. Sammodamāna-Jātaka." The Jataka, Volume I: Book I—Ekanipāta: No. 33. Sammodamāna-Jātaka. January 2006. Accessed June 06, 2016. http://www.sacred-texts.com/bud/j1/j1036 .htm. Originally published: Cambridge: Cambridge University Press, 1895.

Chambers, Robert. "The Paddo." *Popular Rhymes of Scotland: New Edition,* 87-89. London and Edinburgh: W. and R. Chambers, 1870, accessed January 14, 2016, http://www.pitt.edu/~dash/frog.html#chambers.

Clark, Pat. "I Don't Think I'm Biased." *Teaching Tolerance Magazine,* Southern Poverty Law Center. No. 37, Spring 2010. Accessed May 23, 2016. https://www.tolerance. org/magazine/spring-2010/i-dont-think-im-biased.

Clift, Stephen, and Ian Morrison. "Group Singing Fosters Mental Health and Wellbeing: Findings from the East Kent "singing for Health" Network Project." *Mental Health Social Inclusion Mental Health and Social Inclusion* 15, no. 2 (2011): 88-97. http://www.emeraldinsight.com/doi/abs/10.1108/20428301111140930.

Coover, Robert. *Briar Rose.* New York: Grove Press, 1996.

Cressey, Daniel. "Brain Scans of Rappers Shed Light on Creativity." Nature.com. November 15, 2012. Accessed June 03, 2016. http://www.nature.com/news/brain -scans-of-rappers-shed-light-on-creativity-1.11835.

Cudden. J. A. *Dictionary of Literary Terms and Literary Theory.* Revised by M.A.R. Habib. Penguin Group: London, 2013.

Del Negro, Janice. *Folktales Aloud: Practical Advice for Playful Storytelling.* Chicago: ALA Editions, 2014.

Doctorow, E. L. "The Art of Fiction No. 94." *Paris Review*. 101 (Winter 1986). Accessed May 28, 2016. http://www.theparisreview.org/interviews/2718/the-art-of-fiction -no-94-e-l-doctorow.

Doughty, Amie. *Folktales Retold: A Critical Overview of Stories Updated for Children.* Jefferson: McFarland. 2006.

Dundes, Alan, author and Simon J. Bronner, editor. "Folklore as a Mirror of Culture," 55-66. *The Meaning of Folklore: The Analytics of Alan Dundes.* Logan: Utah University Press, 2007.

Dundes, Alan. *Little Red Riding Hood: A Casebook.* Madison: University of Wisconsin Press, 1989.

Dundes, Alan and Carl Pagter. "Prinderella and the Cince." *When You're Up to Your Ass in Alligators: More Urban Folklore from the Paperwork Empire,* 255-257. Detroit: Wayne State University Press, 1987.

Dunst, Carl J., Diana Meter, and Deborah W. Hamby. "Relationship Between Young Children's Nursery Rhyme Experiences and Knowledge and Phonological and Print-Related Abilities." Accessed June 3, 2016. http://earlyliteracylearning.org /cellreviews/cellreviews_v4_n1.pdf.

*Encyclopædia Britannica.* "Point of View." *Encyclopædia Britannica.* Accessed May 31, 2016. https://www.britannica.com/art/point-of-view-literature -and-film.

Elliot-Cooper, Adam. "Moving Beyond 'Igloo Australia'" *Media Diversified* (blog), July 17, 2015. Accessed June 5, 2015. https://mediadiversified.org/2015/07/17/beyond-iggy-azalea/. Part of the Black Friday Series on All Black Everything.

*Encyclopædia Britannica,* s. v. "volta", accessed June 06, 2016, http://www.britannica .com/art/volta-poetry.

Forest, Heather. Story Arts, Aesop's ABC, "The Tortoise and The Hare." Accessed June 06, 2016. https://www.storyarts.org/library/aesops/stories/tortoise.html.

Forest, Heather, and Susan Gaber. *The Baker's Dozen: A Colonial American Tale.* San Diego: Harcourt Brace Jovanovich, 1988.

Forster, E.M. *Aspects of the Novel.* New York: Harcourt, Brace & Company, 1927.

French, Vivian and Stephen Lambert. "The Enormous Turnip." In *The Kingfisher Book of Nursery Tales,* 54-65. Boston: Kingfisher, 2003.

Fyfe, William S., J. Selverstone. "Metamorphic Rock." *Encyclopædia Britannica.* Accessed May 24, 2016. http://www.britannica.com/science/metamorphic-rock.

Geras, Adèle. "The Overcrowded House." In *My Grandmother's Stories: A Collection of Jewish Folktales,* 68-75. New York: Knopf Books for Young Readers, 2003.

Gilbert, Sandra M. and Susan Gubar (1979). "Snow White and Her Wicked Stepmother." In *The Classic Fairy Tales,* Edited by Maria Tatar, 291-297. New York:

W.W. Norton., 1999. Originally published in Sandra M. Gilbert and Susan Gubar, *The Madwoman in the Attic: The Woman Writer and the Nineteenth-Century Literary Imagination*. New Haven: Yale University Press, 1979.

Goding, Anne. *Storytelling: Reflecting on Oral Narratives and Cultures*, 2nd ed. San Diego: Cognella Publishing, 2016.

Gold, Doris B., and Lisa Stein. *From the Wise Women of Israel: Folklore and Memoirs*. New York: Biblio Press, 1993.

Haase, Donald. "Decolonizing Fairy-Tale Studies." *Marvels & Tales* 24, no.1, (2010): 17-38. Web. http://digitalcommons.wayne.edu/marvels/vol24/iss1/1.

Haase, Donald. "Hypertextual Gutenberg: The Textual and Hypertextual Life of Folktales and Fairy Tales in English-Language Popular Print Editions." *Fabula* 47, no 3–4 (2006): 222–30. https://www.degruyter.com/view/j/fabl.2006.47.issue-3-4 /fabl.2006.024/fabl.2006.024.xml

Haase, Donald, ed. *Fairy Tales and Feminism: New Approaches*. Detroit: Wayne State University Press, 2004.

Hamilton, Mary. "The Woman in Brown." On *Live from the Culbertson Mansion: Haunting Tales*. Storyteller. Hidden Spring, 2001. CD.

Hamlet, Janice D. "The Reason Why We Sing: Understanding Traditional African-American Worship." In *Our Voices: Essays in Culture, Ethnicity and Communication*. Fifth Edition, edited by Alberto Gonzalez, Marsha Houston, and Victoria Chen, 112-117. New York: Oxford University Press, 2012.

Haven, Kendall and MaryGay Ducey. *Crash Course in Storytelling*. Westport, CT: Libraries Unlimited, 2007.

Haven, Kendall. *Story Proof: The Science Behind the Startling Power of Story*. Westport: Libraries Unlimited, 2007.

Heckler, Melissa and Carol Birch. "Building Bridges with Stories." In *Storytelling Encyclopedia: Historical, Cultural, and Multiethnic Approaches to Oral Traditions Around the World*. Edited by David Adams Leeming, 8-15. Pheonix. AZ: Oryx Press, 1997.

Heiner, Heidi Anne. "SurLaLune Fairy Tales: Annotated Fairy Tales, Fairy Tale Books and Illustrations." SurLaLune Fairy Tales.com. Accessed June 01, 2016. http://surlalunefairytales.com/. Last updated 12/2/16.

Hutcheon, Linda. *A Theory of Adaptation*. Abingdon, Oxon: Routledge, 2006.

Jacobs, Joseph. *English Fairy Tales*, title page. Accessed December 02, 2015. http://www.sacred-texts.com/neu/eng/eft/eft00.htm. Originally published as *English Fairy Tales*. London: David Nutt, 1890.

Joosen, Vanessa. *Critical and Creative Perspectives on Fairy Tales: An Intertextual Dialogue between Fairy-Tale Scholarship and Postmodern Retellings*. Detroit: Wayne State University Press, 2013.

Knox, R. Seth. C. "Archetype." In *The Greenwood Encyclopedia of Folktales and Fairy Tales*, edited by Donald Haase, 64-66. Westport: Greenwood Press, 2008.

Kreutz, Gunter, Stephan Bongard, Sonja Rohrmann, Volker Hodapp, and Dorothee Grebe. "Effects of Choir Singing or Listening on Secretory Immunoglobulin A, Cortisol, and Emotional State." *Journal of Behavioral Medicine* 27, no. 6 (2004): 623-35. https://www.researchgate.net/publication/8063178_Effects_of_Choir _Singing_or_Listening_on_Secretory_Immunoglobulin_A_Cortisol_and _Emotional_State

Kristeva, Julia, and Toril Moi, ed. "Word, Dialogue and Novel." In *The Kristeva Reader*, 34-61. New York, NY: Columbia University Press, 1986.

Kuo, Louise, and Yuan-Hsi Kuo. *Chinese Folk Tales*, 7-12. Millbrae, CA: Celestial Arts, 1976.

Lang, Andrew, ed. *The Violet Fairy Book.* New York: Dover Publications, Inc., 1966. Originally published in Andrew Lang, *The Violet Fairy Book.* London: Longmans, Green and Co., 1901.

Leach, Maria, and Kurt Werth. "Milk Bottles." In *The Thing at the Foot of the Bed: And Other Scary Tales*,60-62. New York: Philomel Books, 1959.

Leeming, David Adams, ed. *Storytelling Encyclopedia: Historical, Cultural, and Multiethnic Approaches to Oral Traditions Around the World.* Pheonix: Oryx Press, 1997.

Levitin, Daniel J. *This Is Your Brain on Music: The Science of a Human Obsession.* New York, NY: Plume/Penguin, 2007.

Liu, Siyuan, Ho Ming Chow, Yisheng Xu, Michael G. Erkkinen, Katherine E. Swett, Michael W. Eagle, Daniel A. Rizik-Baer, and Allen R. Braun. "Neural Correlates of Lyrical Improvisation: An FMRI Study of Freestyle Rap." *Scientific Reports* 2 (2012). Accessed June 3, 2016. https://www.nature.com/articles/srep00834

Livo, Norma. "The Escape of the Pigeons." *Bringing Out Their Best: Values Education and Character Development through Traditional Tales*, 173-174. Westport, CT: Libraries Unlimited, 2003.

Livo, Norma J. and Sandra A. Ritz. *Storytelling: Process and Practice.* Littleton: Libraries Unlimited, Inc., 1986.

Lommel, Cookie. *The History of Rap Music.* Philadelphia: Chelsea House Publishers, 2001.

Lynch, Jack. "Ballad Stanza." Glossary of Literary and Rhetorical Terms. Accessed January 30, 2016. https://andromeda.rutgers.edu/~jlynch/Terms/ballad-stanza .html.

Macdonald, G. W., and A. Cornwall. "The Relationship Between Phonological Awareness and Reading and Spelling Achievement Eleven Years Later." *Journal of Learning Disabilities* 28, no. 8 (1995): 523-27. http://journals.sagepub.com/doi /abs/10.1177/002221949502800807.

Maclean, Morag, Peter Bryant and Lynette Bradley. "Rhymes, Nursery Rhymes, and Reading in Early Childhood." *Merrill-Palmer Quarterly 33 no.03, (1987): 255-281.*

Maguire, Gregory *Wicked: The Life and Times of the Wicked Witch of the West.* New York: Harper, 1995.

Maguire, Jack. *Creative Storytelling: Choosing, Inventing, and Sharing Tales for Children.* Cambridge: Yellow Moon Press, 1985.

Maguire, Jack. *The Power of Personal Storytelling: Spinning Tales to Connect with Others.* New York: Jeremy P. Tarcher/Putnam, 1998.

"Malapropism" *Merriam-Webster.* Accessed May 27, 2016. http://www.merriam-webster.com/dictionary/malapropism.

Martin, Rafe. "The Wise Quail." *The Hungry Tigress: Buddhist Legends and Jataka Tales,* 71-74. Cambridge: Yellow Moon Press, 1999.

"Mash-up" *Merriam-Webster.* Accessed September 09, 2015. http://www.merriam-webster.com/dictionary/mash-up.

McKee, Robert. *Story: Substance, Structure, Style and the Principles of Screenwriting.* New York: HarperCollins. 1997.

Meyer, Rudolf. *The Wisdom of Fairy Tales.* Edinburgh: Floris Books, 1997. First published in German under the title *Die Weisheit der deutschen Volksmärchsen.* Stuttgart: Verlag Urachhaus, 1935.

Metelerkamp, S. Preface to *Outa Karel's Stories: South Afrcian Folk-lore Tales.* London: Macmillan and Co., Limited St. Martin's Street, 1914. Accessed 5/16/16, http://www.worldoftales.com/African_folktales/South_African_tales_preface.html.

Nardin, Jane. "The Literary Mash-up." *Huffingtonpost.com* (blog), November 27, 2012. Accessed September 9, 2015. http://www.huffingtonpost.com/jane-nardin/the-literary-mash-up_b_2194133.html.

Nelson, Stephen A. "Protolith." In Metamorphism and Metamorphic Rocks. Accessed October 3, 2017, http://www.tulane.edu/~sanelson/eens1110/metamorphic.htm

Nikolajeva, Maria. *Children's Literature Comes of Age: Toward a New Aesthetic.* New York and London: Garland Publishing, 1996

Obermeier, Christian, Winfried Menninghaus, Martin Von Koppenfels, Tim Raettig, Maren Schmidt-Kassow, Sascha Otterbein, and Sonja A. Kotz. "Aesthetic and Emotional Effects of Meter and Rhyme in Poetry." *Frontiers in Psychology* 4 (2013). https://www.frontiersin.org/articles/10.3389/fpsyg.2013.00010/full.

Opie, Iona and Peter. *The Classic Fairy Tales.* New York: Oxford University Press, 1980.

Orenstein, Catherine. *Little Red Riding Hood Uncloaked: Sex, Morality, and the Evolution of a Fairy Tale.* New York: Basic Books, 2002.

O'Toole, Garson. "Jump off the Cliff and Build Your Wings on the Way Down." Quote Investigator. Accessed July 23, 2016. http://quoteinvestigator.com/2012/06/17/cliff-wings/.

Parker, K. Langloh. Preface to *Australian Legendary Tales*. Notes from https://www.worldoftales.com/Australian_folktales.html describe this piece as follows: Folklore of the Noongahburrahs as told to the Piccaninnies. Features 31 Australian folktales, 1896. London: David Nutt; Melbourne: Melville, Mulle & Slade, 1896. Accessed 5/16/16. http://www.sacred-texts.com/aus/alt/alt02.htm.

Pearmain, Elisa Davy. *Once Upon a Time: Storytelling to Teach Character and Prevent Bullying*. Greensboro: Character Development Group, 2006.

Pellowski, Anne. *The World of Storytelling: A Practical Guide to the Origins, Development and Applications of Storytelling*. Expanded and Revised Edition. Bronx: H.W. Wilson Company, 1990.

Phelps, Ethel Johnston. (1978). *Tatterhood and Other Tales*. New York: The Feminist Press, 1978.

Phelps, Ethel Johnston. *The Maid of the North: Feminist Folktales from Around the World*. New York: Holt Paperbacks, 1982.

Pickering, David. *A Dictionary of Folklore*. New York: Facts on File, 1999.

"Plot—Examples and Definition of Plot." Literary Devices. 2013. Accessed June 29, 2016. http://literarydevices.net/plot/.

Propp, Vladimir. *Morphology of the Folktale*, second ed. Revised and edited by Louis. A. Wagner. Austin & London: University of Texas Press. 1968. Originally published in Vladimir Propp, trans. Laurence Scott, *The Morphology of the Folktale*, Bloomington: Research Center, Indiana University, 1958.

Provine, Robert R. "Contagious Laughter: Laughter is a Sufficient Stimulus for Laughs and Smiles." *Bulletin of the Psychonomic Society*. 30, no. 1 (1992): 1-4, accessed May 27, 2016, https://link.springer.com/article/10.3758/BF03330380

"Puns." Literary Devices. 2010. Accessed May 24, 2016. http://literary-devices.com/content/puns.

Ragan, Kathleen., ed. *Fearless Girls, Wise Women & Beloved Sisters: Heroines in Folktales from Around the World*. New York: W.W. Norton, 2002.

Read, Kirsten. "Clues Cue the Smooze: Rhyme, Pausing, and Prediction Help Children Lean New Words from Storybooks." *Frontiers in Psychology*. 5 (2014). Accessed March 14, 2016. https://www.frontiersin.org/articles/10.3389/fpsyg.2014.00149/full

Reynolds, Mary E., Kristie Callihan, and Erin Browning "Effect of Instruction on the Development of Rhyming Skills in Young Children. *Contemporary Issues in Communication Science and Disorders* 30, Spring (2003): 41-46.

"Riding Hood." *Merriam Webster*. Accessed 12/1/15, http://www.merriam-webster.com/dictionary/riding%20hood.

Rogers, Richard A. "From Cultural Exchange to Transculturation: A Review and Reconceptualization of Cultural Appropriation." *Communication Theory* 16, no. 4 (2006): 474-503. https://www.researchgate.net/publication/227630287_From _Cultural_Exchange_to_Transculturation_A_Review_and_Reconceptualization _of_Cultural_Appropriation.

Rush, Barbara. *The Book of Jewish Women's Tales*. Northvale: Jason Aronson, Inc., 1994.

Sanal, A. M., and S. Gorsev. "Psychological and Physiological Effects of Singing in a Choir." *Psychology of Music* 42, no. 3 (2013): 420-29. http://journals.sagepub.com /doi/abs/10.1177/0305735613477181?journalCode=poma.

Schram, Peninnah. *Jewish Stories One Generation Tells Another*. Northvale: Jason Aronson, an Imprint of Rowman and Littlefield, 1987.

Scieszka, Jon, and Lane Smith. *The True Story of the Three Little Pigs: As Told to Jon Scieszka:* New York: Viking Kestrel, 1989.

Schlosser, S.E. "Milk Bottles." In *Spooky California: Tales of Hauntings, Strange Happenings, and Other Local Lore*, 2-6. Guilford, CT: Insiders' Guide, 2005.

Scott, Sophie K., Nadine Lavan, Sinead Chen, and Carolyn Mcgettigan. "The Social Life of Laughter." *Trends in Cognitive Sciences* 18, no. 12 (2014): 618-20. https://www. ncbi.nlm.nih.gov/pubmed/25439499.

Seeley, Tracey. "When Is Lying in Memoir Acceptable? 3 Key Issues | WritersDigest. com." WritersDigest.com. May 31, 2011. Accessed May 31, 2016. http://www. writersdigest.com/editor-blogs/there-are-no-rules/guest-post/when-is-lying-in-memoir-acceptable-3-key-issues

Seifert, Lewis C. "Feminist Approaches to Seventeenth Century *Contes de Fées*. In *Fairy Tale sand Feminism: New Approaches*, edited by Donald Haase, 53-71. Detroit: Wayne State University Press, 2004.

Sexton, Anne. *Transformations.*: Boston: Houghton Mifflin, 1971.

Shepard, Aaron, and Wendy Edelson. *The Baker's Dozen: A Saint Nicholas Tale*. New York: Atheneum Books for Young Readers, 1995.

Silverstein, Shel. *Runny Babbit: A Billy Sook*. New York: HarperCollins, 2005.

Skinner, Charles F. "The Baker's Dozen." *Myths and Legends in Our Own Land*. Philadelphia and London, 1896. Accessed 5/21/16. http://sacred-texts.com/ame/lol/lol009.htm

"Sonnet—Glossary Terms—Poetry Foundation." *Poetry Foundation*. Accessed January 23, 2016. http://www.poetryfoundation.org/resources/learning/glossary-terms/detail/sonnet.

Stevens, Janet. *The Three Billy Goats Gruff.* San Diego, New York, London: Harcourt Jovanovich, Publishers, 1987.

Sutherland, John. *How Literature Works: 50 Key Concepts.* Oxford, New York: Oxford University Press, 2011.

Tatar, Maria. Introduction to *The Turnip Princess and Other Newly Discovered Fairy Tales* by Franz Xaver von Schönewirth, vi-xviii, London: Penguin Classics, 2015.

Tatar, Maria, ed. and trans. *The Annotated Classic Fairy Tales.* New York. W.W. Norton, 2002.

Thomas, Nigel J.T. Stanford Encyclopedia of Philosophy. 2014. Accessed March 11, 2016. http://plato.stanford.edu/entries/mental-imagery/ancient-imagery-mnemonics.html.

Tiffin, Jessica. *Marvelous Geometry: Narrative and Metafiction in Modern Fairy Tale.* Detroit: Wayne State University Press, 2014.

Tolstoy, Aleksey Nikolayevich and Niamh Sharkey. *The Gigantic Turnip.* Brooklyn, NY: Barefoot Books, 1999.

"Traditional and Ethnic—The Library of Congress Celebrates the Songs of America." *The Library of Congress.* Accessed January 30, 2016. https://www.loc.gov/collection/songs-of-america/articles-and-essays/musical-styles/traditional-and-ethnic/.

"Traditional Ballads—The Library of Congress Celebrates the Songs of America." *The Library of Congress.* Accessed June 05, 2016. https://www.loc.gov/collections/songs-of-america/articles-and-essays/musical-styles/traditional-and-ethnic/traditional-ballads/.

Turkle, Sherry. "How to Teach in an Age of Distraction. *The Chronicle of Higher Education,* October 9, 2015.Accessed May 24, 2016. http://chronicle.com.libproxy.ocean.edu:2048/article/How-to-Teach-in-an-Age-of/233515

Turner, Kay & Greenhill, Pauline. *Transgressive Tales: Queering the Grimms.* Detroit, MI: Wayne State University Press, 2012.

United Nations Declaration on the Rights of Indigenous Peoples. United Nations. Accessed May 20, 2016. United Nations. http://www.un.org/esa/socdev/unpfii/documents/DRIPS_en.pdf, March 2008.

Uwujaren, Jarune. "The Difference Between Cultural Exchange and Cultural Appropriation." Everyday Feminism. September 30, 2013. Accessed May 28, 2016. http://everydayfeminism.com/2013/09/cultural-exchange-and-cultural-appropriation/.

von Franz, Marie-Louise. *Archetypal Patterns in Fairy Tales.* Toronto: Inner City Books, 1997.

Wald, Elijah. *Talking 'Bout Your Mama: The Dozens, Snaps, and the Deep Roots of Rap.* New York: Oxford University Press, 2014.

Wan, Catherine Y., Theodor Rüber, Anja Hohmann, and Gottfried Schlaug. "The Therapeutic Effects of Singing in Neurological Disorders." *Music Perception* 27, no. 4 (2010): 287-95. http://mp.ucpress.edu/content/27/4/287.

Warner, Marina. *From the Beast to the Blonde.* New York: Farrar, Strauss, and Giroux, 1994.

Warner, Marina. *Once Upon a Time: A Short History of Fairy Tale.* Oxford: Oxford University Press, 2014.

"Wordplay." *Merriam-Webster.* Accessed October 3, 2017, https://www.merriam-webster.com/dictionary/wordplay.

Wright, Rebecca Hu-Van and Ying-Hwa Hu. *The Three Billy Goats Gruff.* Cambridge: Star Bright Books, 2014.

Yolen, Jane. *Not One Damsel in Distress: World Folktales for Strong Young Girls.* HMH Books for Young Readers, 2000.

Zalka, Csenge Virag. "Representation." Multicolored Diary. April 2016. Accessed September 29, 2017. http://multicoloreddiary.blogspot.com/search/label/representation.

Zemach, Margot. *It Could Always Be Worse: A Yiddish Folk Tale.* New York: Square Fish, 1990.

Zielinski, Sarah. "The Secrets of Sherlock's Mind Palace" *Smithsonian.* February 3, 2014. Accessed May 27, 2016. http://www.smithsonianmag.com/arts-culture/secrets-sherlocks-mind-palace-180949567/?no-ist

Zipes, Jack, trans. *The Complete Fairy Tales of the Brothers Grimm.* Toronto: Bantam Books, 1987.

Zipes, Jack. *Fairy Tales and the Art of Subversion: The Classical Genre for Children and the Process of Civilization.* New York: Wildman Press, 1983.

Zipes, Jack. *Fairy Tale as Myth/Myth as Fairy Tale.* Lexington: University Press of Kentucky, 1994.

Zipes, Jack. *The Irresistible Fairy Tale: The Cultural and Social History of a Genre.* Princeton University Press: Princeton and Oxford, 2012.

Zipes, Jack., ed. *The Trials and Tribulations of Little Red Riding Hood,* 2nd Edition. New York: Routledge. 1993.

Zipes, Jack. *Why Fairy Tales Stick: The Evolution and Relevance of a Genre..* New York: Routledge, 2006

# NOTES

1. Lewis Carroll, Alice's Adventures in Wonderland, Full Text of Alice's Adventures in Wonderland, August 12, 2006, accessed July 10, 2016, https://archive.org/stream /alicesadventures19033gut/19033.txt..

2. Garson O'Toole, "Jump off the Cliff and Build Your Wings on the Way Down," Quote Investigator, accessed July 23, 2016, http://quoteinvestigator.com/2012/06/17 /cliff-wings/.

3. Lewis Carroll, Alice's Adventures in Wonderland, Full Text of Alice's Adventures in Wonderland, August 12, 2006, accessed July 10, 2016, https://archive.org/stream /alicesadventures19033gut/19033.txt..

# INDEX